DAUGHTER OF THE KILLING FIELDS

DAUGHTER OF THE KILLING FIELDS

Asrei's Story

Theary C. Seng

f

First published in 2005 by Fusion Press,
a division of Satin Publications Ltd.
101 Southwark Street
London SE1 0JF
UK
info@visionpaperbacks.co.uk
www.visionpaperbacks.co.uk
Publisher: Sheena Dewan

A catalogue record for this book is available from the British Library.

HB ISBN: 1-904132-70-7
Export PB ISBN: 1-9041-32-78-2

2 4 6 8 10 9 7 5 3 1

Cover photo: Michael S. Yamashita/Corbis
Cover and text design by ok?design
Printed and bound in the UK by Mackays of Chatham Ltd,
Chatham, Kent

In loving memory of

Grandma Hao Yi
Papa and Maman
Mieng Peat and Pou Veng

Contents

Acknowledgements

I am most blessed to have so many wonderful people who through the years have deeply enriched my life. There would be no memoir if not for the love, encouragement and assistance of the following individuals:

I am deeply indebted to my amazing family, who shared with me their deeply held stories amidst my persistent prodding and intrusions, in particular: the incomparable Grandma Hao, brothers Mardi, Sina and Lundi, Aunt Renee, Aunt Ry, Uncle Seng, Uncle Eng, Dr. (Pou) Song Tan, Choulie Hok, Great Uncle (Ta) Ân and his wife Nan, Dr. (Oum) An, Aunt Maly and the Svay Rieng relatives.

Marge and Wally Boelkins are Christian love in action. They have been dear friends to my family since our early days at Millbrook Christian Reformed Church in Grand Rapids. But to me, they are so much more. I called them my 'godparents' for they have not only nourished me materially but spiritually and continue to do so. I stayed with them during countless summer breaks and other holidays in their beautiful leafy estate of Hidden Ridge. Many a morning, I would wake up to a glass of orange juice waiting for me on my bedstand, lovingly placed there by Marge. In June 2005, they celebrated their 51st wedding anniversary. Upon entering the house, daily without fail, the first thing Wally does is to kiss Marge and I remember hearing from Marge a few years ago that they have never gone a day without saying goodnight to each other, even if by phone when he's away on business. I stand in awe of their love for each other, for God and for their 'neighbours', one of whom I am fortunate to be.

Catherine Filloux. Words cannot adequately describe the debt I owe and love I have for this beautiful playwright and friend of Cambodia, for her faith and persistent encouragement. During the moments when I was just content to have written this memoir for my own personal healing and satisfaction, it was Catherine who gently but firmly prodded me to see that it be published because the story needed to be publicly told. I met Catherine and her husband John several years back at a reception in Washington, DC for her play, *Silence of God*, hosted by Cambodian Ambassador, Roland Eng. Since then, she has become my strongest advocate and I her biggest fan. She introduced me to my literary agent, Susan Schulman, who made this book possible. I am very fortunate to have such excellent representation.

Over red wines and Coronas at Doves & Hawks pub in the Capitol Hill neighourhood of Washington, DC, Rebekah Harvey, a friend from law school, generously gave of her time to review and comment on the first draft of my memoir.

Michael Denneny awes me with his editing skills, without which this memoir would be the poorer.

I am deeply grateful to my dear friend Kunno Prak, a fellow survivor of the Khmer Rouge hell, another strong advocate of this memoir and the supreme master of web creation (in particular for www.asrei.net).

The immense generosity and support of the following reviewers (most of whom accepted to read the manuscript without a promise of a publisher and outside review and editing) leave me speechless: Former Representative (NY) Steve Solarz, who not only reviewed the manuscript but invited me to share a Thanksgiving celebration with his family at their McLean estate and shared with me

Cambodia stories; Ambassador Charles Twining, a true friend of Cambodia; Dith Pran, whose life was portrayed in the movie *The Killing Fields*; Ron Abney who was injured in the 1997 Easter Sunday grenade attack; Professor Frederick Z. Brown; Professor David Chandler; Putsata Reang; and Ambassador Ellen Sauerbrey.

If only Cambodia has more of my adopted uncle Soubert Son's compassion and intelligence, the country would not be in its current state. His comments and insight of Cambodian culture and history prove invaluable.

The list would have no end if I am to mention all the individuals who knowingly or unknowingly encouraged and supported me in this memoir, but I would be greatly amiss if I do not mention at least: Ambassador Roland Eng, Prince Sirivudh Norodom, Yann Ker, Ambassador Sichan and Martha Siv, Sereyvuth Veng, Chivy Sok, Chath pier Sath, Arn Chorn-Pond, Sunthary Chhorn, Lisa Davidson, Eva (Katsari) and Erich Hoefer, Kara Odegaard, Sambonn Lek of the Mayflower Hotel's Town & Country and his amazing friends and board members of Sam Relief, Inc. (i.e., Jerry Essenbacher), Adam Fifield, Imran Vittachi, Glenn Kaminsky, Adam Chase, Beverly Watson, Catherine Jones, Professor Stephen Morris, Sybil Hall, Dr. Rasoka Thor, Sorya Sim, Youk Chhang, Sam Mok, Dr. Jonathan Drysdale, Bun Ang Ung, Dr. Rob Garner, Soren Johnson, Bunleng Men, Laura McGrew, Sophal Ear, Damali Sempangi and Shani Warner.

Last but not least, this book would not be what it is without the superb editing of Charlotte Cole, and everyone else at Fusion Press: Emily Bird, Louise Coe, Katie Davison, Sheena Dewan, Sam Evans, Oliver Keen and Paul Swallow, to whom I am immensely grateful.

AUTHOR'S NOTE

It is with some reluctance that I write of my own and my family's history. There are several reasons for this.

First, this literary journey can develop into a showcasing of oneself, either casting positive light or exposing vulnerability that may reverberate hauntingly in the future. Practically, life is to be lived fully in the present; it should not be wasted dwelling in the past. More importantly, implicit in this undertaking lies the belief that my story is sufficiently noteworthy to be put in book form, a medium that inevitably creates an aura of heroism around the author.

In reality, this author has done nothing heroic, only documented events in her life that she never wished for in the first instance. If drama is the litmus test, I'm certain other people have experienced far more inhumanity and have fared better.

Second, by its nature, this story is filtered through a biased and flawed perception: mine. I cannot escape being human. This is not to say I have not made a very conscientious effort to be fair, objective and generous in my assessment. I have. Nonetheless, it is only one perspective – my perspective – one tainted by human depravity and an instinctive want for self-protection.

I am reminded of the famous sketch of a woman, at once beautiful and ugly; which image one sees (either the beautiful or the ugly) depends on a prior exposure of the woman from a similar sketch of only the beautiful or the ugly image to establish a schema. Once established, this schema controls the interpretation; it takes a deliberate training of the mind to shatter the schema in order to see the other perspective.

Moreover, I wield the power of the pen and the medium does not allow for immediate rebuttal and clarification from those involved in my story which might provide a more balanced, full view.

Nor does it help to know that the story is based on memory, always selective, which is my third concern. I could not have been more than four years old when my father disappeared. I have almost no memory of him. My clear memories of my mother are limited to our time spent in prison. In recalling my early memories, I found that many times, rather than sequential and profound recalling of situations, stray images floated in and out of my head, giving me a glimpse here and there of my past. This past is comprised of detached and undatable flashes, of an event, of a face, of a smell/sound/feeling, which would in turn trigger other flashes of event, person, and smell/sound/feeling.

For example, I remember a man who lived next to our house in Chensa village. I remember him as a romantic figure, a learned poet, a political dissident who whispered coded instructions and wise sayings to me. Even though I didn't understand the politics of those days, I had complete confidence in him, that he somehow would rescue us. One day he disappeared. This man made such an impression on me that I carried his memory with me all these years and assumed that my older brothers remembered him as well, until one day I asked them whether they recalled any such man, and they could not.

And other times, I find it difficult to distinguish my personal memory from the countless Western accounts I have read and the stories I have heard in various informal family conversations or more public Cambodian social settings.

Only recently, I decided to conduct formal interviews of my relatives and tape-record their memories. Cambodians follow an oral tradition of storytelling; thus, a lot of the events beyond the personal memories of living relatives may well fall into the category of hearsay. Moreover, a suspicion of mine was confirmed during this process of writing: Cambodians – in this case, my relatives – are more concerned with getting the spirit of the situation correct than with the minutiae.

Let me clarify with a true example: in a draft of a previous autobiographical essay, I had written that '[We] not only had to endure travelling a long distance and on rugged terrain with an aunt who was in her third trimester of her pregnancy but dangers of banditry, Khmer Rouge soldiers and mines as well.' In reality, it was not the case that my cousin Visal was in her mother's womb; she had been born one year earlier. This essay had been intended for publication, and all my family who read it failed to raise the huge factual error with me. It could be that no one noticed the misstatement. But more likely, my relatives were focusing on the spirit of the account and that spirit was correct: we were travelling through dangerous terrain; and it mattered little to them that I had written about the pregnancy instead of the factually correct 'many little children and a one-year-old baby' that I would write later.

Fourth, I am concerned with the finality of putting something onto paper; it gives the false impression that one has gained some sort of higher ground or achieved some mentioned goals. On the contrary, to state the obvious, we are all works-in-progress and my espoused principles are more aspirations than fait accompli. I believe it is important to have dreams and ideals, for every achievement begins with them.

But several reasons impel me to overcome these concerns.

I promised my grandma before she passed away that I would

write her life story. Her life embroidered my life. In a story drenched in death, her life provides an aroma that lingers to this day.

In addition, numerous people through the years have encouraged me to write about my experiences under the Khmer Rouge regime and in the United States. Up until this point, I had neither the tools, energy, nor the time to begin writing seriously.

Finally, it is time that I practice what I preach. I am constantly urging my brothers and relatives to put down their thoughts on paper. Beside the fact that this disciplinary exercise is therapeutic and personally rewarding, I am a strong believer of George Santayana's adage that those who forget the past are condemned to repeat it. From April 1975 to January 1979 a thick cloud of evil blanketed the whole of Cambodia, wherein the Khmer Rouge communists targeted bourgeoisie principles by successfully killing off Cambodia's educated class. In addition, they obliterated all infrastructures, including education, with the goal of reverting the country to the year zero.

I have always been haunted by this fact. Present-day Cambodia continues to reap the legacy of this intellectual deficit. Imagine such a country existing in this 21st century global world of porous borders and hi-tech machinery. Imagine the exploitation. Now that I have an opportunity to contribute a book to the rebuilding of its resources, I am redoubling my efforts.

If for nothing else, I pray this story will provide, for the members of the new generation in my family who are growing up in American decadence, a bridge to their roots and a way to understand their parents' sacrifices for them.

Addresses and honorifics
Cambodians rarely address each other by name; the honorifics and addresses below are used instead. Names are added only to clarify and specify, and by adults for children. Moreover, descriptions

or relational phrases are often employed as well. For example, many people would address and refer to my mom as 'the mother of Mardi', as usually the firstborn is named. But sometimes, if I am present at the conversation, 'mother of Asrei' is used. Another example, Aunt Ry has reddish tint in her hair, so she is known as 'Red-head'. Or, my cousin Vannak, is known as À Barang (or Frenchie) because of her more westernised, narrow nose and fair skin.

It is not uncommon for people, especially the young, not to know the official names of relatives and other people. In a close-knit village, a person can be readily identified relationally or by a physical description so the need for someone to be formally addressed hardly arises. This provincialism affects the way that Cambodians give directions – by physical signposts, rather than by street names (even when they're literate and street names are high-ly visible), as villages do not have street names. When names are used, they are often shortened to only the last syllable: Mardi becomes 'Di' or 'Dee'; Sina 'Na'; Daravuth 'Vuth'.

When used, Cambodian names are written and given with the family name preceding the given name. For example, in Cambodia, I would introduce myself and others would refer to me formally as 'Seng Theary'.

Bong: Specifically, a wife (woman) uses this address for her husband (love), it means 'darling'. In a family, it is also an address for an older brother or sister. When generally employed, it is a respectful address for someone of your generation who is the same age or older than you (but not used by a woman for a man not her husband/love).

Aun: The feminine opposite of *Bong*. Specifically, a husband (man) uses this address for his wife (love); it means 'darling'. Generally, it means 'younger'.

Pou: In a family, it means 'uncle'. When employed generally, it is an address for a man of your parents' generation.

Mieng: The feminine opposite of *Pou*. In a family, it means 'aunt'. When employed generally, it is an address for a woman of your parents' generation.

Oum: In a family, the address is reserved for the 'aunt' or 'uncle' who is an older sibling of your parents. Generally, it is an address for a man or woman who is of your parents' generation, but older than them.

Ta: In a family, it means 'Grandpa' or 'Great Uncle'. When employed generally, it is an address for a man who is of your grandpa's generation.

Yay: The feminine opposite of *Ta*. In a family, it means 'Grandma' or 'Great Aunt'. When employed generally, it is an address for a woman of your grandma's generation.

Lauk: It is an honorific that means 'Sir'. It is also commonly used with the other addresses to make them more formal (and polite), i.e., 'Lauk Yay', 'Lauk Oum', 'Lauk Pou', etc. In this case, it can be both feminine and masculine.

À: Pronounced 'ah', it is used with a name or an address. Generally, it means 'contemptible', especially when used by a younger person to address any male, older or with status, i.e., À Pot (in reference to Pol Pot). (The feminine derogatory version of *À* is *Mi*.) Another example, it is normal for my older relatives, but unthinkable for me, to address any of my older brothers with an À; however, it's fine for me to call my youngest brother, À Vuth. In reference to a woman, it is used generally in an endearing manner, as in my nick-name, Asrei (or Asei, to make it even more familiar).

Asrei: My nickname is very common among Khmer girls; it comes from two words *À* and *Srei*, which means girl or female (a bit comparable to the French word *elle*).

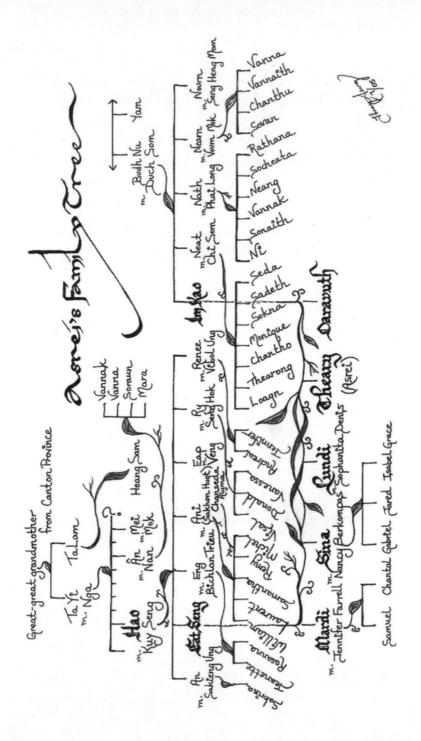

Sovry's Family Tree

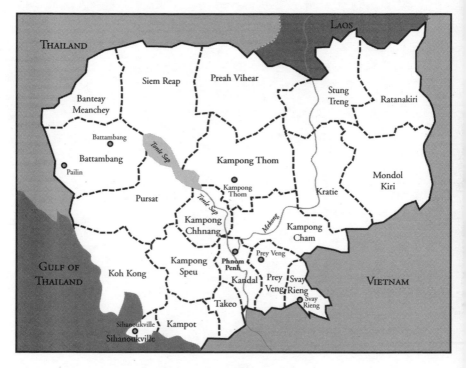

Map of pre-1990s Cambodia

DAUGHTER OF THE KILLING FIELDS

PROLOGUE

I am an orphan of the killing fields. As a toddler, the Khmer Rouge executed my father. A few years later, my last night in prison, my mother disappeared from my embrace into the night. Twenty-three years later, I confronted the public face of the regime, the Khmer Rouge head of state to Pol Pot's prime minister, Khieu Samphan. I hold him accountable for the deaths of my parents. I hold him accountable for the deaths of my relatives. I hold him accountable for the blood of 1.7 million others. He bears direct responsibility for these lives. The indirect damages he caused are beyond calculation. To this day, Khieu Samphan lives freely among his victims.

I met him in his house, an ostensibly humble wooden dwelling in Pailin, the regime stronghold in northwestern Cambodia. A few months before my encounter, Khieu Samphan had written an open letter to The *Cambodia Daily* proclaiming his innocence. He did not know that I was the author of the response to his open letter published in the same English-language newspaper, calling for his apprehension, as a moral imperative, a legal obligation and a strengthening of democratic governance.

I had arrived the day before into the mountainous, once gem-rich Pailin to train political party agents on the laws, regulations and procedures for the 3 February 2002 commune elections, a first in Cambodia's modern history. I flew on the dilapidated Presidents Airlines from Phnom Penh to the country's second largest town,

Battambang, and rode in a taxi for over two hours on remote newly built roads to forested Pailin. I had been to this jungle hamlet before.

In July 1998, I had joined the campaign trail of Cambodia's pro-democracy party and rode with its leader, Sam Rainsy, in his Landcruiser, among a caravan of political activists, international observers and rights workers. The vehicles gingerly manoeuvred on the war-shredded road the width of a wagon. Pockets of sedan-sized craters, several feet deep, marred the dirt path every few feet. Miniature red flags, ubiquitous as poppies in a field, warned passers-by of the danger of mines hiding in the thick side brushes and dense jungles hugging the narrow road. The Pailin hamlet had been opened to outsiders only a few weeks before our visit.

Three-and-a-half years later, the Pailin I encountered had new energy. The recently paved road had opened up this former guerrilla hideaway to more than a few adventurous souls and risk-taking journalists. This time I stayed on the top floor of a newly refurbished multi-storied hotel, prominently situated in a wide open field, replete with a garden and amenities only recently available – air conditioning, a telephone, colour television, flushing toilet and hot water. Rather than being grateful for these amenities, I missed the view of the mountain ranges on the other side of the wall. Even though I had a corner room, the window opened in the wrong direction, to the tail end of the silhouetted mountain vistas where only half a decade before thousands of Khmer Rouge soldiers roamed and strategised their comeback.

I learned of my meeting with my parents' murderer less than 24 hours before it was to take place. Over dinner, my seminar facilitator and host nonchalantly asked whether I would like to meet Khieu Samphan. My jaw dropped. 'Really?' I repeated, my gasp drowned by the loud band playing on stage a few feet away from our table.

'Yeah. I know him quite well. He's very impressed with democracy and could not have imagined its success a couple of decades ago,' explained my charismatic, young, handsome host.

I had yet to plan for the full-day seminar that was scheduled for 8 a.m. the next morning, but I had to speak with someone to release the overpowering weird, entangled sensation of giddiness, numbness and surrealism I felt. I could not grasp nor comprehend the magnitude of such an encounter. I telephoned my oldest brother in Massachusetts to talk, to give form to what I had been promised – an opportunity to meet face-to-face the architect of history's most heinous crimes against humanity.

In light of the region's sensitive political history, the next day I had to concentrate on the contents of my seminar and had little unfettered time to think about Khieu Samphan, but the impending meeting punctuated my thoughts. *Khieu Samphan, the world's madman. Khieu Samphan, the intelligent one among the mad brothers.* I had more immediate concerns regarding the potential explosion among the warring parties in attendance. *I've lived with a mentally incapacitated woman in prison, but have never met a madman before, especially one that is infamously so.* Two top former regional Khmer Rouge leaders, known for their brutality, shared the dais with me for the first half of the day. *Khieu Samphan, the popular teacher and government minister who shunned corruption and humbly rode rickshaws to work.* Khieu Samphan's closest aide, as I found out later, attended the seminar. He confirmed the meeting during our lunch break. *Khieu Samphan, always smiling in pictures. How could we have known there were so many daggers hidden in those smiles!* I ended the seminar by 2.30, an hour earlier than usual.

A colleague, my host, the driver and I jumped into our sedan and headed for Khieu Samphan's house on the outskirts of Pailin. *In a few minutes I'm going to be face-to-face with my past, the man of my nightmares, the killer of millions.* As the sedan pulled out of the temple gate, we ran into his aide, walking in his flip-flops to the same destination. He was at least 60 years old, taut, with leather skin, browned from the oppressive sun. At our invitation, he rode with us in the car. Five minutes later, we pulled into the dirt courtyard of a typical Khmer village dwelling, one in a row of similar simple blockhouses.

A man walked out of the wooden structure when he heard our car pull into his flimsily fenced-in dirt courtyard. My heart skipped a beat. I immediately recognised him as someone I knew well, even though we had never met. Of course, the familiarity came from public pictures. I stood face-to-face with evil incarnate, my parents' murderer. Instead of revulsion, a perverse sense of awe initially captured my emotions – for evil was not mad, but charming, gracious and grandfatherly.

CHAPTER ONE

The Deaths of Papa and Maman
(April 1975 – 1978)

The deaths of our parents drew my brothers and me close together; a common void pierced our souls. My youngest brother, Daravuth, had probably just reached his first birthday when my teacher-turned-soldier father was executed.

On 17 April 1975, a once rag-tag band of young soldiers triumphantly paraded through Cambodia's capital to the cheers and euphoria of the city's war-weary residents. '*Cheyo! Cheyo!* Victory! Victory!' shouted ecstatic Cambodians, as they waved makeshift white flags to welcome the war heroes. Some of my relatives joined in the jubilation. Peace was finally at hand. Like ostriches with their heads stuck in the sand, they were too intoxicated by the illusion of peace to be prescient of the awaiting evil.

The celebration was short-lived. The ill-humoured 'liberators' (known as the Khmer Rouge, although they had yet to obtain global notoriety) did not share in the people's ebullience. In fact, they disdained these city dwellers.

They had already consolidated their positions. Next, they ordered an immediate evacuation of Phnom Penh. 'The Americans are planning to drop bombs on the city,' they propagandised, 'so everyone must leave.'

Residents of Phnom Penh, including my relatives, did not need much convincing of the truth of American bellicosity. For five years, the United States had made an indelible impression on the Cambodian landscape and psyche. Craters the size of satellite dishes dotted the outskirts of Phnom Penh. No one knew for certain if it was the handiwork of the Americans, for determining who is friend or foe can be confusing during wartime. However, despite the people's ignorance of the perpetrators, the effects left no room for dispute.

Unlike a farmer's daughter, who at birth is greeted by the chirping of crickets and croaking of frogs, when I, kicking and screaming, entered the world, in 1971,* it was into a restless Phnom Penh that had already learnt to calibrate its existence to the cadence of war. The whistling, thunderclap and rhythmic pattering of the instruments of war provided the city's residents the background music for their daily existence.

On the morning of 17 April 1975, I woke up to something wonderfully different, a quietude palpably strange to those used to the clamorous sounds of war. A celebratory mood intoxicated the air. I could not have been more than four years old, but I sensed in the expressions of the adults a dramatic uplifting of spirit.

I love having Papa home, even though Maman keeps telling me not to bother him because he is not altogether well. I should go play with my brothers instead. I am so happy to have everyone so happy. Even Grandpa Kuy is in a good mood.

'We will now have peace, *santepheap*,' beamed my mother, floating about our apartment, freed from the tremendous weight that had been continually on her shoulders. It mattered little to her and our relatives that the victors were the same people against whom my father's battalion had been fighting. 'The shelling and

---

* My birth year was established from memories of my Uncle Ani Seng. He left for France in September 1971 and he remembers me as a baby who had not yet learnt to crawl.

bombings have ceased; that's all that matters now,' Maman concluded.

My relatives must not have been listening to radio broadcasts that had begun at 6.45 a.m.: 'Our party has gained victory 100 per cent over the traitorous Khmer Republic led by Lon Nol,' crackled the voice over Phnom Penh radio. 'Our party obtained this victory at gunpoint. Our party doesn't need to negotiate with any individual or party. Traitors have to be defeated. No one will receive the failure for them.'*

My mother went outside to cheer on the grim-faced newcomers, 'Cheyo! Bravo! Cheyo! Victory!'

A few Cambodians – and the foreigners in the diplomatic corps – knew better. Cambodia's head of state, General Lon Nol, had fled the country two weeks earlier. The flight of other members of Cambodia's political elite ensued, as they found safety in France or the United States. Others walked across borders into Thailand or Vietnam. Many of the Western embassies had already evacuated their essential and non-essential personnel. On 12 April, the Americans had folded their flag, closed down the embassy and left the country.

'Evacuate!' various voices shrilled through hand-held bullhorns, fanned across the capital. 'The Americans are going to drop bombs on the city!' Three-wheeled, motor-driven carts carrying megaphones were employed to disseminate the message: 'All people, please don't be chaotic, crossing here and there. Be prepared for moving out of the city for a period of time, maybe three days. Angkar needs to sweep up enemies.'**

From the rooftop of our penthouse apartment, just south of Wat Koh, we could see the young soldiers parading below, in eerie silence, on Monivong Boulevard.

* Documentation Center of Cambodia (DC-Cam), *Searching for the Truth*, 4 April 2000, p. 3–4.
** Ibid., p. 4.

Within hours, the mood of the adults quickly darkened. *I am confused by the confusion on the adults' faces. Why is everyone fretting about the apartment? Why are they packing? 'Maman, are we going somewhere? Mieng, Auntie, where are we going? Lauk Yay, Grandma, can I come along?'* The adults continued to pack frantically, and I wandered amidst the chaos, my queries left unanswered. *I hate it when big people ignore me. I will never be like that when I am bigger.*

'Evacuate!' persisted the voices shrilling through the same handheld bullhorns and wheeled megaphones.

A sea of faces filled the boulevards of Phnom Penh.* Pandemonium seized the city once known as the Paris of Southeast Asia, as its two million bewildered residents exited to the countryside. (Ironically, the fighting and explosions in the countryside during the previous five years had resulted in a steady stream of refugees into the capital, burgeoning the city's population of a little over half a million more than fourfold. Now, by fiat, they had to leave it again.)

Except for the staff of a few foreign embassies sympathetic to communism, the Khmer Rouge cadre and the so-called 'anti-Angkar elements', Phnom Penh was literally transformed into a ghost town within three days. (The meaning of the word Angkar is the omniscient, omnipresent Khmer Rouge authority or 'Organisation'.)

Similar outward migration occurred in other towns and cities throughout Cambodia. No location was exempt. Thereafter, for a period of almost four years, all the towns and cities across Cambodia stood vacant, as their former residents slaved away in newly-created labour camps in the countryside.

My family drifted along with the ebb and flow, joining the

---

* For the November 2004 Boat Festival, I witnessed from the third-floor apartment balcony overlooking the river near the palace an inkling of what the exodus of 17 April must have been like. A current of human bodies, moving shoulder to shoulder, flowed on Sisowath Quay for miles along the river.

stream of people leaving the city. From our house, we turned right onto Trasak Paem Street, away from the central market, where a group of Khmer Rouge soldiers was setting up a security checkpoint for enemies, *khmang*. Upon reaching Sihanouk Boulevard, we weaved left among the heavy traffic of human bodies. Independence Monument, with its naga motif, was in front of us. Upon reaching this landmark, we turned right, onto Norodom Boulevard, which took us south to the 'head of road', Kbal Khnal.

Patients evacuated from the city's hospitals limped along; some still strapped in their beds were pushed by relatives. The old and the infirm tried desperately to fight off the heat, the deluge of bodies and carts, and exhaustion. The crying of babies and outbursts of young children contributed to the cacophony.

Some 20,000 Cambodians died in the mass exodus from Phnom Penh.

The journey weighed heavily on my father, who had yet to recover from his war wounds. He had been hospitalised since the beginning of March, and it was only at the request of my mother that he had been released a few days prior to the exodus. With the increase in bombing attacks on Phnom Penh, she wanted all of her family together. White gauze patched the left eye he lost in combat.

My mother carried baby Daravuth, and different relatives took turns carrying or pushing me on one of the mopeds. The rest of the family – my maternal grandparents, my three aunts and my three older brothers, Mardi, Sina and Lundi – carried the belongings we had hurriedly packed in the exigencies of the moment required. Grandma and Maman took with them US dollar bills and all the family jewellery, secreting gold, diamond and other valuable pieces inside their bodies and clothes. (My mother's three brothers and their maternal uncle had left for France and the United States to further their studies in the early 1970s.)

My eyes absorbed the scenes around me. Immediately to my right, a mother carried on her hip – in traditional Cambodian manner, the way my mom was carrying Daravuth – a daughter not much younger than me. The slight frame of the woman leaned steeply to one side under the weight of the little girl. The girl shifted her head to rest on the shoulder blade of the mother, facing me. Tears stained her face, as her body heaved back and forth from the choking motion of her crying.

'I'm going to pinch you again if you don't stop crying,' threatened the woman. 'Do you want to be left here by yourself?' Strains of exasperation dribbled out of the woman's voice.

I quickly averted my eyes, embarrassed to be caught witnessing her distress. I returned to surveying the crowd. With amazing ease, women balanced baskets heaped full of housewares, while expertly dodging cars, mopeds, bicycles, carts and people. The relatively few motor vehicles manoeuvred their way through the sea of pedestrians, honking all the way. The wrangling and discordance of the moment enchanted me.

Along the boulevards, young men, toting guns, yelled out orders. Their loose, black uniforms mirrored the dark grimace of their countenance. *Why do they look so angry?* I wondered.

My eyes rested on my father. I studied his handsome face with its perfectly shaped nose and large almond eyes. Little bubbles of perspiration were evident where his black silky hair met his forehead. His worried face suddenly lit up into a broad smile as he caught me observing him. I returned the smile.

The travel moved laggardly. We walked for half a day and hardly covered a noticeable distance.

Out of nowhere, a Khmer Rouge soldier accosted our group and jerked my father by the arm. 'You're a Lon Nol soldier?' he flashily accused.

'No, I am a teacher,' my father replied.

'Why the patch over your eye?'

'A rocket landed in my school and debris hit my eye,' my father lied.

The soldier stood there for a few seconds, weighing the plausibility of my father's answer, and then strutted away as quickly as he had arrived. We heaved a collective sigh of relief. The chill subsided. And we continued on.

The tropical sun beat down on us, and hunger racked our exhausted bodies. April is the hottest month in Cambodia, with temperatures often above 100 degrees Fahrenheit. My father had tried removing his eye patch to decrease suspicion of his military background, but the dust and oppressive heat quickly irritated the vacuous eye and he had to cover it again.

'My feet hurt,' grumbled an aunt, joined by a chorus of others.

Grandpa Kuy suggested we rest and directed us to a small, beautiful white house to the side of the street. As we neared, we noticed a few broken windows and several families resting in the courtyard.

We proceeded inside. We could see no one. Strange. Why were the families resting outside under the humid sun and not finding shade inside the house? As we turned into the living room, the answer confronted us in the rawest form of human savagery. On the floor sprawled a family of five bodies, soaked in blood from head to toe. We quickly exited and joined the other families in the yard. The civil war of the last five years had numbed our emotions and the bloody scene failed to elicit any visible sign of stupefaction from us.

Soon after we left that white house of dead bodies, less than a quarter of a mile away, Lauk Ta (Grandpa) asked Mardi to fetch water for the family, especially for the children who were grumbling with thirst. He headed for the nearest house. Along the way, he noticed a boy not much older than himself, not yet a decade old.

The boy had on an adult, green camouflage army jacket too large for his thin frame. A Khmer Rouge soldier walked up to him, grabbed him by the collar, held a pistol to the boy's temple and fired.

Stragglers and dissenters were usually executed on the spot.

Life is but a breath.

When night descended, we camped along the road and huddled together to sleep as comfortably as we possible could under the circumstances. An aerial view would have shown thousands of clusters of weary travellers sprawled on all the major arteries leading away from Phnom Penh, resting for the night, stitches on a social and political fabric that was quickly unraveling.

'I want to go home,' I pleaded. I fidgeted from the great discomfort caused by the mixture of dust and extreme heat in the flowery sundress my mother had made for me.

'Stop being a baby!' came a sharp rebuke from one of my elders.

Three days later, we arrived at Wat Champa, an ornately decorated temple complex located off National Route One, about ten miles from Kbal Khnal, where the city limits of Phnom Penh end and Kien Svay in Kandal province begins. My family entered a pathway lined by tall trees, which led from the welcoming temple archway to a fenced-in plot of levelled ground the length of a soccer field. There was a forest of stupas and mausoleums of various sizes in the area to our immediate right.

We proceeded further and found space in the main temple, a low, concrete building that was the nucleus of the temple complex. Adjacent to this building was a wooden structure, raised on stilts, that proudly boasted the date of its construction, 1960, in blue ink on the post of the stairwell; it provided shelter to a number of other families. We unloaded our belongings and slept on mats amidst the patchwork of other mats on which other families unpacked their belongings and slept. Many families who arrived after us could not find room in the sheltered buildings and stayed in the courtyard, propping up their belongings against the many elegant trees that shaded the temple grounds.

News of a resistance movement captured my father's attention. Different theories about the political situation were circulating. Soon, announcements requesting the return of all former civil servants and military personnel to central Phnom Penh blared through loudspeakers; their assistance was needed. Moreover, if the head of the household returned to the capital, Angkar would feed and take care of his family during his absence.

My father heeded the call, partly out of curiosity, to obtain more information, and partly to stock up on food and various other provisions the family had neglected to pack for the trip. It was now the third day of what we had been told was a three-day evacuation, and we were out of food. We had eaten all the cooked rice that we had brought along, packed in the ornate, stacked, silver containers customarily used to hold food for temple offerings.

Papa reasoned, 'Let me investigate the situation. If nothing else, I'll bring back rice sacks from our house and we'll have food.'

'Darling, *Bong*, don't go,' my mother beseeched my father, with visible concern etched on her face, which was still elegant despite the trauma of the past weeks and the dust and heat of the journey. 'You're not fully recovered yet.'

'Papa, where are you going, *tuy na*?' I enquired.

He picked me up. I leaned my face into his and our noses touched. 'Oh, you're getting to be a lady. Soon, I won't be able to pick you up anymore.'

'Please, don't go,' I repeated my mom's entreaty and gingerly caressed the patch covering his eye.

'Papa has to go. But I will come back. Do you know you're my most favourite daughter?' I broke into giggles and feigned embarrassment, a child in complete confidence of her family's love and attention.

'Papa,' I chided him, 'but I'm your only daughter.'

'Be a good girl for Papa. Now, give Papa a big kiss.' I promised him I would, pressed my face against his, and rubbed my nose against his cheek.

Not until several months later did it dawn upon us that the Khmer Rouge had lured former Lon Nol soldiers and civil servants – the enemies of the new regime who had betrayed the nation *(kbot cheat)* – to their death.

≈ ≈ ≈

The Khmer Rouge executed many of these men immediately.* They transported them west in military convoy trucks and disposed of them at Pich Nil.** Their remains testify to unspeakable barbarity.

The other men, once captured by Angkar, atrophied for a time in Tuol Sleng prison before they were executed. Tuol Sleng, or 'S-21' (Security Office 21), was the name of the Khmer Rouge's premier security apparatus; it was housed in a former high school in southern Phnom Penh.*** It served as the interrogation, torture and extermination centre of those 'elements' who were thought to oppose the new Democratic Kampuchea, the ironic nomenklatura of the Leninist-Marxist regime. Other branches of S-21 existed elsewhere around the outskirts of Phnom Penh, but Tuol Sleng

---

* I learnt this in conversations I had with Craig Etcheson, who worked from its early days with the Yale Genocide Program, which created the Documentation Center of Cambodia.

** Conversation with Ung Bun-Ang. Pich Nil is half way between Phnom Penh and sea resort Sihanoukville. Now, whenever I escape Phnom Penh for Sihanoukville, I am constantly reminded of Papa as I pass through this lush mountainous part of Pich Nil.

*** Information on Tuol Sleng prison retrieved from the Documentation Center of Cambodia.

served as the nerve centre. It covered an area of 600 by 400 metres and was enclosed by double sheets of corrugated iron topped off with electrified barbed wire. Nearby, what were once residential homes served as offices or interrogation sites.

At Tuol Sleng, the classrooms were converted into prison cells. Iron bars and barbed wire blocked the windows. The Organisation sectioned off the ground floor into tiny cells for individual prisoners. Other prisoners were crammed en masse into cells on the top floor. Female prisoners were held on the middle floor – and were regularly raped.

The authority trained children to serve as guards and medical personnel; these young revolutionaries used their unbridled power with exceptional savagery and childish ignorance.

The Tuol Sleng prison administrators, under the infamous prison director Duch,* kept meticulous records. During their four years in power, the Khmer Rouge fastidiously recorded the inflow and outflow of prisoners. Many files are lost, but documents survive for some 16,000 inmates. This figure also does not include the large number of children who were killed at the prison. Less than a handful of prisoners are known to have survived this reign of terror.

The prison administrators photographed each of the inmates and through torture extracted 'confessions' from which they compiled detailed biographies for their records, before the prisoner was stripped down to his or her underclothes and shackled to the iron bars that ran across the classrooms' chequered floors.

Possibly my father was one of the countless undocumented prisoners detained in 1975. Records survive for only 154 of the prisoners incarcerated that year.

The life span of a prisoner in Tuol Sleng averaged two to four months, or six to seven months for important political prisoners.

---

* His official name is Kaing Khek Iev.

On 27 May 1978, Director Duch signed 582 death warrants, the highest number for a single day.

During this time, all prisoners were awakened every morning at 4.30 for inspection and were ordered by the prison staff to pull their underpants down to the ankles. While chained, prisoners defecated into small iron buckets and urinated into small plastic ones; permission for relief was required in advance. Twenty to forty strokes of a whip awaited those who failed to follow orders.

Posted on blackboards in each cell was the following:

1. You* must answer accordingly to my questions. Do not turn them away.
2. Do not try to hide the facts by making pretexts of this or that. You are strictly prohibited to contest me.
3. Do not be a fool for you are a man who dares to thwart the revolution.
4. You must immediately answer my questions without wasting time to reflect.
5. Do not tell me either about your immoralities or the revolution.
6. While receiving lashes or electrification, you must not cry at all.
7. Do nothing. Sit still and wait for my orders. If there are no orders, keep quiet. When I ask you to do something, you must do it right away without protesting.
8. Do not make pretexts about Kampuchea Krom [now southern Vietnam] in order to hide your traitorous jaw.
9. If you don't follow the above rules, you shall receive many lashes of electric wire.
10. If you disobey any point of my regulations, you shall receive either ten lashes or five shocks of electric discharge.

* The derogatory form of 'you' and 'me' was used.

Life is but a breath.

I have visited Tuol Sleng, which is now a genocide museum, several times. Each time, I have studied the photographs of the faces of the prisoners – some of them looking terror-stricken, some languid and some impassive – searching for one particular sweet countenance to match the few grainy, black-and-white pictures I have of my father.

I have yet to find a match, for I have yet to finish viewing the many haunting expressions covering the walls of the memorial. I have yet to build up a sufficiently strong resistance to human agony to satisfy my curiosity.

If I could not grieve for you then, a lifetime since then I have grieved, and I am grieving for you now, dear Papa. You, who gave life to me, had but a breath to live yourself. Did the toddler-me grieve your loss, for certainly the moment you bid the eternal farewell a light in me must have been extinguished?

It is only in the wistful memories of others that I have come to know you, to construct a caricature that is limited by the simplicity of my imagination. At times you are but a character to me, as with a hero I love in the pages of a good novel. But at other times the thought of you excites such personal feelings, for no fictional character can evoke this knowledge that I am half of you.

≈ ≈ ≈

My family restlessly waited for Papa, camping on the outskirts of Phnom Penh where he left us. Most of the population had moved on, many to their ancestral villages, many to their deaths. But many families also stayed to await their loved ones, crowding the spacious Wat Champa.

The Khmer Rouge soldiers stayed true to their promise to provide us with an adequate rice ration. For one month. It was now the middle of May; and the start of the monsoon season dashed to pieces their promise of food. Our hopes of home and the embrace of Papa were crushed under the weight of thundering torrential rain that daily flooded a swath of our earth. Sheets of rain swayed in and out of the open arches of our temple home.

The soldiers stopped giving us rice grain. Instead, they gave us *samlay*, grain of cotton, an inedible diet that quickened the deaths of first the children and the elderly, then the rest. As certain as the coming of the rain, and the rising and setting of the sun, death struck these listless waiters of loved ones, ticking off one child by illness followed by one woman by starvation, first once or twice a week, then every other day. Not long after, Death knocked as a daily occurrence.

Many more weeks passed.

Once healthy strong bodies transformed into ghost-like figures stripped of dignity and grace, no longer recognisable as human beings. Even their defecation resembled that of animal and bird droppings.

The living dead buried the physically dead on the temple grounds. For the children, these new cemetery grounds formed part of our playground, for those of us who had energy left to play.

As much as possible, my family avoided eating the *samlay* grain. Even at our nadir of desperation, we would at least cook a mixture of the *samlay* with rice grain. My mother put her business acumen to good use. She would cross the nearby river to trade with villagers gold and silver for food, to supplement the meagre diet. Despite the supplementary portion, our family was not saved from the fury of diseases that was befalling the other families.

Aunt Ry fell gravely ill with a very high fever. The crown of Khmer beauty, her long black silky hair, fell out; the sister who always had been popular with the boys was now bald. Rey, the youngest sister, also became deathly sick. As the oldest sister, Maman pushed both of them in a wheelbarrow to neighbouring Kien Svay, several miles away, to find medicine and get treatment. They were too sick to walk, waiting only to die.

Death surrounded us; hunger suffocated us and made us delirious. A child immediately to our right starved to death. A woman in front of us died in her sleep. Each family, save ours, experienced at least one or two members who died during the duration of our stay in Wat Champa.

One day, a Khmer Rouge soldier, a security officer, *nek santisok*, quietly approached my mother. '*Bong Srei,** move on. Take your family to your village. There will be food there. Don't stay here too long. Don't wait for *Bong Proh*** any more. If I wanted to kill *Bong Proh*, I could have shot and killed him a long time ago. But I refused to kill him because he treated everyone so well.'

It turned out that this sympathetic Khmer Rouge soldier had infiltrated the battalion under my father's command and had recognised my mother from her field visits to the trenches. He detailed how my father used to take my mother on motorbike joyrides to Neak Loung. He convinced my mother that he knew her well.

He never expressly told my mother the fate of my father, but he did urge her to leave and not wait any longer, because 'most likely, he will not be coming back.'

A few days later, the authority ordered us all to evacuate Wat Champa to go work in Neak Loung, the transit port where National Route One and the Mekong River intersect, between Phnom Penh and Vietnam. But we received news from different sources – first a maimed escapee from Neak Loung and then the whisperings that rustled with the monsoon breeze of those who had secretly been listening to radio broadcasts – which converged in a

* A generic, respectable address for an older female.
** A generic, respectable address for an older male.

uniform interdiction: 'Don't go to Neak Loung.' The place was soaked in landmines. Only suffering and death existed there.

That evening, the black pyjama-clad soldiers herded everyone in the direction of Neak Loung, along National Route One. The first time the soldiers looked away, all my family members quickly ducked into the side brushes in the direction of the river, a short journey of half a kilometre from the temple's back gate.

Maman went with Ta Kuy to hire a boat from a fisherman; she had done this on numerous prior occasions during her excursions to trade in precious stones for food. She knew her route and the terrain on the other side of the river.

Initially, it was questionable whether the canoe-shaped boat could carry everyone. It teeter-tottered as the five adult women, three children, one toddler and a baby either jumped or were carried onto it with their belongings. The weight nearly levelled the edge of the boat with the river's surface.

Already dangerously full beyond capacity, the boat could not accept the weight of another person, Grandpa Kuy. Fortunately, he knew how to swim, the only one in the family who did, and so helped the owner of the boat steer by pushing it from the water. The monsoon rain of the last few months expanded the width of the already-wide section of this body of water to half a kilometre, from Kien Svay in the direction of Prey Veng province.

'Maman, I'm afraid,' I pierced the tense air with my small voice, snuggling against the side of my mother.

'Ssshhh. It's okay. There's nothing to fear,' she comforted me. But I could feel the tension in her body.

'Where's Papa?' I enquired. 'I miss Papa.'

'Stop talking,' hissed an older relative.

Maman remained quiet. Her body quivered and she tightly squeezed hold of me at her side, bones against bones, for both of us had lost a lot of weight waiting for Papa.

Having arrived safely on the other side, we walked to the nearest village. A villager, a complete stranger, gave us shelter in his humble dwelling. At night, we squeezed under the small thatched hut with his family to sleep away from the torrential downpour.

We stayed with him for a little over one week. Grandma and Grandpa went with him to the village chief to ask for permission to settle in the village. Although sympathetic, the chief refused the request because the village was already full. There were no available dwellings to house us.

The saintly villager packed a lot of food for us as we prepared again to move to an unknown destination.

We tried the next village. The grandparents vaguely knew someone there. Again, the village chief turned us away because of lack of space.

A dilemma confronted the family: where should they go next?

One or two voices suggested an escape to Vietnam, 'We already have some relatives living there.'

Grandpa Kuy and Maman wanted to go to Svay Rieng, a province about 90 miles southeast of Phnom Penh, where he had spent his boyhood years and she had lived during a more idyllic time. He wanted to return to Prey Roka, a village in Svay Rieng, to be among relatives and familiarity. My mother insisted that we go to Chensa, a village two miles from Prey Roka, where her in-laws were a prominent landowning family. She secretly clung on to the hope that her husband was still alive and would come to find us there. He never came.

Grandma, in exasperation, chimed in, 'Let's just stay here. They're not just going to let us die! We're in the middle of the monsoon season.* Our childhood village is too far away. Travelling will be difficult. And what if our relatives are no longer living there?'

* The rainy season is May to October.

The irascible Ta Kuy hotly concluded, 'We have many relatives there; at least one person we know will yet be alive.'

Of course, everyone knew the decision had already been made when Ta Kuy spoke the first time, because whatever he said goes.

We took the wheels of a moped and made an ox-cart out of them to carry all our belongings.

Deep in melancholy, my family rejoined the tail end of the exodus heading southeast in the direction of Svay Rieng. We marched to the rhythm of the falling rain drumming in our ears and soaking our bodies. The torrents swallowed little Daravuth's crying sounds. Maman wrapped him tighter and pressed him closer to her body in an embrace to provide a human shield against the blustering monsoon downpour. The monsoon whipped its fury in the whimsical manner and capricious direction of a force of nature that knows it has bowed trees and fields to its will, unchallenged for centuries.

'I'm hungry,' I groaned, barely audible in the heavy rain, into Sina's ear. He had been giving me a piggyback ride. He remained silent. He must not have heard me.

I repeated myself, 'I'm hungry,' and then started to whimper. No one took notice as the rain drowned out the sound.

The family silently and listlessly marched on to the pitter-pattering of the raindrops, replacing the previous swooshes and howlings.

≈ ≈ ≈

'Did you know Maman was raped?' Sina quietly asks me 25 years later, in a rare moment of brother-sister bonding in front of the television set in his newly-built home in the heart of mid-western USA. He had safeguarded the secret until now. The revelation dealt a blow to my inner core; the loss of air leaving me temporarily devoid of reaction.

'During our exodus from Phnom Penh to Svay Rieng, we often

had to trade gold for food along the way. On one occasion, Mardi and I went with Maman. A soldier accosted us. At gun point, he took her behind a bush and violated her.'

'Where were the two of you?' I ask him accusingly.

I have never thought of my mother more beautiful and noble than I did that moment. St. Augustine's wisdom echoes in my mind, that violation of chastity, without the will's consent, cannot pollute the character.* My mother never mentioned the crime to any of her sisters.

The boys were under ten years old.

'We just stood there,' he replies, keeping his solemn monotone. 'Maman reported him to the village chief, but he was nowhere to be found.'

≈ ≈ ≈

Having walked 90 miles, through most of the monsoon season, my mother, four brothers, maternal grandparents, three maternal aunts and I arrived at Prey Roka, one of the poorest villages in Svay Rieng province, a condition besetting the villagers even before the Khmer Rouge era.

Hearing of our arrival, my father's father, Ta Duch, who lived in *Phum* (village) Chensa, came to greet us.

'Upon hearing of the fall of Phnom Penh, I went to look for you, bringing you food. But it was impossible to find you amidst the crowd of people,' he ruefully related his failed expedition.

'All of you cannot stay here. Come, live with us in Chensa, where it is more prosperous. The situation in Prey Roka is not good,' he said ominously.

---

* St. Augustine, *The City of God*, Book I, Chapter 16. This explains my inclusion of this revelation in this memoir, not to disrespect the memory of my mother, as thought by one incensed aunt when she first learnt of this incident upon reading a draft of this memoir, but precisely for the opposite reason. If we say no shame befalls the woman, why then should we act and react as if that was the case?

The two grandpas were childhood best friends and they decided that everyone would move to Chensa. However, in a society where the exercise of power is arbitrary and often overreaching, they first needed to procure the permission of the village chief, Lo, a child-hood acquaintance of our family.* Lo refused. He could not believe his luck upon the arrival of these uppity relations and former neigh-bours from Phnom Penh, who now had to bow to his authority. The situation was too delicious for him to allow to escape through his fingers.

More on *À* (contemptible) Lo later as life under Angkar unfolds.

After a bit of wrangling, he finally relented to Ta Duch's subse-quent request that his daughter-in-law and grandchildren come to live with him in Chensa.

At that moment, my immediate family parted ways from my maternal grandparents and three aunts, as they settled into life under the watch of À Lo in Prey Roka, and we in Chensa. During the next three years, even though we lived only two miles from each other, we would see them only on a few occasions and mainly in secret.

We arrived at the farmhouse of my father's parents in Chensa towards the end of the monsoon season, November 1975.

Naturally, my mother's in-laws enquired the whereabouts of their son and oldest brother, my father. We had no answer for them.

My mother, a very successful businesswoman, joined my father in the after-world two years later. For the first seven years of my life, I had a mother. The year my mother died was 1978; the place: a prison compound somewhere in western Svay Rieng, Cambodia,

---

* My maternal relatives in the United States described Lo as a nephew of Grandma Hao by marriage. Relatives in Cambodia described him more ominously as the 'man who takes other men's wives', who was the lover of Mok, Grandma Hao's sister-in-law.

known as Bung Rei. According to the Documentation Center, 20,000 to 30,000 people were believed to have been killed there.

The story begins six or seven months earlier. During this time, Cambodia and Vietnam were caught in a full-scale war in Svay Rieng province, part of what the Khmer Rouge designated the Eastern Zone. The rank-and-file and residents of the Eastern Zone became the victims of Pol Pot's paranoia as the Central Committee in Phnom Penh carried out internal purges.

According to Elisabeth Becker's *When the War Was Over*, '...the Center decided the entire zone was tainted as a haven of traitors. Whole villages were emptied and slaughtered ... The Eastern Zone erupted with waves and waves of butchery. Whole villages of people were moved to nearby fields and clubbed to death. The thick whacking sound of axe handles bludgeoning people at the neck was heard over and over again.'*

Phum Chensa sits less than 15 miles from the border Cambodia shares with its aggressive eastern neighbour, Vietnam. Around the turn of the new year, 1978, until Vietnam's full-scale invasion into Cambodia, the battlefront deadlocked a few miles away from our village. According to Elisabeth Becker,** in December 1977, Vietnam committed 60,000 soldiers into Cambodia against the Khmer Rouge's 28,000. It used sophisticated helicopter gunships and tanks, while the Khmer Rouge resorted to guerrilla tactics. The Vietnamese soldiers pushed across Svay Rieng province all the way to Neak Loung, the main Mekong River crossing point to the capital. When they decided they had made their point, they retreated. There were three main incursions.

The first was in late 1977/early 1978. The receding Khmer Rouge soldiers took refuge in my village of Chensa. All the villagers were pushed inwards to another village away from the new battlefield.

* Elisabeth Becker, *When the War Was Over: Cambodia and the Khmer Rouge Revolution*, Public Affairs, New York, 1998, p. 313.
** Ibid., p. 310–11.

Each time there was an incursion, we would be uprooted for a day or a couple of weeks from our village home.

On this occasion, they granted permission for my paternal grandfather Duch to stay in order to attend to his tobacco crop. One day, the soldiers occupying our house offered Ta Duch a bowl of soup. He accepted their generosity. Because the soup brimmed to the top, Ta Duch reflexively poured out some of the broth onto the dirt courtyard. The soldiers took offence at this act as condescension. They arrested and bound him, and hung him upside down off a tree on his property.

Several days later, we returned to our village because the Vietnamese soldiers had pulled more back as the Khmer Rouge soldiers advanced on them. Ta Duch was nowhere to be found.

In the afternoon of that first day, we were told news that my mother, brothers and I would be killed.

Mardi, Sina, and Lundi arrived home that evening from attending water buffaloes. They at once noticed the authority, including two or three faces they hadn't seen before, from the gate.

Upon seeing their presence, Lundi immediately jumped off his water buffalo, dropped whatever he was carrying, shrieked in terror and ran. 'I don't want to die!'

Sina stood there expressionless. The boys knew what their presence meant because they had seen friends who had been visited by the authority disappear. The next day they would find their friends' clothes worn by children of Angkar.

There was a large gathering of people at Ta Duch's farmhouse, in the dirt courtyard in front of the raised wooden dwelling. Maman and my paternal aunts convulsed with tears. Lauk Yay (our paternal grandma) tried to comfort little Daravuth and me. We were understandably disturbed by the funereal scene and joined in the wailing. My frail, thinly-framed, 80-something-year-old great-grandmother sat there, moved into silent paralysis.

Maman approached the boys. The corners of her mouth trembling, she informed them, 'They will take us tonight.'

The boys did not question the 'they' of her statement for Mardi and Sina automatically understood. It was the same elusive 'they' the family had encountered since that first day Phnom Penh fell.

The boys' strength left them.

Maman encouraged us to eat.

The sun was setting and Lundi was nowhere to be found. Sina and Mardi went to look for him and found him asleep in an old storage hut. He had cried himself to sleep, hiding there.

No, he had not dreamt the last couple of hours. Sleep only temporarily suspended the inevitable. The two older brothers brought Lundi back to the house.

Darkness descended. A large gathering of family members joined in the mournful congregation to bid us goodbye.

Finally, the armed men dressed in their signature black pyjamas appeared. They had Grandpa Duch with them. His arms were tied at the elbows behind his back. They had aimlessly led him on a walking tour the last three days, extracting information from him on the background of his new relations, my family.

'I don't want to die! Don't let me go! ' Lundi choked with spasms. He clung onto and wildly pleaded with my great-grandmother to save him, as fresh tears streamed out his eyes.

Great-grandma stared blankly into the darkness of the night; her lined sunken cheeks and thin, aged lips trembled. Her fingers ran through his hair. Stricken with grief, she passed away later that night. Infinite sorrow broke her heart.

Two men tied my mother's arms behind her back, above the elbows. Mardi carried my youngest brother Daravuth, who could not have been more than four years old at that time. Sina held my hand. Lundi carried a sack of extra clothes. Four armed men led the seven of us, including Grandpa Duch, into the night.

We proceeded in a line, sandwiched in by the black-attired men.
We walked.
And stumbled.
And groped.
And walked some more through the pitch-black night.
Eventually, our eyes adjusted to the darkness.

Barefoot and in complete silence, mother, children and grand-father submissively resigned to death and helplessly tottered towards its beckoning. The gods had refused salvation, and the power of the darkness ever more strongly enveloped us into its fold. We were invisible to human eyes as half of the world slept and the other half busied themselves handling modernity – all oblivious of the evil convulsing Cambodia, in particular, the drama played out that long, lonely night. The night obscured us from the gods, from all hope.

But we still had our breath. We continued walking. Our silhou-ettes outlined against the midnight sky, we marched to the throbbing of our individual heartbeat.

How many times had this scene been played out before, in our village, in Svay Rieng, in the whole of Cambodia? Who at that moment shared our paralysing fears, the thumping in our hearts and our unutterable scream for life? What is it in the human make-up that tells us we prefer life over death? Is the unknown death not better than the known life, which is an idiot's tale, full of sound and fury?

It was unknown territory, even to my older brothers who had wandered far and wide tending to water buffaloes. We lost all sense of direction. My seven-year-old body ached with pain from walk-ing across endless rice fields. Several times, Maman and Ta Duch lost their balance as they staggered on the uneven narrow earth paths without the use of their arms.

An eternity later, we noticed the shadow of a structure. It was a prison. The face of death was postponed to be encountered another night. But fatigue offset any inclination we may have had to be jubilant.

They chained the ankles of everyone save Daravuth and me. We fell straight to sleep, drained of emotions and physically exhausted, in the middle of that night, in a prison somewhere in Svay Rieng province, not knowing nor caring what the future held. We were grateful for relief, no matter how precarious and slept soundly the night through.

We woke up to a brilliant morning. Life! We are alive, this beautiful phrase whispered in each of our ears.

We took note of our surroundings. We were in the middle of nowhere; no signs of village life could be detected from the prison. We stayed in a cabin, among several other cabins, made of split bamboo shoots, raised above the ground. We were among 40 other prisoners from what we could perceive; this number waxed and waned immeasurably during our stay.

They separated my grandfather from us and we found out later that the authority released him only a few days before the disappearance of my mother.

My four brothers and I were the only juveniles detained in the prison. At night we slept in a room shared with other prisoners who were given more freedom. A rusted, long iron pipe ran across the room, holding pairs of shackles. They clamped both ankles of each prisoner each night. Side by side, flat on our backs, chained, we would sleep the night through. Daravuth and I were free of shackles because we were very young and our bony ankles could slide in and out of them. Consequently, our freedom secured us the job of bringing a toilet bucket to prisoners at night.

In our room lived a mentally insane woman. She had coarse, knotted un-kept hair and possessed an appearance of one completely devoid of human capacity. She often foamed at the mouth. She would wake us up periodically with her nonsensical babbling. One night she startled us with her delirious shrieking, 'I'm thirsty! I'm thirsty!' Since the toilet bucket was within her reach, she wildly took hold of it and swallowed the excrement and urine from it. I reacted too late to pull away the bucket from her.

Later in our stay, the guards publicly killed her. They sat her in the middle of the central courtyard, tied up. Then they took the wooden coconut cruncher and squeezed her head until her cranium cracked.

It was an experiment in cruelty, a virus of death plaguing the land. Possibly, a new form of creativity. More likely, an amusement to pass the languid day. Did an eruption of laughter and merriment ensue or is it only a figment of my dulled memory?

'As flies to wanton boys are we to the gods; they kill us for their sport.' The sentiments of blinded, old Gloucester echoed from Shakespeare's *King Lear* through the ages, across the continents, against the cultural morass, to the heart of darkness that was the Cambodian experience.

She was a daughter, possibly someone's sister or wife – what must have become of them? What is the threshold for pain before a constitution breaks down to pure incapacity? Maybe it would have been better if she had not felt so intensely, if she had not loved deeply, if she had not desperately missed her loved ones. Maybe she would not have suffered so much if she had been less than human, if she had steeled herself against all feelings, all emotions. How many deaths did she die before that final crack?

And what to think of the monsters who became less than human. How will they account for their action before the all-consuming Judge? What could they possibly say? Is there not a limit to human degeneracy?

Death is a mystery. And life is but a breath.

*

During the day, my chores included picking up dried cow and buffalo manure for fertiliser. I carried a basket against my hip or balanced on my head like the older women. Sometimes, I would pick up dung that I believed had dried but it would split in half as I dropped it into the basket. The inside of the green dung was yet too moist.

I had much time to myself during these days as I wandered alone among the gravesites and blood-drenched fields, eyes darting back and forth in search of animal dung. I had gotten so used to the stench sizzling out of the ground that I didn't have to wrinkle my nose as much anymore. Rather, at times, gaiety freed my spirit that I would hum tunes Angkar taught us and practiced vocabulary new to my seven-year-old mind.

> Our red flag is born from the blood of workers, peasants,
> intellectuals, monks, youth, and women who
> have sacrificed themselves to free our people.
> There it is waving! gloriously!
> Comrades, ahead! Smash the enemy!
> There it is waving! gloriously!
> Our implacable hatred towards the enemy embraces our heart.
> There it is waving! gloriously!
> We annihilate the imperialists, the reactionaries!
> We scour the soil of Kampuchea!
> Ahead! Ahead! We wrest victory!*

I liked the tune. Singing put a spring into my steps. The meaning eluded my comprehension. I didn't care. The polysyllabic vocabularies escaped my pronunciation. I didn't care. It was often difficult to make my tongue correctly pronounce certain words the way the

* Khing Hoc Dy, 'Khmer Literature since 1975' in *Cambodian Culture Since 1975: Homeland and Exile*, May M. Ebihara, Carol A. Mortland and Judy Ledgerwood, eds., Cornell University Press, 1994.

adults pronounced them. But I had the privacy of the open fields to say the words over and over again to loosen my tongue into the right pronunciation. I hummed over those words my young mouth could not form.

When I was not in the fields searching for animal manure, I helped my mother out in the central courtyard of the prison compound. As my mother stepped up and down on the wooden grinder to pound on the bushels of rice stems, I sifted the beaten rice. Customarily, Cambodians pour two or three cups worth of grounded rice grain onto a tightly woven bamboo plate. The wooden plate is slightly tilted and shaken in a circular motion to separate the rice grain from the chaffs. I made an art form out of it and fluidly swirled the rice grain.

All the while, little Daravuth played on the dirt floor nearby. Maman also served as one of the cooks.

One morning, I did not feel like getting up to look for dried animal manure. So I pretended I was not feeling well. Because my brothers and I were the only children and I was the only little girl in the prison, the guards periodically teased us playfully and we sensed they had taken a liking to us. I decided to exploit this sentiment. The guards were not amused nor moved. They came to look for me and carried me outside, as I kicked and screamed. They forced me to come back with a quota of animal manure; I obeyed and trudged along carrying the basket I needed to fill.

My three older brothers looked after water buffaloes.

Every morning, two guards accompanied the three boys to watch water buffaloes. One time, lightning almost struck Mardi and Sina while out in the fields.

At this first prison, every day the boys walked past one particular tree and saw women's breasts and vaginas, old and new ones, hanging off the branches.

At one point another boy, all alone, lived in our prison and watched over water buffaloes with the three older boys. One day, as they were all out in the fields, the new boy decided to escape and ran wildly in the direction of a patch of bamboo trees. The guards aimed and shot him, leaving him to die in the bamboo brush.

Every night, the guards came to inspect the chains on our ankles.

On one occasion, in our cabin but in the next room, one prisoner's ankles were not properly chained. The guards beat him; Sina, and certainly everyone else in our room, could hear him moaning, screaming and begging not to receive more blows. Death met him and his roommates another night when one prisoner attempted an escape; the authority accused the other prisoners in the room of collaboration and killed them all.

The Khmer Rouge normally were very judicious in their use of bullets. Usually, they saved bullets for *À khmang* (contemptible enemy).

Average Cambodian victims encountered their premature death in more economical, systematic ways. Often death occurred at night. Angkar rounded up a group of people, bound in the same manner they had done my mother, above the elbows. A mass grave, possibly one that several of the victims had dug themselves the day before, awaited them. There the authority forced the victims to kneel in front of the grave before being struck by a blow to the head with a shovel or pickaxe. The momentum pushed the victims into the grave's abyss, one body on top of another.

Afterwards, the perpetrators shovelled the nearby mound of dirt to cover their crime. Many of the victims died not from the blow but from later asphyxiation. During the day, the scorching sun pierced through the thinly covered mound of bodies, brewing an acrid odour of death that saturated the fields, my work and play ground.

Other individuals died by having plastic bags tied over their heads, cutting off all flow of air. Yet others had their bodies disembowelled.

Principally, the city people were the victims – people who wore glasses, who spoke a foreign language, whose hands were smooth and skin was pale because they 'haven't laboured a day' in their life but rather 'leisured like pigs in their air conditioned villas'. At one period, the Khmer Rouge targeted people tainted with Vietnamese blood – Vietnam being the historical, more aggressive, more powerful enemy of Cambodia. Then they added to the list those with Chinese blood, paradoxical given the fact that the Khmer Rouge based its movement on the teaching of Mao Zedong and China served as the Organisation's patron.

But then again, the Khmer Rouge was riddled in paradoxes.

At other times, a killing had no rhyme or reason (not that having rhyme or reason necessarily justifies the taking of life), but resulted solely from the whim of an angry village boy, girl, man or woman who now possessed unrestrained power. As power corrupts, absolute power corrupts absolutely, so too a Khmer Rouge not uncommonly wielded his power to exact a revenge or to whimsically test its outer limits simply because he could.

A few months later, they transported all the prisoners to another compound, known as Bung Rei, in Kraul Kor commune, in Svay Chrum district, about 15 kilometres from Phum Chensa.

The second prison compound was similar to the first one, comprised of three main buildings. Countless massive graves covered the grounds surrounding the compound. By this time, the Khmer Rouge had had three years of unrestrained mayhem. New graves heaved up in a mound and oozed blood; the stench of fresh blood reacting to the penetrating tropical sun permeated the fields. In contrast, old graves could be identified by a depression in the ground because the bodies forming the mound had decayed to simply bones.

Over time, during our first prison stay, the guards trusted the boys enough to confide in them about killings they had done.

They told my older brothers who they had killed and detailed how they went about killing them. Even some of the freer prisoners participated in the killing. There was this one outlaw – everyone nicknamed him 'À Mop' and chubby he was – who boasted about having participated in killing other prisoners.

However, at the second prison, a set of new guards replaced the old ones, most likely as part of the internal purges. At the whims of the new guards, À Mop and a few of the old prisoners who had experienced relative freedom in the first prison were put back in our cabin, in a room adjacent to ours, with other prisoners, separated from us only by a woven dried-leaf partition.

A couple of days before the disappearance of my mother, two prisoners from the adjacent room attempted an escape. It occurred in the evening as all the prisoners congregated for dinner. That day, the heavens opened up and drizzled down tears onto our patch of the earth. The men ran with all their heart in the direction of freedom, the open field. The guards opened fire in front of everyone. The tall one dropped dead in the field. They captured the other one; it was À Mop.

'Are you scared?' a guard asked him.

'No, I'm not scared, *bong*', he quivered his reply. A shot rang out and pierced into his skull.

Life is but a breath.

Later that same night, the guards came into the adjacent room where À Mop had been and took all the other prisoners. Sina, undoubtedly as well as everyone else in our room, could hear the scuffling next door. These prisoners were never to be seen again.

Life is but a breath.

The day following the attempted escape of our cabin mates, my mother distributed her belongings to other prisoners in our room.

Like Sina, she must have heard and understood what had occurred the previous night in the room next door. She sensed Death's propinquity and calmly prepared to meet it. This time, the encounter would not be postponed.

Late that evening, a prison guard called for my three older brothers.

'À Kdee, À Sina, À Nong,* come with me. We're going to the next village to look for stranded water buffaloes.'

It was an unusual order.

A pounding thought flashed through Mardi, 'This is not true; all of the water buffaloes are accounted for.'

The guard unchained my brothers' ankles and two guards escorted them away from the prison compound. The two older boys had a premonition of the evil confronting them.

Sina leaned towards Mardi and whispered, 'Did you see, there were a lot of guards with ropes, guns and shovels outside the prison compound?'

The two brothers exchanged furtive knowing glances, their hearts heavy with grief as they once again marched in the shadow of the darkness, this time away from personal danger. They remained silent the rest of the journey, isolated in their individual thoughts.

The beautiful countryside contrasted with their souls' upheavals. The stars sparkled their radiance. The glowing moon beamed its incandescent rays onto the earth, creating shimmering sheets of glass on the water-covered fields.

When they arrived at their destination, a house from where the boys could still see the main prison compound the next morning, Mardi and Sina confided in Lundi their fears. They tried to comfort each other in their forlorn silence. Each wrestled with his thoughts in the night and experienced little sleep.

Back at the prison compound, later yet that night, two prison

* Mardi, Sina, Lundi.

guards peeked in our room in the partitioned cabin. This too was unusual. They had already secured the shackles on the big people's ankles for the night. The guards gave a cursory glance across the room to find Daravuth curled up against my mother on one side and me on the other, he caught my eyes and quickly exited.

'Mom, why were those guards carrying wet ropes?'*

'My daughter, *kaun srei*, go back to sleep.'

The guards returned later that night. Little did I know that that would be the last time I would see my mother.

The light went out. Night. Eternal night.

Life is but a breath.

Early the next morning, Daravuth and I woke up sobbing hysterically as we clung to each other in a foetal position. I felt weightless, an empty frame floating. I could not comprehend what had happened, but a deep, deep sense of loss of agonising proportions pervaded our little frames and pounded into our hearts. To choke out, 'Mom, Mom,' in between crying was all we knew to do. Simultaneously, two worlds battled within me; in my levitation experience, it was as if my being wanted to be transported to the new world my mother had entered, to follow and join her, but the old world clung onto my material body. The spirit and the material wrestled; in this convulsion, the material won; it was not yet my time to leave this world.

'Stop crying. Your mom is working in another building.' But we were inconsolable and they did not persist in lying to us, as if they realised we needed this grieving period.

What seemed like several hours later, Mardi, Sina and Lundi returned to us. Vuth and I experienced pure exhaustion from the morning's emotional outburst. Clearly, the older brothers from their listless saunter had encountered similar emotional fatigue. As

---

* They wet the ropes to make them more malleable to knot.

39

they neared, I wanted to convey to them my hollowness, only to see the same hollowness reflected in their faces. Mardi subtly shook his head to silence me.

The prison was eerily empty.

'Here, take your crying siblings with you. You're free to go home,' a guard instructed my older brothers.

My mother's blood purchased our first freedom.

Lugubriously, the two oldest brothers picked up their younger siblings and started walking away from the compound. We did not know where we were going. My older brothers waited to ask for direction until we reached the nearest village. 'Which way is Phum Chensa?'

Hunger pains jabbed at us new orphans, ranging from ages five to thirteen, as we trudged along in the direction pointed out to us. Weightless and numb, subdued yet animated at times in conversation, we attempted to piece together the last 48 hours of our changed identity.

We conjectured that had Daravuth or I awakened that night when the prison guards came back for my mother and the others in the room the second time around, they would have taken us along to be killed as well. The guards left empty-handed on the first visit because they noticed I was still awake. They separated my older brothers from the group marked to be killed. They wanted to preserve us, the children. Why? A thin strand of compassion existed at that moment amidst their perfect cruelty and it acted to save us.

Maman had at least 36 hours to think of her violent end, about what it means to cease to be human – materially, emotionally, intellectually – never again to be caressed by her children, by the velvety wind; never again to see, to smell, to touch, to feel. What brave thoughts entered her mind, the mind that would soon be emptied of thoughts, and vanish altogether? Nothingness.

All the adults in the room that night must have tiptoed to their graves in fear of waking Daravuth and me from our sleep. How did Maman disentangle her body from our embrace without waking us? In her silent goodbyes and fervent prayers for our safety, could she have any inkling that her children would be alive 25 years later, one to write about it, to attempt to understand her beauty amidst this pure collective insanity?

It is believed that the guards tied up these individuals, stuffed them in gritty rice sacks, carried them to an open field under the starlit night, beat them into unconsciousness and disposed of their bodies in shallow graves. During the insanity of the Khmer Rouge years, our scope of knowledge and experience was limited to our immediate person, but nonetheless, there were things that we just knew, from the air we breathed and from an upbringing of always relying more on intuition, of unconsciously connecting events and conversations, than on rationalised verbal arguments.

Ripped apart from us were the two most fundamental, profound connections experienced by a human being – these givers of life, our mother and father. How much of the loss did we process at that time? How could Maman be there one moment and the next moment be eternally erased from the earth? Eternal separation. It is too long to bear. How much can a seven-year-old comprehend of death?

How can an emptiness, a void, a nothingness be so acutely powerful and viscerally present in this material, human body? Is a body not simply a combination of joints, sinews and tissues clothed in flesh, and once these decay, we die? But what is this haunting air, this spirit, that allows us to feel the exquisitely painful or the achingly beautiful? A joint cannot feel. A sinew cannot be moved to emotions. What then?

Philosophers tell us about, and experience confirms, the existence of the soul – the spirit, the core essence of who we are as human beings. Did those guards not know they were treading on sacred ground? Did they not know that in extinguishing one life, 20 other spirits are sucked out as well – spirits, forever battered and bruised?

Papa, Maman, may you arrive in fertile Phthia on the third day.*

How I wish for one last glimpse of Maman and Papa. I wonder how she said goodbye to us that lonely, ominous night. I wonder about his thoughts before he passed into the other world.

---

* A quotation from the ninth book of *The Iliad* (363), referenced by Plato's *Crito*. Achilles refused to return to battle and hoped to arrive on the third day (the day after tomorrow) 'in fertile Phthia', his home.

CHAPTER TWO

The Wedding Banquet of Papa and Maman
(late 1960s – 1970)

My grandfathers, Kuy Seng and Duch Som, arranged my parents' marriage before either of them were even born. My parents' fathers befriended each other during their childhood years in Svay Rieng province and avowed to be blood relations through the marriage of their firstborn daughter and son. The oddly-matched best friends each had a son as their firstborn. The first daughter to be born for either man would now marry the firstborn son of the other man. Kuy Seng was the first to produce a daughter, Eat Seng, my mother. Now, a marriage could be arranged and the verbal agreement sealed: the son of Duch Som will marry the daughter of Kuy Seng.

My father, Im Kao, who was given the last name of his grandfather rather than that of Som,* grew up in a relatively well-to-do landowning family in a rural village in Svay Rieng province, in southeastern Cambodia, bordering Vietnam. An established family of farmers in Chensa, the Soms had lived off the land for generations. They hired hands to help plant and harvest rice in their many

---

* Usually, Cambodians are known first by their family name followed by their given name, thus in Cambodia, my father was known as 'Kao Im'. Also, my siblings and I have my mother's family name of Seng, instead of Kao, changed in order to expedite the paper process to the United States when we were living in the refugee camps. Since we were with my maternal relatives, we needed to appear to be related.

hectares of rice fields and raised various livestock, such as water buffaloes, cows, pigs and chickens, for both trading and food. Their bucolic existence provided them the basic necessities of life, peace and security.

Compared to other villagers in the region, the Soms were well-to-do; to Phnom Penhians, they were peasants; to the developed world, they were an indigenous and exotic group of Khmer people living in a backwater, an interesting research study.

My father passed his elementary school years in the local village school, attended middle and high school in central Svay Rieng, and then went off to Phnom Penh for a two-year teacher training programme in an institute located on the boulevard to Pochentong Airport. After graduation, he was offered a teaching position in Kratie province, north of Phnom Penh, which he accepted. During this era, all parents wanted their daughters to marry a 'professeur', men who practised a well-respected profession, received a handsome salary and were well educated.

Im Kao was a man who loved life. His relatives nicknamed him 'Dim'. To his friends and acquaintances he was 'Im Prum Prey', for he was always seen smiling, grinning or joking. His sanguine nature and light-hearted outlook on life put people at ease and gained him many friends and admirers. His younger sisters remember a loving brother who bestowed on them gifts of make-up and clothes upon his visits from Kratie or Phnom Penh.

My mother, on the other hand, grew up in the same southeastern province, which bulges into Vietnam, but came from a lineage of Chinese immigrants. She started out life in the dull, poverty-stricken village of Kampong Marek and she began her education in the Khmer elementary school in her village. But at an early age, Eat expressed a desire to visit China. A distant relative had just returned from a visit to China and filled the curious mind of young Eat with stories and adventures. At the end of her elementary school education, her parents, second-generation immigrants from China, transferred her to the private school in central Svay Rieng, where all the subjects were taught in Chinese. However, one hour every day was devoted to teaching the Khmer language in order to conform to a government law.

She studied there throughout high school. She grew up speaking several languages – Cambodian, Vietnamese, French and different Chinese dialects. Her fluency in Chinese, the language of trade, would prove to serve her well in the mercantilist racial hierarchy of Cambodian society in that period, where the Chinese merchant class controlled local businesses.

Her siblings recall a soft-spoken, kind-hearted, well-mannered older sister, who became a mother figure to them while their mother was eking out a living, trading and selling in the local open markets. Eat herself was still a child. In later years, her personable character gave her an edge in her business dealings.

Eat and Im were officially engaged when they reached their late teenage years. A long, official courtship period ensued, whereby my father had to work for a period of several years for my mother's family as an indentured servant, for a few months each year during school holidays from university and then from his teaching position in Kratie.

Grandpa Kuy loved my father, his future son-in-law. Whenever my father saw Ta Kuy, he would jump off his bicycle and bow, *krahp*, to the ground to greet his future father-in-law. But this affection in no way altered Ta Kuy's strict, controlling nature. Even after their betrothal, and even chaperoned by family members, he refused to permit Im to take his daughter to the cinema. My father ended up taking all her siblings and mother to the movie, while Ta Kuy and my mother stayed behind at home.

My mother's sister Renee* recalls: 'Even before the marriage of

*   Aunt Rey changed her name to Renee when she became a naturalised US citizen.

Asrei's parents, both families were very close. We would call his parents "Mother" and "Father".'

The affection and affinity between the families, however, did not stop Ta Kuy's shrewd calculation. Towards the end of my father's service in my mother's household, Ta Kuy had a last minute change of heart. He called off the engagement, even though preparations had already been started for the wedding celebration. A more prominent man of higher social standing – a doctor – had fallen in love with my mother.

My father's family cajoled and pleaded with the ever-mercurial Ta Kuy, until he finally relented and agreed to the original arrangement, allowing the wedding to proceed. But he refused to drop the subject matter and let the Soms forget the sacrifice his daughter had to make to marry their son. Not uncommonly, he would cruelly draw attention to the contrasting features between my mother and father and likened them to 'a black crow carrying a white egg'.

Aunt Renee remembers: 'Of all the sisters, Bong Eat was truly the most beautiful. She had many admirers. Petite. Fair skin. And always elegant.'

A brother, Eng, interjects: 'Although, there was a period in her youth when she broke out with terrible acne.'

When my father was officially betrothed to my mother, his acquaintances would compliment him on his luck. Later, his students would run to glimpse at the white porcelain, *saw skuoh!*, Chinese woman, who is the wife of their *Kru* (Teacher) Im. She certainly did provide a contrast to his very Cambodian, sun-kissed, dark-skinned features.

(Cambodia, then and now, is a country obsessed with equating beauty, status, and wealth with the hue of one's skin. Differences translate to value-laden superiority–inferiority gradation.)

The union broke class barriers because by the time of the marriage, my mother's family had moved to Kampong Speu province and joined the prosperous Chinese merchant class, while my father's family continued to live off their land as peasants in Phum Chensa.

(Hindsight on these matters of class and status never fails to amuse me. People can carve out distinctions to one-up each other out of most anything, even when appreciable differences do not even exist.)

One month before the start of the wedding celebration, most likely during the dry season after the rice harvests, my father's family, friends and musicians journeyed west to prepare for the wedding, past Phnom Penh, from Svay Rieng province to the Sengs' residence of Svay Kravann in Kampong Speu province. All 30-something of them filled one rented city bus. A second rented bus carried the necessary wedding materials: tents, musical instruments, decorations, various Cambodian delicacies and sweets, other gifts-in-kind and personal necessities for the wedding party to exist until their return home when the festivity ends.

My mother's sisters remember: 'Mardi's grandma from Svay Rieng baked delicious *noum tr'uom*, Cambodian sweets made of baked flour or sticky rice wrapped around fillings and sprinkled with sesame seeds.'

My father's father, Ta Duch, sold a lot of land, many sacks of rice grain and livestock to pay for the wedding celebration and the dowry. He wanted to put on a lavish wedding for two reasons. First, my father was his oldest child and the first one to be married. Second, he did not want to lose face in light of Ta Kuy's constant reminders that a doctor had been turned down for his son.

The Soms erected the wedding hall and started their wedding preparation as Ta Kuy lorded it over them in his exacting manner. If it had not been for the affable and easy-going nature of Ta Duch and the quiet intervention of his wife, Grandma Hao, the ceremony would never have taken place and I would not be here to tell this tale.

Ta Yam, the younger brother of my paternal grandmother in the Svay Rieng clan, took responsibility for the traditional wedding music, *areak' ka*. The ensemble of instruments consisted of the three-stringed fiddle, musical bow or monochord, longneck lute, double reed shawn and goblet drums. He arranged all the music and hired the musicians. Every day during the month prior to the ceremony, he played tapes of Cambodian wedding music over a loudspeaker; the music could be heard miles away.

The Svay Rieng musicians performed only during the actual wedding ceremony. A local band was hired to play contemporary music for the dance parties held every night in the weeks preceding the wedding. The Sengs had to request the permission of the provincial governor to have music played past the already generous curfew.

The wedding celebration, a fusion of traditional Chinese and Buddhist customs, lasted three continuous days and nights, comprising of many symbol-laden ceremonies.

My two grandmas busied themselves directing relatives and hired hands on food preparation and looking after the welfare of the monks. Throughout the house and inside the tent, bundles of incense sticks burned continuously around a few miniature Buddha statues.

The day began at five in the morning, before the rising of the sun, to pray when the air was considered religiously pure and the temperature was still cool. Early on the morning of the first wedding day, all the relatives from Svay Rieng queued up in pairs, with the groom and his attendants at the head of the line, each individual holding a tray of food or material offering. After a bit of chaos, everyone found a place. The musicians near the head of the line began bowing and drumming their instruments and the procession began.

The groom processional paraded through the main road of Svay Kravann and stopped in front of the bride's house. The bride attired in beautiful wedding clothes went to meet him at the door. She bent down to help the groom to take off his shoes and dark socks. Someone then handed Eat a bowl of water and she symbolically washed Im's feet by gently dabbing them with the wet cloth in her hand.

Inside the crowded house of relations and guests, monks chanted prayers and incense fumes ascended into the air.

The following day, the wedding opened with a ceremony to 'enter into the marriage court'. A group of hired monks chanted the appropriate mantras as the bridesmaids accompanied the bride Eat to the awaiting audience already assembled under the tent, where it was more spacious than inside the house.

The bride found everyone seated in rows before the chanting monks, turning to face her, as one of her brothers at the entrance repeatedly clanged the cymbals to announce her coming. The women had on their best custom-made, folded, ankle-length Khmer skirts. The skirts differed only in colours, fabric and fabric designs. Most of them were cut from the best Khmer hand-woven silk. Some women wore matching tops. Others preferred beautifully knitted, form-fitting, pastel-coloured blouses that accentuated their hour-glass petite figures, open necks and bare arms.

Khmer women then and now love jewellery and weddings provide the perfect occasion to show off their wealth on their wrists, necks and earlobes. Sapphires, gold, silver, diamonds competed in brilliance. Their finger and toenails were perfectly manicured and brightly painted in various shades of red. Their faces were painted with heavy make up, over evenly-blended pale liquid foundation, powdered by an even lighter shade. For the Svay Rieng relatives, the fairer the better, to hide their brown, sun-kissed skin – a noticeable give-away that their existence was lived in the fields and not in air conditioned rooms. It was not very often that the women have occasions to wear make-up, escape their mundane lives and feel glamorous.

The men had on slacks and tucked-in light shirts.

The bride was ornately and richly wrapped in a body-hugging glittering gold sequinned top; the extra material was swung across one shoulder to drape down the back, in the tradition of Khmer royalty. On the bottom half, she was wrapped in the customary Cambodian manner for such occasions in a corresponding brilliant fabric; the extra cloth was artistically folded into several layers of pleats in the front. An ornate gold belt held the outfit together.

Some of the guests who had not seen Eat in a long time commented on her svelte figure. Eat had lost a lot of weight prior to the wedding and dropped several sizes.

A tiara towered her silky coifed up hair. Several pieces of gold wedding jewellery adorned her wrists and ankles. Heavy make-up accentuated her elegant facial features.

The outcome was neither gaudy nor overdone, a commonly committed sin in Cambodia. Several gasps could be heard in the crowd, proclaiming her beauty. The bridegroom Im had already fixed his gaze in the direction of her coming. At her entrance, he tried to catch the eyes of his bejewelled bride. Not surprisingly, being the perfectly proper Cambodian woman that she was, young Eat cast her eyes on no one in particular. Demurely, she softly lowered them as she entered the court, head slightly bowed to show respect to the elders in the room. It was learnt submission, born not from weakness but quiet strength. Confident of her position, she could afford to be self-effacing without compromising any moral or social ground.

She made her way to her groom already seated at the front of the room, near the monks and the presiding minister who would give them their blessings. The bridesmaids followed her. Along the way they passed the guests seated directly on the matted floor and rows and rows of food and material offerings, some wrapped in shiny gold cellophane, others served on silver trays: twin trays of all the seasonal tropical fruits, various baked Cambodian delicacies and different types of Khmer hand-woven silk.

The bride and groom sat on the floor next to each other, with impenetrable expressions, facing the monks and minister. They exchanged little between them throughout the wedding celebration except stolen glances of each other. Their palms were raised between their breasts and chins, in praying position, facing each other slightly. The monks resumed their chanting, lit several candles, passed them in a circular motion to the others in the room, who in turned passed them on to the person next to them, but not before waving one hand above the flame, something to do with keeping away evil spirits.

The bridesmaids and groomsmen sitting behind the couple massaged their numbed feet. Grandma Yi Hao periodically leaned over to adjust her daughter's skirt or shawl.

Some time later, two of the monks each took a bundle of slivered banana stems or reeds, dipped it into a silver-plated bowl of holy water and repeatedly sprayed their blessings onto the couple, accompanied again by hypnotic chanting. The older people in the room who knew the Sanskrit-based chants joined in with the monks. Eat and Im kept their statuesque, praying postures.

When this particular ceremony ended both the bride and groom were led to their separate dressing room to change into another brilliant matching outfit, costumes rented specifically for the occasion. The owner of these costumes took responsibility for dressing the couple.

While they prepared for the next ceremony, family members and guests stretched their aching bodies, cleared the silver trays with the food and material offerings and prepared the room for the next event. The groom came first into the room, followed by the bride. Again, the clanging cymbal announced their arrival. They were attired in complementary costumes to represent a royal couple. They assumed the same sitting positions as before, their legs folded to one side – inconspicuously switching them when they numbed. This time the minister addressed them with blessings, admonitions and worldly wisdom. Im and Eat thanked him by bowing three times to the floor, each time separating and pressing their palms downwards.

Then the presiding minister asked both sets of parents whether they have gifts to present to their son- or daughter-in-law. Grandma and Grandpa Sam approached their daughter-in-law Eat, dispensed blessings and welcoming remarks to her as she faced them in a prayer-like position with palms raised to her nose and head bowed to receive their blessings and wisdom. Grandma Som then present-ed Eat with a gold necklace and gingerly placed it around her neck, careful not to disturb the tiara and coifed up hair. My maternal grandparents in turn and in a similar manner presented their son-in-law Im with blessings and a gold necklace.

Once again, the couple were led to their respective dressing room and changed into another set of matching outfits, as brilliant, ornate and royal.

Those near the front helped to arrange the room for the string-tying ceremony to symbolise unity and the oneness of mar-riage. Two silky golden pillows were placed near the front for the bride and groom. The clanging cymbal signalled the start; every head turned in the direction of the entrance. Im and Eat assumed their previous position on the matted floor. This time, however, their bodies leaned forward, their elbows cushioned by a pillow, palms again in prayer-like position. Again the monks chanted and blessed them, throwing aromatic jasmine petals on the couple between chant intervals. The presiding minister gave a short ser-mon on marriage and love, and approached the couple with a handful of red soft strands of string. He separated one from the bundle, which he laid near them, and loosely tied Eat's right wrist with Im's left. The parents, relatives and guests followed his example. Im and Eat's bodies paralleled each other, in an incredibly uncomfortable position, with their folded legs cast to one side and their strained faces lifted up towards the monks and presiding minister. By the time everyone had his or her opportunity to unite the couple with a red strand, a large lump had accumulated on the couple's joined wrists and their feet, lead-heavy, had gone to sleep.

It must have been about 11 a.m., and the monks had left to have their only meal of the day.

Children ran and laughed outside throughout the celebration. Some of the adults entered in and out during the ceremonies – to stretch, to gossip, to rest and to help the hired hands with food preparation and setting up for the informal breakfasts and lunches. A formal dinner celebration was scheduled for the last night, where the guests presented the couple with envelopes full of cash.

The hair-cutting ceremony was to represent physical cleanliness and grooming in the marriage. The couple sat in the two chairs, which were placed before the monks and presiding minister, covered with traditional brilliant Khmer fabric. A hired couple danced and sang in exaggerated movements to music specific to this ceremony. The woman led, carrying a bowl of water, a mirror, a bottle of perfume, among other things, followed by the man with a pair of scissors and comb in his hands, all the while encircling the couple, pretending to snip at Eat and Im's hair and perfume their heads. After five minutes of this, the grooming materials were handed over to the couple's parents as they similarly pretended to cut the couple's hair and perfume their heads. Traditional instrumental music accompanied their actions. Adult relatives and guests lined up as a family unit to do the same, many whispering their blessings, others cracking jokes to the couple and some holding the mirror for the couple to see their work, asking whether they were satisfied with the result. Frequent bursts of laughter filled the room amidst the loud music and various private conversations.

The end came when everyone who wanted to participate in this ceremony had a chance to groom the couple with hair cutting and perfume.

Again the bride and groom were led out, signalled by the loud banging cymbals, to change into another set of wedding attires for the last ceremony where the couple were led to their marriage bed. Halfway reclining on the bed, the couple eyed each other and the relatives and guests who crowded around them. A relative teased the couple by holding a cluster of grapes between them and asking them to eat one simultaneously without the use of their hands. As Im and Eat leaned forward, the relative pulled away the clump of grapes. The crowd erupted into laughter as the couple's faces brushed into each other, the first time Im and Eat had touched romantically after all these years of betrothal. Eat's face turned several shades redder than her powdered blush. A few in the crowd exchanged some earthy jokes; Eat and Im were teased again and again.

After the long, rambunctious formal dinner party on that third and last night, the couple consummated their love for the first time. At the age of 21 my mother wed my father, who was one year older than her.

Aunt Renee remembers: 'I can still picture Bong Eat in this one exquisite outfit; it was a peach-coloured top, dotted with glittering pearls. It really complemented her fair skin. She looked radiant.'

My paternal grandparents presented my mother's family with the customary gifts of cash, gold and diamonds. The other guests presented the newlyweds with cash, a continuing custom to the present day among Cambodians. Rarely do guests give gifts-in-kind. That last night at the formal dinner party, everyone stayed up later than usual dancing to the music of the live band, interspersed with everyone's favourite 'raum vuong' and various other Khmer traditional dances, and those of western cha-cha-cha, the twist and good old-time rock-and-roll. The couple went around to each table and thanked the guests for attending as the guests presented the couple with more envelopes of cash.

The wedding stirred a little bit of attention because some guests were 'excellencies' and came in chauffeured, black, shiny sedans. The Sengs also owned a car, but it was a used one.

One guest predicted to the Seng sisters, 'None of you will have as extravagant a wedding ceremony as your sister Eat.' If only the speaker knew the truth and gravity of her statement.

Up until the time of the wedding, Im had been teaching in the capital of Kratie province, a sleepy town, situated northeast of Phnom Penh, lined by tall, elegant trees along the raised bank of the Mekong River. Grandma Hao did not want her daughter to live there, so she decided to pay a visit to Ta Yuman, an acquaintance and the superintendent of the Svay Rieng school system, whose house had many chapu fruits. Grandma knew her feudalistic society well and was too clever to visit him with empty hands.

(She got her oldest son An out of prison for his political activities against the monarchy by similar means. In 1962, An's vocal opposition to Prince Sihanouk landed him in jail where he languished for a year. Grandma Hao assessed the system; it was corrupt and it was not her role to change it. As a mother, she only wanted her son, who had been unlawfully imprisoned by the quixotic authoritarian Prince Sihanouk, out of jail. She knew the right people to see and the right gifts to bring.)

Ta Yuman said it was beyond his power to transfer my father directly from Kratie to a good position in central Svay Rieng. However, he could transfer him to a smaller town, Prasot, in Svay Rieng province. Once in the province, it would be easier for my father to make the move to the central school if he later desired.

Thus, after the wedding celebration, the newlyweds settled in Prasot. My father taught natural science to junior high students.

My mother designed and sewed clothes on order at home. Periodically, she ventured into Vietnam to buy and trade fabric and other materials.

While there, Eat gave birth to her firstborn, a son. Grandma Hao came to care for her daughter and witness the birth. She served my mother pepper ginger soup – a customary dish she was to make for other pregnancies. She had the fully pregnant Eat lie on a bamboo bed over a burning bed of charcoal. The heat loosened the tension and muscles of the expecting mother.

The proud new parents named their first-born son after the French word for the day of his birth, Mardi. (Cambodians tend to be Francophiles and adopt an affectation of anything *barang*, the Khmer appellation for the country's former imperialists. My parents were not unaffected by this. Now, *barang* refers to any Caucasian person.)

According to Chinese custom as practiced by Chinese-Cambodians, one month after birth, because of the nine months the baby is cocooned in the mother's womb, the child is considered a year old. Usually, the parents throw a lavish celebration to commemorate the occasion. All other birthdays hold little meaning in comparison. It is also customary to shave the baby's head in order to rid him of the impurities during his time in the womb. Additionally, so goes the belief, a child will grow to have a thicker head of hair if his head has been shaven at birth.

My mother stayed true to her Chinese roots. She shaved Mardi's head and threw an extravagant party for him. After all, he was their first child, a son, and the first grandchild to both sets of grandparents. She ordered about 40 tables, each table seating eight to ten people. Grandparents, aunts and uncles from both sides of the family attended the celebration. They travelled the long distance from Svay Kravann in Kampong Speu province and Chensa village to attend the celebration. They ate boiled eggs that had been painted red and *Ee* cakes, both essential to carrying out the tradition.

The paternal grandparents presented him a pair of cows and a pair of water buffaloes. My mother's parents, not to be outdone, gave him the same. The other relatives and guests presented him with gold and silver anklets, bracelets and necklaces. He collected a basketful of them.

After teaching two years in Prasot, my father accepted a position that opened up in central Svay Rieng, located about ten kilometres away. My mother opened a tailoring school and business, *Neary Niyoum* (Modern Woman), the first and only school of its kind in the province. Her brothers helped with radio and television advertising. The business quickly prospered.

Prominently situated in a three-story building in the centre of the provincial capital, on the main national route, *Neary Niyoum* catered to a society continually in demand of new custom-made costumes and outfits for every holiday and festivity. Cambodians will celebrate any occasion, foreign or not. People always needed a new outfit to attend a wedding or a son's one-month birthday. Additionally, parties existed to celebrate Cambodian-Chinese New Year, Independence Day, the King's Birthday, *Bon Pchum Ben* (Soul Day) and the myriad of other Buddhist remembrances. All said, my mother struck the right social and business cord.

On the ground level, two rows of 30 sewing machines stood on the chequered floor, extending to the back of the building. The second and third floors served as the living apartment for my parents as well as boarding rooms for students who came from the outskirts of the province.

Seng Hok, not yet then a relation, recalls: 'My family lived nearby, so I would periodically pass by *Neary Niyoum* on my way to or from my Chinese school because it was rumoured that Kru Im's wife is *sa'art nah!* (very beautiful) and successful. She was quite the talk of the town. My mom would also do business with her, at times bringing fabric from Vietnam to sell to her.'

Soon after, Im and Eat bought and moved into a concrete house a block away from the central market. At different times, Papa's sisters lived with them – it was understood that richer relatives should care for less well-off members.

By this time, Im and Eat had sent their baby to live with her younger sisters in Kampong Speu, not an uncommon arrangement in the Khmer society of extended families. Through Mardi all of the other siblings would come to know Ry as *Ma-Mieng* (literally, 'Mom-Aunt').

Aunt Ry remembers: 'When À Kdee, Mardi, napped, he would twirl his finger around the hem of my *sarong* so that I could not leave without waking him up.'

As a teacher, Papa received a handsome salary. Nonetheless, Maman was the breadwinner whose business success allowed the young family to live comfortably. The school charged a student more than the monthly salary of Papa. At any one time, Eat had 30 students studying under her and she employed several teachers. When she was not teaching, she worked on the orders from ladies of high society to design, cut and sew their outfits.

In the Chinese calendar year of the horse, Im and Eat had their second child, another son. They called him Sina. It was also the year torrential rain flooded the region. Knee-deep water occupied the ground floor of city buildings, including *Neary Niyoum*.

A midwife came to the house to deliver the 12-pound baby, who appeared 'as black as charcoal', an exaggeration to contrast his milk-chocolate skin to Mardi's fair skin. After he was done with breast-feeding, Sina also went to live in Kampong Speu with Mardi and the maternal relatives. The youngest girl, Rey, took care of him.

As the family grew in wealth, Im, the ever-charming *bon vivant*, decided to share these riches earned by his wife with other women. He lived in a society that permitted him to indulge in such liaisons without social disapprobation.

Aunt Ry explains: 'Your dad was a spender. Your mom was very gentle and kind. She would have her moments of frustration and out-bursts, but overall was very good-hearted. Almost to the point of naiveté whereby people would take advantage of her soft-heartedness. So many people borrowed money from her and never paid her back. Not surprisingly, she was born in the year of the horse.'

I enquire: 'But I heard that she would physically beat up my father's mistress?'

Aunt Ry continues: 'Who wouldn't be angry in that position? Some people had the mistresses killed.

'One time, when your uncles visited your parents from universi-ty in Phnom Penh, your dad took all of them out to a local pub. He also took along five-year-old Mardi.

'Little Mardi ran home to tell your mother that he saw Papa give money to some strange woman there. Immediately, your mother left for the tavern and had a cat-fight with the other woman. Of course, all the men, including her own brothers, found great amusement in the whole incident.'

According to my father's sisters, if Maman had a fault, it was her burning jealousy, for 'she loved your dad too much'.

Eat had many reasons to be jealous. Another time, according to her cousin, Mieng Maly, when they arrived together at Eat's home in Prasot, Eat caught her husband in bed with another woman. Upon her violent protest, my father took my mother aside and brutishly beat her. He must have reasoned that she was irrationally spoiling his entitlement.*

---

* In June 2005, family and friends from all over the world gathered for two wed-dings, that of my brother Lundi to Sophanita and of cousin Visal to Abraham. In between wedding preparations, conversations strayed to our days in Cambodia and under the Khmer Rouge. I asked about Mieng Maly's account, and Great Uncle (Ta) Ân confirmed that yes, my father was certainly a woman-iser: 'during his wedding soiree of the last night, he went up on stage to sing and dance with the female singer, but immediately your Mom went up to drag him away by his tie. However,' he cautioned, 'take what Mieng Maly says with a grain of salt.'

These social and family interactions of the late 1960s occurred within a broader political framework of instability and warfare. The American war in Vietnam had spilled into Cambodia and both North and South Vietnamese soldiers occupied almost half of Cambodian territory. The situation severely affected the citizens of Svay Rieng, because the province shares a border with Vietnam. A huge population of legal and illegal Vietnamese immigrants lived there. Inevitably, many Cambodians viewed people with Vietnamese ethnicity with suspicion.

Aunt Ry explains: 'Despite his womanising, your father had a very generous, compassionate and tender heart. A lot of killing occurred of ethnic Vietnamese by Cambodian soldiers. Your father gave shelter and hid many of these people, especially in 1970 during intense fighting in Svay Rieng. He didn't turn away anyone who came to him for help.

'The soldiers tried to make trouble for your mother as well. In part, because of her fair skin, believing her to be a Vietnamese woman. But also to extract money from her because they could see that she was successful.'

For a period of time, my mother went with her two sons to stay with her in-laws in Chensa. Somehow, the fighting missed Chensa. Also around this time, General Lon Nol assumed power and his army conscripted my father into its rank.

Around the middle of 1970, the military transferred Papa to Kampong Sala, west of Phnom Penh, on the way to the sea resort Sihanoukville (Kampong Som). My mother moved her family to Phnom Penh.

When the family moved to Phnom Penh, the French-influenced capital had a population of little more than half a million. Founded in 1372 by Lady Daun Penh on a hill (*phnom*), the city did not find permanence as the country's capital until the end of the 19th century. In 1970, the royal Norodoms and Sisowaths and their acquaintances such as the Sams, Tioulongs and Kheks comprised the decadent, educated elite citizenry. They lived in a Phnom Penh that was a melange of Asian artefacts, traditions and modern structures; a colonial oasis of lined spacious boulevards, charming villas and a demurred population. Along the western banks of the Tonle Sap, east of the city, the golden spires of the enclosed Royal Palace drew attention to its grandeur. Half a mile south of the palace grounds, bridged by open parks and opulent villas, stood the Independence Monument. Many temples, each the size of a city block, dotted the city, surrounding the Olympic Stadium, the nucleus of the capital. The temple Wat Phnom formed the highest building in the city. The city's low-lying structures offered the citizenry an ambience of managed comfort and amiability.

My mother settled into her new life in the country's capital with her three sons. She rented a two-story wooden house next to her uncle's family, next to the pagoda Wat Mohamintrei. Eat's other siblings had already moved to Phnom Penh for university. The three sisters shared an apartment of their own in the eastern part of the city, while their older brothers lived in a rented dormitory run by the French priest, Père François Ponchaud. Their parents continued to live in their home in central Cambodia, Kampong Speu.

Before the move to Phnom Penh, probably in 1969, my mother gave birth to her third son. She encountered complications because he came out feet first. However, the doctors at the hospital near Psah Thmei, the circular landmark market, were able to deliver him without having to do a caesarean section. He was named for the French day of his birth, Lundi.

During the era of King Sihanouk's Sangkum Reastr Niyum, in the 1950s and 60s, Cambodians looked to their monarch as their Papa and he viewed them as his children, effeminate and sheltered. Amidst the warfare and trauma, amidst the instability, my relatives join the chorus of other Cambodians who remember this epoch as idyllic and peaceful, a roseate perspective of life accurate only in degree to what was later to unfold.

Chapter Three

The Rise of the Khmer Rouge
(1953 – April 1975)

On 9 November 1953, Cambodia gained independence from France. Two years later, King Sihanouk adeptly abdicated his throne to pursue an active political role as the head of state. Although he acquired the new title 'prince', ordinary Cambodians continued to revere him as their 'god-king' and Father of the Nation, Samdech Oeuv.

During late 1968, the United States' war in Vietnam spilled into Cambodia. Despite his public stance of neutrality, Prince Sihanouk either granted permission to Viet Cong soldiers to establish sanctuaries within Cambodia along its border with Vietnam or he passively closed his eyes to their presence. Regardless of his actual actions, the presence of Vietnamese communist soldiers inside Cambodia unleashed the aerial bombing power of the United States. President Richard Nixon, as part of the 'Nixon Doctrine in its Purest Form', secretly ordered 540,000 tons of bombs dropped on neutral Cambodia (a country not at war with the US), more than twice the amount dropped on all of Japan during War World II. These policies emanated from his national security adviser Henry Kissinger. These two players of realpolitik conducted their power games without the knowledge of the

United States Congress, from a 'menu' of choices – 'Breakfast', 'Lunch', 'Snack', 'Dinner', 'Dessert' and 'Supper', as these bombardments came to be known. The B-52 bombers were flown at high altitude and could not be observed from the ground. Consequently, they were incapable of accuracy and could not discriminate between a civilian and military population. No matter. It was understood in diplomatic circles that the country was to be bombed 'to the last Cambodian'.

On another level, the United States used Cambodia as testing grounds for developing its bombs. It implanted tapes in certain bombs to record the degree of their destructiveness. Donald Dawson, an Air Force captain flying these missions, was court-martialled when he refused to drop any more bombs on Svay Rieng. He heard cries of children and women on these tapes and realised these bombs were killing the civilian population.* Cambodia, politically neutral, became a sideshow to the US–Vietnam War and bled profusely as a result.** The unrelenting bombing carpeted Cambodia's lush emerald-green rice fields, defoliating the countryside, uprooting hundreds of thousands and killing thousands more Cambodian villagers in the process. Rural Cambodians rushed into the capital. With no one left to farm, the population went hungry. It was in this period that my mother, too, moved her young family to Phnom Penh.

* Journalist Imran Vittachi alerted me to these facts. According to Vittachi, Donald Dawson now works as a public defender in Nashville Tennessee. *Thank you for your humanity.*
** For those interested in a more comprehensive look at the abuse and arrogance of power during this period, William Shawcross' celebrated *Sideshow* is highly recommended. Actually, the book is a must-read for all students of history who believe morality can be divorced from politics. As he concluded, the US foreign policy in Cambodia during this period was not a mistake but a crime. The secret bombings violated international law of national sovereignty and the destruction of Cambodia amounted to crimes against humanity. But as often the case, might makes right and the demagoguery of politicians is assuaged by lip service to higher ideals. Machiavellian politics, devoid of morality and decency, informed Nixon and Kissinger. (Mr. Shawcross' father served as one of the justices of the Nuremberg Trial.)

As US B-52 bombs rained on Cambodia, an obscure small group led by French-educated Cambodian intellectuals, schooled in Maoist ideology, found its political mandate: liberate Cambodians and rid the country of all traces of western imperialism. They found the official Cambodian royalist government too corrupt and self-absorbed to be competent, and had taken up an armed struggle against it almost immediately following independence. As early as 1958, Sihanouk conducted a search-and-destroy mission against his opponents, during which he first gave them the French moniker 'Khmers Rouges'.

Since then, the ragtag band of revolutionaries transformed into a powerful insurgency, as they galvanised support among Cambodia's poor, the majority of the country's population. Their ultra-nationalistic, anti-Western rhetoric resonated with the common people at a time when the population needed a political saviour to pull them out of the mire of warfare and starvation. Initially they gained the support of rural villagers. But over time this once unknown group took control of major villages and towns across Cambodia and ultimately, on 17 April 1975, the capital city of Phnom Penh. Later, the world would come to know them by the term derisively coined by Prince Sihanouk, Khmers Rouges or Red Cambodians, the colour red to connote their communist ideological affiliation. History would come to designate Pol Pot, the *nom-de-guerre* of the elusive leader of the Khmer Rouge, in the same special category as Germany's Adolf Hitler.

In April 1970, General Lon Nol, a hopelessly incompetent sycophant and mystic, reluctantly but successfully severed his allegiance to Prince Sihanouk in an American-supported coup d'etat. At the commencement of Lon Nol's Khmer Republic, North and South Vietnamese soldiers had already occupied half of the country's territory, and although the South Vietnamese were a Cambodian ally, they ravaged the land and population with a fervour almost exceeding the purported enemy from the north.

The new establishment of power brokers did nothing to eradicate the graft and excesses they abhorred in the monarchists. To the contrary, they managed to out-do those they ousted for venality in their looting of the national coffer and exchange of favours. They ruled with a reckless abandon. The intoxication of power dulled their high-minded principles, and they engaged in corruption and licentiousness with a fervour tenfold that of their royal predecessors.

Aunt Renee recounts her family's ordeal during this period: 'We had been living in Phnom Penh, for university. One weekend in the early part of 1970, all the siblings visited home in Kampong Speu.'

Her brother Eng interjects: 'When we rode our mopeds from Phnom Penh, we encountered a roadblock into Svay Kravann.'

Aunt Renee continues: 'While we were there, the North Vietnamese soldiers invaded our town. A long line of tanks, at least 30, possibly 50 of them, rumbled through it on the main paved road.

'First, the South Vietnamese soldiers had sought sanctuary in Svay Kravann. They rounded up all the town leaders, bound them with electrical cord in a line and paraded them through the centre of town on the main thoroughfare. They kept the men inside a house directly across from ours and left them there as they retreated further into Cambodia.

'But before they left, they had strategically placed loudspeakers all over town in trees and buildings. At night, they played tapes of the sound of gunfire, explosions and the whistling of rockets into a microphone connected to all these loudspeakers.

'Of course, the approaching North Vietnamese soldiers retaliated to the fighting sound with real ammunition aimed directly into the civilian population, concentrated in the town. A bomb directly landed on our neighbour's house and decimated it. Nothing was left standing except for ashes and soot. By the time the tanks rolled in, most of the buildings had already been destroyed and the town flattened to the ground.

'The soldiers barked directives to the remaining residents in Vietnamese. Most of the people had already fled. My parents refused to leave their home; they relied on their fluency in Vietnamese to translate for the soldiers. They grew up in Svay Rieng where everyone knew Vietnamese.'

Before the soldiers reached their house, as the gunfire and bombs exploded around them, my maternal relatives had taken shelter under their firmly built beds, made of dark wood. The surface of the thigh-high heavy beds measured four to six inches in thickness. During the day, these beds served as tables or seats. Ta Kuy placed sandbags around the beds to fortify against gunfire and other shrapnel.

Three neighbourhood girls also took shelter with them under these beds. Some of the other female population were not so fortunate; the soldiers raped many of them.

Uncle Eng continues: 'Our house was the strongest in town. The North Vietnamese soldiers used it as their headquarters. Besides, many of the other houses had already been destroyed. They ransacked and looted the ones left standing. Those items they could not transport due to lack of space, they piled in the middle of the road. Then they drove the tanks and crushed the piles.'

Aunt Renee adds: 'The children lived under these beds, made cavernous by the surrounding sandbags. Our parents and the servant Gnat moved about the house with the soldiers. For at least one week we stayed crouched under there. We relieved ourselves into a bowl. Afterwards, Pou Gnat would empty it.'

At night, the soldiers would peak into the hideaway and taunt Grandma Hao to give over one of her 'beautiful virgin daughters' to them. In exchange, they would give the family meat to eat. At other times, they demanded that the daughters come out to cook food for everyone. Grandma deflected their designs by asking instead for Gnat to prepare their meals, adding that none of her daughters know how to cook. All the while, Grandma blocked with her heavy-set body the one entrance into the cavernous hideaway. Grandpa would accompany Gnat outside to cook and run errands for the soldiers.

The North Vietnamese found the bound leaders who had been left inside the house directly in front of my grandparents' house. They proceeded to pour kerosene on the house and light it on fire. Upon seeing this, Grandma ran out to them and pleaded for the lives of the men.

The soldiers asked Grandma, 'These leaders, did they mistreat their subordinates?'

Grandma replied in Vietnamese, 'Never. These are good men.'

Whether or not they believed my grandmother, the soldiers did grant her entreaty and released the men. Afterwards, they burned down the house.

The residents of other houses were not so fortunate.

Uncle Eng recalls: 'The soldiers burned one house with the people tied up in it. A corps of foreign journalists had arrived. By this time, the soldiers had already left. Ani, my youngest brother, and I took a few of the American journalists around the decimated town. The bodies inside one house singed into charcoal.

'Near our house, the soldiers bulldozed a large hole and dumped countless bodies into it. Bodies were strewn everywhere. On the fence. On the road to the temple. Only two families were left alive. Death met the others or they fled.'

The Khmer Rouge continued their armed struggle against this corrupt, new republican government.

My father had been conscripted into Lon Nol's army several weeks before the family moved to Phnom Penh. As a *professeur*, he was immediately put in charge of hundreds if not thousands of people. He spent many months at the battlefront. He came to stay at home only three to five weeks out of a year.

Sometime during this period, most likely mid-1971, my mother gave birth to me, the first daughter in the family. Technically, my parents had another girl before me, but a stillborn. (Maman was already eight-months pregnant when she bumped into the edge of a table. She did not realise the child was already dead when she went to the hospital.)

I take it as a truism now, after hearing people's repeated recollections, that my mother possessed strength, commercial deftness, innate intellect and impeccable style. Not a bad combination of qualities to have had. In Phnom Penh, Maman had put aside her tailoring business; she often travelled to be with Papa. Over time, she shrewdly made a business out of her trips with him. She noticed that the war had cut off certain regions from supplies. The fighting and bombing had damaged a lot of roads. Maman took advantage of the situation. She contacted Buny,* a family friend and pilot, and asked him to fly merchandise to these isolated areas.

Aunt Renee vividly recalls: 'One day in 1973, at the height of the intense fighting, Bong Eat left on the helicopter for Kampong Som. That evening, she returned home with literally sacks full of cash.'

During this time, the dispossessed from the countryside continued to stream into Phnom Penh in droves. Squatter camps and makeshift shelters went up, quickly marring the aesthetics and charm of the capital.

---

* Buny, Mr. Harrison Lee, was a close family friend, in particular to my parents. He would have left Phnom Penh with us during the evacuation had he not left our apartment that morning to run an errand. He first came to the United States in early 1974 to study, and returned to Cambodia in February 1975, two months before the fall of Phnom Penh. When he was sponsored a few years later as a refugee, he lived in Oklahoma. Curious to make friends and discover his new country, he visited a tavern, eliciting many stares from the rowdy regulars there. From nowhere, he felt burly hands strangling him from the back. He was soon surrounded by other burly 'red necks' who made a punching bag out of him with their fists and pool sticks. He struggled home and returned with nunchuks; he waited outside. Upon seeing his nemesis, Harrison, a martial artist, took his revenge. The police was called and he was jailed for a day or so until the tavern owner came to his defence. After this incident, he moved to Michigan. Currently, he lives with his family in southern California.

In December 1973, my uncle Eng, as a Cambodian Air Force officer, received a grant from the US government to train in Lackland Air Force base in Texas.

Mardi recalls my father's military service: 'Maman would take Sina and me to visit Papa in the trenches. On the first visit, we were so excited at seeing the war machines: artilleries, rocket launchers, bazookas and M-16s.

'But that first night, terror and fear gripped us. The Khmer Rouge bombarded our camp with rockets and artilleries. We took cover in an earthy trench, huddling with Maman. Papa went to command his company.'

Sina remembers: 'At the army base, I remember Papa handing out money to his troop. I rode with him in his jeep that was pulling artillery. Another time, soldiers came out to warn him to turn around because the enemy had been spotted.'

My father received a modest military salary. The money for comfort came from other sources. First of all, he controlled the purse strings. He handled the distribution of salaries for his men. In her business, my mother had a captive clientele among the families of my father's men. Those who did not have the finances right away to pay for Maman's merchandise owed my father money, which he docked from their monthly salary.

Also, at one point, he was charged with manning the 'fish route', where fishermen and non-fishermen alike were charged a fee to cross.

In May 1974, my father's company and three others were laid under siege in the mountains. For the next 11 months, Khmer Rouge soldiers kept them hostage in trenches covering no more than one square mile. Day after day, night after night, the Khmer Rouge shelled their location; they were confined to the trenches and could not walk on level ground.

During this time, my mother was very pregnant with Daravuth. She gave birth to him either in late 1973 or early 1974.

In September 1974, my mom's uncle, Ân Seng, left to study at the International Institute for Public Administration in Paris on a scholarship. His wife, Nan, visited him in Paris one month later. When Phnom Penh fell in April 1975, Ân and Nan were separated from their four children. They lived next door to us in Phnom Penh.

My family moved into the Sengs' residence, a top floor apartment with a rooftop terrace that allowed for a spectacular view of central Phnom Penh. With the increased fighting, Maman wanted everyone to be in one location. In late 1970, the Seng daughters asked Buny to fly my grandparents from their Kampong Speu home. The road from Phnom Penh had been greatly damaged and was impassable by car.

Relief for Papa came in late March 1975. The Khmer Rouge army left the stranded Lon Nol army to assist their comrades in capturing Phnom Penh. Over the military transistor radio, my mother heard of Papa's injured condition. He was deeply wounded in the bombardment in Kampong Sala. He lost his left eye and had to be hospitalised.

Aunt Ry recounts the ordeal: 'I drove Bong Eat on my moped to Pochentong Airport to see her husband. We were told he had been transported from Kampong Sala to Phnom Penh. On the way there, explosions went off everywhere. The smoke blackened the sky. The whistling of rockets criss-crossing above us shrilled in our eardrums. Flames from the surrounding fire caught the bottom of my bell-bottom pants' leg. We had to stop the moped several times to hit the ground as bombs exploded around us.

'Upon our arrival to the airport, we failed to find Bong Im. Fortunately, Bong Eat recognised her husband's military friend, Srey Meas, who told us that Bong Im had already been transported to the military hospital on Monivong Boulevard.'

They left for the hospital and found my father unconscious, crusted with blood and dirt-ridden. They met Buny, who contacted his medical friends there, including a young medical intern, Ngor Haing. Through him they procured a bed and medical treatment for my father's injuries. Without that crucial contact, it would have been impossible to receive medical attention amidst the sea of men in need of treatment.

Aunt Ry continues: 'The wounded sprawled all over the hospital floor and hallways. Pools of blood splattered the facilities. So much suffering confronted us in that hospital ward.'*

On 17 April 1975, the Khmer Rouge toppled the Lon Nol regime. Soon followed by Vietnam and Laos, Cambodia was the first domino to fall to communism. Upon the surrender of Lon Nol's republican government, Pol Pot immediately implemented an eight-point programme:**

1. Evacuate people from all towns.
2. Abolish all markets.
3. Abolish the old currency; retain the revolution's currency that had been printed.
4. Defrock Buddhist monks; put them to work growing rice.
5. Execute all leaders of the Lon Nol regime beginning with the top leaders.
6. Establish high-level co-operatives throughout the country with communal eating.

---

* My aunt's description of the hospital scene reminds me of my visits to several hospitals a few hours after the grenade attack on peaceful demonstrators on Easter Sunday, 30 March 1997. The four grenades killed at least 17 people and wounded over 100 others. Because it was Sunday, very few hospital staff were on duty to treat the wounded and the almost-dead. Some of the very few doctors who were on duty refused to treat them because they reasoned that these people did not have money to pay them. The hospitals also lacked adequate facilities and equipment to handle the emergency. Many of the patients sprawled on the dirty, chequered hospital floors in their own pool of blood. Witnessing one man dying in front of me, I never felt so helpless as I did during those visits.

** A long time ago, I retrieved this eight-point summary from an internet essay on Cambodia. I have since been unable to retrace the piece for the title and author in order to give proper credit.

7. Expel the entire Vietnamese minority population.

8. Dispatch troops to the borders, particularly the Vietnamese border.

Pol Pot loved mankind. It was individual man that he could not stand.* He loved humanity, for it was on behalf of the suffering mass, the hapless victims of foreign superior war machines, that he took up arms. His biographers describe an affable, soft spoken, self-effacing, *sa'art s'om*, an elusive man.

But those individuals who perturbed him – the educated, the arrogant, the wealthy, the foreigners, the foreigner-wannabes, the city dwellers, the challengers, the religious and everyone else – he destroyed.

Pol Pot wanted to reinvent the wheel and revert the country to year zero. In April 1975, he had his chance.

Ideas have consequences, writes theologian Francis A. Schaeffer. Thirty years later, the consequences of Pol Pot's ideology continue to sear the hearts and minds of all Cambodians.

* Paraphrasing Fyodor Dostoevsky in *The Brothers Karamazov.*

Chapter Four

Life in the Killing Fields: Chensa
(November 1975 – December 1978)

My mother, my brothers and I reached Phum Chensa, northwest of the provincial capital, around November 1975, almost seven months after we first evacuated Phnom Penh. Apart from the five months spent in prison, where my mother died, we lived with my paternal grandparents for the duration of the Khmer Rouge regime in their sizeable, firmly built, raised wooden house, in the style of well-off villagers in Svay Rieng province of that era.

In case our modern Western affluence should confuse what I mean by 'well-off', permit me a description of this house and the village it is situated in.

Unlike many other villages in the region, Chensa was not concentrated in a hamlet of trees. Rather, many simple stilt houses, raised off the ground, dotted the left side and right side of a raised main dirt road that stretched north-south for several miles. One-room huts composed of woven dried leaves sat exposed and off-balanced as islands, embraced by open low-lying fields for wet-rice cultivation. Other dwellings were more formidable because they were enclosed by a fence, tall trees and lush vegetation on a large raised plot of land and had tiled roofs. Each house or hut was placed at intervals of one-fifth to one-half of a mile from each other.

The width of the main road was the width of a sedan during the rainy season. But the size of the road never posed a problem for the villagers because cars made rare appearances in their part of the world. This hamlet was surrounded by miles and miles of open rice paddies. Flat land of lush emerald green fields – tinted by golden rice grain at the tips of the thin reeds in season, swaying, rustling to the brush of the cool breeze – made up my village of Chensa.

Ta Duch's blockhouse with tiled roof sat on raised wooden stilts eight to ten feet off the ground; the adults could easily walk about underneath the house without worrying about bumping their heads. A large rectangular bamboo bed stands in the middle of the dirt floor. Here, everyone found shade during the day from the oppressive sun, to gossip and nap. The kitchen with all its earthen stoves and grills stood to one side of the dirt floor. There is one stairwell in front of the house that we took upstairs. An open, airy space greeted us, devoid of any furniture. In the back were two lightly sectioned off rooms, one my grandparents' bedroom, the other storage. During the Khmer Rouge era, my mom, brothers and I slept on the open floor, in the open, airy space that served as the main part of the house.

Fresh air and light flowed through two windows on each side of the house, vertically grated with shutters. Through the windows on one side of the house, our eyes rested on an outhouse and a circular concrete well. On the opposite side, there is a corral for the larger livestock. The pigs and chickens roamed freely under and around the property, fenced in artificially and naturally with trees and various brushes. A garden sat in the back.

We found deep respite in our life the first few months in Phum Chensa. After our long arduous journey from Phnom Penh – the fighting of the last several years, the sea of human suffering confronting us along the way, our own hunger pangs and the disappearance of my father – the vast open sky of village life suited us perfectly.

We had plenty to eat – fresh fish from the nearby ponds, periodically supplemented with chicken, pork and beef from my grandparents' farm. Vast emerald-green rice paddies, dotted by long, elegant palm trees, provided us more than the daily dietary staple; their gentle rustling, kissed by the fresh clean air, calmed our souls. Beauty surrounded us – the expansive, pristine sky above greeted by the unadulterated, verdant open fields and clear ponds below. We found contentment in the simplicity of farm living. Life was sublime and picturesque.

All the while, my mother continued to wait quietly for her husband's return.

Lundi, Daravuth and I enjoyed meeting my father's family for the first time. Our childhood notion of family expanded. The last time my mother had paid a visit to her in-laws in Chensa, Mardi was four years old.

Grandpa Duch's house loomed largest in the village, surrounded by acres of flat, low-lying rice fields. Many of the villagers were related to him in one way or another. His lineage to the land extended back many generations. His family was part of the established base people, *nek moulitharn*, whose lives are tied to the land and subsistence wet-rice cultivation, the pinnacle of Cambodian village life.

According to my father's younger sister who continues to live there to this day, when we arrived at Chensa, each of the 70-plus households that comprised the citizenry of the village housed two to three new families. During this time, Eam ruled our village of Chensa as the chieftain. He was a distant relative and a member of the Khmer Rouge.*

---

* Distinctions should be noted regarding the use of the elusive term 'Khmer Rouge'. At the official level, there existed the ideological Khmer Rouge, the small band of ideologues who ordered the social engineering of Khmer society. However, many 'Khmer Rouge' cadres existed at the grassroots level. These included the base people who carried out the orders or who passively joined the ranks of the regime. Loosely speaking, many of my paternal relatives could be called 'Khmer

That first day on the farm, my youngest aunt took the three older boys to care for the family's water buffaloes, many of them belonging to Mardi. The pairs of buffaloes and cows the grandparents had given him on his one-month birthday celebration had procreated.

Many children ran to greet the newcomers.

Mardi recalls: 'Their vocabulary awed me; they were strange to my ears, very proper. They addressed each other as "comrade", *met*.

'One of them asked me, "Comrade, what is your name?"

'"Mardi. And these here are *met* Sina and *met* Lundi."

'A chorus of laughter erupted. My brothers and I joined them in their laughter, but we did not understand the reason for it. Later, my aunt educated me that I should not address my siblings as "comrades".'

Nor should we continue to address my mother as 'Maman' and use other foreign words.

Peace and tranquillity existed ephemerally and changed within a matter of months. As we entered the hot and dry months, in February or March, Angkar ordered that everyone in each village eat together at a common dining hall. The directive had been given earlier by the Central Committee in Phnom Penh, but our zone was late in complying with this. The authority turned our elementary school building into the village cafeteria. They demanded that all the families turn in their kitchenware and all foodstuffs. No one was permitted to eat outside the dining hall. They reasoned equity and practicality, so 'people would not have to cook for themselves'.

Rouge'. One can imagine the challenges confronting the seekers of justice at the soon-to-be-established war crimes tribunal (legitimate or otherwise). On this slippery slope of culpability, where do we draw the line in holding someone responsible? What if the person did not engage in the actual killing but aided and abetted the commission of the crime? In criminal law, a person must have committed an act, *actus reus*, and possessed the requisite intent, *mens rea*, before he could be found guilty of a crime. Regardless the high threshold of this standard, nonetheless many Cambodians can be found guilty under doctrines of individual responsibility and/or *respondeat superior*.

In reality, Angkar wanted control of every aspect of life, to be the almighty provider for Cambodians.

A barrage of other changes ensued, following the establishment of the dining hall. People worked longer hours. Young people 15 to 25 years old worked in the fields from sunrise (around 5 a.m.) until sundown or late into the recesses of the night if adequate moonlight existed or the work quota had not been met. Their humanity stripped from them, they existed only as automatons, for the good of the elusive Angkar. Each solitary figure mechanically moved in death-like silence back and forth, up and down, side by side with other solitary automatons against the burning saffron sky. From above, they formed black specks, like ants, labouring away in camps, awaiting their turn to be smashed, *kumticht*.

Food became scarce although we had just harvested a good crop. The Organisation demanded unrealistic quotas of rice to be delivered to its centre in Phnom Penh. The authority exported the rice to China and North Korea in exchange for armaments. Fulfilling the quotas took precedence over feeding the people.

Of course, each village chief and his family ate well. The pecking order next favoured those 'base people' who had good standing or relations with the authority. Then the regular base people. At the bottom of the totem pole stood the vulnerable 'new people' from the cities, new to rural life, new to poverty, new to hard labour – so the Khmer Rouge assumed.

My paternal grandparents by nature of their indigenous status received favourable treatment in the new social hierarchy. The fact that we lived in their household provided us with a special buffer not available to the other new people. But as the arrest of Ta Duch and the death of my mother attest, loyalty rendered little significance in the face of hysteria of the power-that-be.

The authority restricted our travels. A person must have a permit to travel outside his village. The new people faced visible contempt from the indigenous villagers. Fear etched its poison into the features of the adults' faces.

Clang, clang, clang! The bell of the dining hall called out to the labourers across the fields and ditches. My mother and the other labourers suppressed the aches and pains of having bobbed up and down in the leech-infested rice fields or having dug and carried heavy baskets of dirt from one location to another all morning on empty stomachs. They dropped their scythes or dirt-filled baskets to stretch and loosen their tightened muscles.

Everyone shook with hunger and welcomed the clanging bell with alacrity. Little children, who had been tending small gardens or collecting animal manure for heat and fertiliser, hurried from their straw huts and wooden homes to meet their parents.

'Vuth, come on. Let's go find mom. I'll give you a piggyback ride.' He jumped on my back and I carried him halfway to the dining hall, but then changed my mind. 'Get off!' I snapped in my clipped Khmer, forgetting that it was I who extended the offer. 'You're getting to be too heavy.'

The adults, dressed in the Khmer Rouge's signature uniform of loose fitting, black hospital scrubs with chequered red-and-white *kramas* (scarves) wrapped around their necks or heads, filed along on the narrowly raised dirt paths marking the boundary of each rice paddy towards the dining hall. Individuality had no place in the revolution.

We found Maman amidst the crowd in the dining hall.

In the dining hall, everyone lined up to receive a scoop of cooked rice. Of course, the authority only placed trusted base people in the enviable position of cooks or rice scoopers. The person dishing out the rice possessed complete discretion. Those he favoured received the rice ration tightly packed into the half coconut shell. The others received a thinly and loosely dished portion.

The children sat among themselves on long tables with benches in one end of the room. 'No manners,' complained the adults.

'They fight for the meat and leave only the broth for *chah-chah*, old people.' At the other end of the room huddled the new people, eating in muted silence. Fatigue had sapped every ounce of their energy for conversation. But they had also learnt the less they speak, the less evidence the authority had against them.

At each meal, a group of ten people shared a bowl of vegetable soup and a plate of stir-fry vegetables to accompany their apportioned individual plates of rice. The meat tasted by the lucky few came from the two or three chickens diluted into the big pot of soup serving the 500 famished souls at each lunch or dinner.

I commonly found leeches hidden in the vegetables of our soup. Despite my age and ignorance of the social and political situation, I knew enough not to jump and make a fuss upon discovering one. 'Maman, look, there's a leech, *chleurng*, in our soup,' I nudged and whispered in my mother's ear. She quietly took her spoon, scooped the cooked bloodsucker out, and everyone continued eating. Just another meal at the dining hall.

'*Kaun srei*, eat well. Try to eat well,' encouraged my mother. 'You're only a slip of a figure now.'

The month of May ushered in the rainy, monsoon season. Torrents of water poured on this part of the world almost daily. Within the blink of an eye, rays of glorious sun pierced through the sheets of refreshing rain, their interaction creating majestic beauty. Lightning struck and the thunder clapped. Fields turned into shallow lakes. The lush rice paddies teemed with life – frogs, tadpoles, large and small fish jumped and played in their life-giving habitat. Water buffaloes and children splashed and swam alongside them. Velvety wind glided across the expanse, caressing the faces of those in its path, and continuing aimlessly onwards to the horizon.

The croaking of frogs and chirping of various insects produced melodic harmony that contrasted with the storms churning within each of our souls. It seemed the gods were playing a cruel game with us because the beauty before us belied the evil and fear that was within us. Somewhere, someone – a Khmer – would be brooding and conspiring against his next victims, other Khmers.

Cambodia has always been a land of extreme contrasts. Cambodians' trait of deep passivity informed by Theravada Buddhism foils the ferocity displayed during this period. Once King Sihanouk's Eden, Cambodia turned into Beelzebub's Pandemonium, his palace of utter darkness and pure chaos; Cambodia became Milton's earthly paradise lost.

A paradox separates modernity's progress from Pol Pot's reversion to the year zero.

An incongruity exists between the miserable squalour of Cambodia even today in the 21st century and the awe-inspiring majesty of ancient times. The immense scale and glory of the Angkor ruins easily rival any one of the Seven Wonders of classical antiquity. Now they sit amidst growing jungles of landmines and giant trees, slowly being choked of life by the passing of time, the roots of banyan trees, the greed of marauders and the current phenomenon – the trampling of a million tourists a year.

Foreigners passing through the 'gentle land' over the years have commented on Cambodians' softer qualities in comparison to their neighbours to the east and the west. The sensuousness of its people – captured in the stone carvings of voluptuous Apsara (celestial dancers) on temple walls and in the insouciant, prevailing Khmer smile – beguiles visitors and masks the darker side of the population's psyche. Cambodian mythology has it that these graceful nymphs danced to please the gods and to keep the cosmos moving in an orderly fashion.

A spectacular freak of nature distinguishes the Tonle Sap's unique mid-year reversal from the natural flow of the world's rivers. The Mekong River, originating from the mountains in

China bordering Tibet, converges with the Tonle Sap flowing from the northwest, in Phnom Penh. During the annual monsoon season, the immense rise in volume of the mighty Mekong forces the Tonle Sap to back up and reverse its course. This northwards reversal in turn floods a huge pocket of lake water, also known as the Tonle Sap, trebling its size as much as 3,100 square kilometres. When the rainy season ends in mid-October, diminishing the Mekong's water level, the flow of the Tonle Sap is reversed again.

I was only six years and too young to understand. So I did not try or even care to understand the antinomies of the present life. Instead, little Daravuth and I ran through the sheets of hard rain, gleefully splashing and chasing each other.

'You can't catch me! You can't catch me!' I taunted my little brother with the bloated stomach, who hopelessly teetered-tottered after me.

'Vuth, see if you can catch the rainwater with your mouth. Look at me.' Then I showed him as I tilted my head backwards to face the torrential downpour, scrunched my eyes shut, opened my mouth wide and stuck out my tongue.

Boredom of playing with Daravuth quickly set in so I wandered off to our backyard and chased after the many frogs that lived there. The rain had now stopped and I formed a solitary figure against the magenta-hued sky. My seething, suppressed hunger pangs surfaced, reminding me once again how hungry I was. But I had just had dinner and there was not much I could do about the aches in my stomach. Back to chasing after the frogs.

I wonder when Papa will return to us again. He's been gone for so long. I miss him.

Does he still have that patch over his eye? It must hurt him so much.
Back to the frogs. I just saw one. Where did it go?

*

Mardi remembers a haunting encounter during this time, our first monsoon season on the farm: 'I was watching my two water buffaloes some distance from my village when I noticed a frog. Angkar forbid us to supplement our diet, but I was hungry so I chased after the frog. The frog jumped into a newly dug hole. Too excited at the prospect of having meat for dinner, I jumped into the hole after the frog, failing to notice the depth and size of the hole until I had to get out.

'As I tried to hoist myself out with my new catch, I noticed the lip of the hole stood above my head. The hole was rectangular and probably measured two-and-a-half by two metres.

'In the dining hall two days later, I noticed the absence of a group of Chinese new people. I asked Maman their whereabouts but she did not know.

'The following day, I returned to the same hole in hope that I would catch another frog. I found the location but did not find a hole. Rather, the hole had been filled up with putrefied bodies, stacked one on top of another, and gave off this rancid odour.'

Life is but a breath.

Sina had a friend whose family lived by the dining hall. The friend's father wore very thick, dark-rimmed glasses. Both parents spoke Cambodian with a very heavy Chinese accent. The little boy often joined my brothers watching over water buffaloes. Other times, they helped the adults to plough the muddy fields by riding on the buffalo-pulled contraption to give added weight.

One evening, Sina looked for his friend at the dining hall but he never showed up. He asked Mardi and Lundi but they too did not know his whereabouts. They glanced around the dining hall for his parents. They were nowhere to be seen.

As they proceeded home after dinner, the boys passed Sina's friend's thatched hut. The sounds of a despairing, anguished, staccatoed requiem filtered out through the leafed walls to the boys' ears. The family huddled inside, lambs waiting to be slaughtered. In the meantime, they mourned.

Resist. Fight back! But this would run contrary to their nature, to that ancient belief that is Taoism – the espousal of action through inaction, of letting go, of resigning oneself to fate. Additionally, to fight back would be as futile as battling against shadows, as successful as beheading facelessness.

Instead, they took this time to mourn together, to comfort each other in their grief, to savour each precious second in the fellowship of suffering. For in a little while, they would be no more.

The brothers dejectedly moved on, laden with heavy thoughts of life and death, in this cruel and never-ending tragedy that was their world. From then on, Sina no longer saw his friend, the friend's sister and parents. The family 'disappeared'.

Life is but a breath.

The ensuing months witnessed many more disappearances of new people. The threnody of death replaced the forgotten laughter, the insouciant Khmer smile, the carefree spirit of young love, the rhapsody of lovemaking. If we communicated at all, we did so in hushed tones. Fear and terror reigned in the hearts of Cambodians with the coming of night. Angkar, it was believed, had as many eyes as a pineapple, *mean pnai doich mnu'oh.*

One night, Daravuth needed to go to the bathroom. 'Do you have to go number one or number two?' asked my mother half-asleep, hoping that she did not have to lead him downstairs and into the night to the outhouse. He only needed to pee so he went to relieve himself from our second story sleeping compartment. Little did he realise he was urinating on an eavesdropper below, as the former informant sheepishly revealed to us at the end of the Khmer Rouge reign. Poetic justice?

Little Daravuth provided us with much amusement. After watching his older brothers enjoying the spiciest, hottest pepper, he too wanted to eat it. 'Vuth, you can't eat it. It's very spicy, too spicy for you,' everyone told him.

He took the prohibition as a challenge and began to nag for it all the more.

'Okay. But don't say we didn't warn you.' We all looked at each other, greatly amused with anticipation of his reaction.

Vuth took the biggest, reddest pepper he could find and plopped it into his mouth whole. Our eyes widened with disbelief; his bravado startled us.

He took his first bite, followed by some chewing. His face contorted. Tears began to stream down his face. We could tell hell was brewing fire inside his little mouth. But he refused to spit out the cause of his torture.

We continued to watch him with incredulity at his chutzpah. Then he swallowed the whole thing and immediately ran for a tin cup of water. Then another cup. And a third cup.

Everyone burst out in laughter at the hilarity of his passage into manhood, at the full age of four years old.

The lack of nutrients, compounded by the unsanitary environment, produced extremely sensitive skin for little Vuth. Mosquitoes loved his sweet skin and made their marks on it. Numerous bites from other insects bespeckled his body, the scars remaining for years after.

During this time, my chores included taking care of the village garden, transporting water from one field to another and working on whatever miscellaneous projects the authority delegated. I became quite adept in pulling water from one field over the raised-dirt pathway to the other field. All the older people whose work it was thought so.

A bucket is attached to four long ropes, each with a handle at the end. One person takes two ropes and the other person takes the other two ropes. When the ropes are pulled taut, the bucket suspends in the middle. Both people stand on the raised-dirt pathway. At the same time, they bend forward to dip the bucket into the watered field and, immediately after, pull the ropes to lift the bucket over the raised-dirt pathway and dump the water from the bucket into the other field.

This activity requires coordination, rhythm and upper-body strength, which I quickly acquired and mastered. Barefoot and raggedly clothed, oftentimes topless, I would draw the water with my youngest aunt, Aunt Nourn, Papa's adopted sister. I found the work greatly satisfying and fun. Afterwards, I would splash in the watered, leech-infested field.

It took me a while after our arrival from the city, to overcome my fear of the ubiquitous leeches living in field water. The first time a leech clamped onto my leg, I shrieked with terror and splashed wildly for help. Fortunately, my mother was working in the nearby rice paddies and ran to my aid. She pulled the fat, glossy, black bloodsucker from its food, my leg.

The dot of blood from its prick ballooned and deflated into a line down my leg, but washed off easily with the splash of water. The creature's repulsiveness rested more with the thought of a blood-filled, living, black blob sucking my blood and inching up my leg than the pain that it actually caused. Relatively speaking, the pinprick didn't really hurt.

One time, the authority gathered all the little girls my age, five and six years old, of the village to transport palm leaves. They rounded us up early in the morning and the group of 20 of us went with the several men in charge of the project to the outskirts of the village where a patch of palm trees stood.

Smiling my insouciant Khmer smile, I skipped along with the other little comrades, soothed by the morning breeze. One of the adults led us in a chorus, one of the Revolution's popular tunes.

Ruby blood that sprinkles the towns and plains
Of Kampuchea, our Homeland
Splendid blood of workers and peasants,
Splendid blood of revolutionary men and women soldiers!
This blood changes into implacable hatred
And resolved war,
April 17, under the flag of the Revolution.
Freedom from slavery.

Refrain:

Live, Live, glorious April 17
Glorious victory of greatest importance
For the epoch of Angkor!

We come together to build
A new Kampuchea and a new society
Splendid and democratic in equality and justice,
Steadfastly bestowing the heritage of independence,
sovereignty
And relying on our own strength.
We resolutely defend
Our homeland, our sacred earth
And our glorious Revolution!

Refrain:

Live, Live new Kampuchea
Democratic and prosperous!
We resolutely lift high
The Red Flag of the Revolution,
We build our Homeland,
We cause her to progress in great leaps,
In order to render her more glorious and more marvel-
*lous than ever!**

---

*   Khing Hoc Dy, 'Khmer Literature since 1975', *Cambodian Culture since 1975: Homeland and Exile*, op. cit.

None of the children knew all the words, nor could we pronounce them. But it was a catchy tune so we hummed along. I temporarily forgot the grouchiness of that morning, of having to wake up early and the nagging of my ever-hungry stomach.

Initially, I did not mind the work. However, the morning breeze quickly turned dead calm, replaced by the penetrating tropical sun. All day along, we carried the palm branches back to the village where we soaked them in mud. Afterwards, we drew the mud-covered branches and laid them out to dry.

We finished the project that evening. By then, all of us were crusted in mud from head to toe and exhausted from carrying heavy loads and the long hours. They gathered us around the village wells and poured water on us to clean us.

During this time, one of the men who poured water on me poked my right eyelid with his long-nailed little finger. It pierced into the skin and barely missed the top of my eyeball. I screamed and howled, writhing with excruciating pain as the other people gathered to find out the cause for the explosive outburst.

The screaming and howling, as can only be produced by a six-year-old, who just had her eyelid pierced into by a man's fingernail, continued. With both my palms covering my right eye and the other eye blinded by tears, the authority led me home.

The man with the long pinky fingernail explained to my family that an 'accident' had occurred. 'As I tried to wash the crusted-mud spots from her face, she moved and my finger inadvertently went into her eye. A bad little girl! If she had stayed still, this would not have happened.'

No one contested the power-that-be. In private, my family believed the man wanted to disfigure my face.

Maman broke down in tears, believing I had lost my eyesight. 'Oh, my daughter, my only daughter, your eye ...' she repeatedly moaned, letting her words trail off, 'your eye ...'

Over the next few days my eye ballooned to the size of a base-ball. My mother grounded various herbs to suck out the puss and other infection and to cool my eye.

'I am now like Papa,' I sprightly told my mother one afternoon. My face lit up at the clever revelation. 'We both have patches on our eye.'

My mother did not find the comparison at all clever as her eyes glistened and her face darkened. She broke down in tears. *She cries so easily these days.* Sometimes, at night, I heard muffled sniffling when she thought we were asleep. Grandpa Duch's loud snoring filtered through the airy house, partitioned only by silky pink curtains. The noise normally drowned out other noises, but small ears learnt to ignore it for other sounds.

My mother applied the home-made medicine on my eye day after day for the next few weeks. One month later, the swelling completely disappeared and I regained my eyesight. Everyone rejoiced at the miracle. To this day, the man's imprint indelibly marks the 'accident' on my eyelid with a half-inch scar.

Sina carries to this day his own physical scars from the Khmer Rouge years. While watching water buffaloes among a group of 15 other boys, one of the older boys of the base people pushed Sina off a tree branch. He scratched against and landed on other branches as his flailing body made its way to the hard ground. The other brothers carried the broken-up Sina home. A darkened line runs across his back to mark the fall.

We had a pet dog. Lundi grew the most attached to it, so every-one referred to it as 'Lundi's dog'. I was working or playing in the field one late afternoon, when I heard a great commotion coming from the gated courtyard of my house. Lundi's dog yelped and yelped. I ran to see the cause of this painful squeal.

For one reason or another my three older brothers were within hearing distance and they too ran over to investigate the situation.

Lundi screamed out in hysteria upon seeing his dog being roped, beaten and pulled into a rice sack.

Two men of the village authority had come to our house and without permission chased after Lundi's dog and captured it. Once they had the dog inside the rice sack, they repeatedly struck the sack with heavy wooden sticks until the yelping subsided.

They killed our pet dog for food. This occurred soon after the authority enforced the communal eating edict but when rules and regulations remained yet malleable. Later that afternoon, the authority gave a huge portion of the dog meat to our family to eat at home. Somehow, my mother must have sent word to my relatives in Prey Roka because that night my aunt Ry traversed through knee-deep watered fields to our house to eat meat again. She risked violating an infraction of the travel restriction that could have cost her her life.

My family had a feast on the ground floor. 'I'm not hungry for the meat,' I told them as I headed up the stairs. I could hear everyone enjoying the feast beneath me, as I lay down to sleep on the matted floor.

A little while later, I heard my mother asking one of my brothers to fetch me. 'Asrei, *kaun*, come eat with us,' she persistently refrained from downstairs. I reluctantly got up to join them. I took a bite of the dog meat and headed upstairs again. During the night I fell ill with a high fever.

One evening, a great commotion arose in the house. Anguished groaning and screaming filtered through the sectioned-off room upstairs. The older female adults scurried anxiously back and forth. I hardly got one step up the stairs, when my grandmother sternly warned, 'You cannot go up there!' while she herself hurried up the stairs passed me with a pail of water. One of my aunts had gone into labour. *Why the secrecy and anxiety?* I wondered. *Adults can be so irrational and mean.*

I had intense feelings of jealousy towards the children who had sandals to wear, ones fashioned out of car tires. I had outgrown the nice strapped, made-in-China sandals I wore from Phnom Penh. Now barefoot, I wanted so badly to have a pair of sandals, any pair, but had to be satisfied with trying them on or borrowing a friend's pair to wear for an hour or so. I took great delight in strutting around and admiring myself in them.

At night, Maman would point to the moon above. 'Those are bonsai trees,' she would tell us of the craters on the moon.

'Look, I have a loose tooth,' I informed my mother. I wiggled the tooth to prove that I wasn't joking.

'Let me see.' I opened my mouth even wider for my mother's inspection. '*M'en*. You're right,' Maman confirmed. 'It's very loose, ready to come out. Let me pull it for you.'

She pulled out the tooth and told me to hold the salt pebble in its place. Later on, she showed me how to brush my teeth. We had run out of toothpaste and toothbrushes a long time ago, since our stay in Wat Champa, waiting for Papa. Instead, during the Khmer Rouge period, we brushed our teeth with either charcoal or grains of sand. Our finger served as the tool we used to rub the charcoal or sand on our teeth.

Another time, I tried to hold back the tears from a fall off Lundi's water buffalo.

For an unknown reason, the authority enlisted little Sina to join the adults in *kang chalot*, the travelling work brigade. They transported him to a different village to dig dirt. When he returned to us one week later, he had almost died from starvation.

Sina recalls: 'I not only ached from the heavy labour, but constant sharp hunger pains jabbed my stomach.'

Malnutrition hit everyone; the most severe form befell former city dwellers. During every second of our waking hours, hunger preoccupied our thoughts.

Of all the siblings, the other relatives fussed the most over the welfare of Lundi and me; they argued over which of us was more anorexic. They poked and snapped the latex skin hugging our bones to make their point and sometimes yelled at us in their clipped Khmer why we don't take better care of ourselves, as if it was our fault that we should find ourselves in this state.

Around the turn of the new year, 1978, Vietnam invaded Cambodia, which was when my mother, brothers and I were arrested and experienced our long walk to prison.

Fast-forwarding, my brothers and I returned alone to Chensa following our release from Bung Rei prison. The tension between Vietnam and Cambodia remained intense, and Pol Pot continued his purges of the Eastern Zone leadership and people. The whistling of rockets and the clapping of explosions frequently rang in our ears. Incessantly, guns coughed fitfully into the majestic sky. Once or twice a week we cowered in trenches until jumping into trenches became a normal part of daily life.

Amidst this backdrop, we had returned from Bung Rei forever changed. The house was so empty without great-grandmother (who had passed away the night they arrested us) and Maman. My siblings and I never ever discussed the disappearance of Maman. We did not possess the words to do so. Even if we did have the words, our sixth sense suppressed us into muted silence. Who is friend? Who is foe? We did not know. It was better to remain silent and not trust.

Even the wind and the sunrays, once refreshing and life giving, felt cold and untrustworthy. They, too, could be working for Angkar, absorbing and transporting our conversations to the authority.

Even though we did not communicate in words with each other, we looked at each other differently. The older brothers in their clumsy, macho ways took on the care-giving role of Maman. My paternal grandparents also extended to us compassion and love. During that first week back, everyone spoke to us softly and quietly.

Nonetheless, life was not the same without Maman. The world was so empty without her presence in it. The Khmer smile disappeared from my face. I sulked and brooded. A morose film cascaded over the beautiful pristine earth and my whole outlook. Very often, the admonitions of the relatives in the house would send me running away from home to live in another relative's or neighbour's house down the road. 'Beware. You are now an unruly waif, living at our mercy. You better behave!'

Running away became an every-other-day ritual, a spiritual cleansing, for I became easily distraught and provoked. I was a chaff floating in the wind, to and fro, in search of safety and tranquillity. None was to be found, because Maman was no longer. I would inevitably return a couple of days later, believing I had given the relative inflicting the misery enough time to feel sorry. Also, I thought, the other family members must miss me terribly.

However, when I did return, instead of the pity I tried to elicit, I always got a whipping. Worse than the whipping was enduring the long tirade of how unruly and sassy I'd become. 'Just you wait. Already you are a little whore! Go, put on a shirt. You're already seven years old. Do you have no shame?'

But I did not learn my lesson. I would have imploded from the tumult of tension, anger, confusion and despair if I did not run away. Evil swirled within me and found a welcome home in the fibre of my being. It rocked the foundation of my world. I abandoned myself to pity and grief.

I feel so alone. I miss the embrace of Maman and snuggling close to her when I sleep. I miss her lullabies. I miss her protection. I want to scream. I wish I could shake off these strange feelings. I wish the ringing in my head would stop. People are so mean. They know no one will come to my rescue. Oh! How I despise all of them!

My chaotic inside mirrored the exploding, whistling, spitting sounds of warfare fought on the outside. Blinded either by tears, rage or both, I would run and run, until my exhausted seven-year-old body and mind could carry me no longer. I would enter whoever's house was closest to me at that point, unless it was a house I'd already visited and overstayed my welcome. *Well, I hate her too! They're all against me!*

At the other houses, I had whoever was available pinch the lice that nestled in my head. '*Mieng*, Auntie, my head itches. Could you *gnitch chai* for me?' Combing through my head with her fingers and upon finding a louse, the *mieng* would then squeeze the little troublemaker between the nail tip of her two thumbs. Often she would lick her thumbs afterwards to suck in the nutrients.

My three older brothers, along with the village children, periodically visited the campsites of the Khmer Rouge soldiers and mingled with the soldiers among the cannons, artillery and various other explosives and gunfire. One time, several Khmer Rouge soldiers tried to enlist my three older brothers to join them. Sina, the second oldest, seriously entertained the idea until Mardi categorically blocked the possibility.

At other times, the boys used hand grenades to fish. It worked potently well.

Mardi recalls this period of escalation: 'Sometimes we had to sleep in trenches because of the artillery bombardment.

'Vietnamese planes usually attack the Khmer Rouge camps during the day. Sina, Lundi and I witnessed spectacular aerial views of warplanes and bombing raids as we watched our water buffaloes out in the fields. Every afternoon, for a duration of one to two months, planes dove towards the Khmer Rouge camps and rained down bombs. In return, anti-aircraft guns from the ground rattled bullets in their direction. The exchange of gunfire and explosions fascinated us.'

Every time the Khmer Rouge soldiers fired rockets in the direction of the Vietnamese enemies, the group of children jumped into nearby trenches.

Mardi continues: 'One afternoon, we assumed our position a quarter of a mile away from the Khmer Rouge camp, watching our water buffaloes with other children in the grassy field. We took shelter from the scorching sun under nearby trees in a wooded area.

'I noticed my water buffaloes, on the opposite side of the open field, leading away other buffaloes from the herd. Lundi and Sina walked towards the water buffaloes to stop them from straying. I followed them a few minutes later.

'We had walked a quarter of a mile from the wooded area, when Sina and Lundi, about 50 metres or so in front of me, pointed towards the eastern sky. Against the backdrop of a deep blue cloudless sky, four World War II T-28 planes made a dive directly in our direction. We stood there, in the open field, paralysed, too dumbfounded to react. Even if we had thought to react, there was no cover. The pilots had mistaken the black water buffaloes for Khmer Rouge soldiers, since they too dressed in black.

'As the planes continued to dive towards us, we heard the release of anti-aircraft missiles fired into the air and watched the shells exploding in the air.

'The planes dove so close to us that we could see the pilots and noticed writing on the bombs.

'We fell to the ground and covered our ears with our hands because of the loud noise from the plane engines and the explosions.

'My blood ran cold; I thought that was the end of all three of us. I can still picture those bombs attached under the planes' wings.

'The rapid firing of anti-aircraft shells forced the planes to fly away.'

In December 1978, the third and final Vietnamese incursion once again uprooted the people in our village from their homes. Planes overhead hummed louder and louder above us as we scurried away from the oncoming planes that were dropping bombs on our village. Along the way, Sina witnessed a stranger struck by flying shrapnel. My paternal relatives, my brothers and I took shelter in a house of the next village, half emptied of its former residents. We cooked the duck and chicken we found there and enjoyed a bittersweet feast in the hell that was brewing around us.

CHAPTER FIVE

Life in the Killing Fields: Prey Roka
(November 1975 – December 1978)

In the village of Prey Roka, two miles east of Chensa, my maternal relatives underwent their own personal ordeal under the Khmer Rouge. Whereas in the beginning my family and I found respite in Chensa, the Seng family immediately encountered the idiocy of village life in a time of oppression. Old family grudges of generations past came back to haunt them. Many of the indigenous base people in that region had worked at one time or another as hired hands on the farm of my grandfather Duch in Chensa.

À Lo, in his early thirties, was chief of this poor village of Prey Roka, comprising of very closely-built, flimsy one-room shacks, some raised on stilts, some not, amidst denser vegetation than my village of Chensa. This was the same À Lo who had at first refused permission to have the newcomers move to Chensa. Already living in Prey Roka were Grandma Hao's father, Ta Yi, and his younger son, Mei. Lo was Mei's nephew, on his wife Mok's side – a connection Mok shrewdly flaunted.*

Upon the family's arrival into Prey Roka, À Lo sarcastically snickered at Grandma Hao, 'Where are all your big cars, small

---

* Or, as mentioned earlier, according to two relatives in Cambodia Lo may have been Mok's lover.

cars, long cars, short cars?' We had pulled into the village with an ox-cart after having travelled several months through the monsoon rain from Phnom Penh. Everyone appeared exhausted and sickly. À Lo's facetious comment upon our arrival harked back to the time Grandma Hao arranged her mother's funeral service. As a dutiful daughter with sufficient means, Grandma hired several cars to transport musicians and 63 monks to perform the mournful rite.

Now, they faced rural living without basic mosquito nets, pillows or blankets. The village chief beamed with sinister glee at the irony of the situation.

In this same village lived the Hok family, who had arrived five months earlier. Altogether, 15 new families, mostly of mixed Chinese blood, arrived into Prey Roka among an existing population of 50 base families. Most of the new people had been killed by the end of the Khmer Rouge period.

Seng Hok, one of my father's students, would later marry my aunt Ry in a communal village ceremony.

Seng remembers: 'One week after our arrival, a short, stout man came to enquire about my family's background. At the time, we did not know to hide our educational background or to dumb ourselves down. So I answered truthfully.

'Of course, given the circumstances, even at that time, it was always better to talk in generalisations and be vague, since you don't know exactly what it is they're looking for. But who would have thought that to be educated would turn out to be a fatal sin?

'It turned out that anyone with an education beyond the fifth or sixth grade was taken to prison. Soon after, the authority took my brother Peng and me "to a place to further our education".

'We joined other men in our same position, gathered from different villages, and arrived at a temple. Shouting to the group, the authority pointed to a shovel, "That's your pencil." And to a basket for holding dirt, *pra'kear*, "That's your book." And to the open fields, "That's your classroom".'

The Khmer Rouge divided them into groups of ten people, watched over by one base person. At one point, there were 263 men. The men worked in the fields during the day. At night, they sprawled on the second floor of the temple. Four soldiers, *yo'thear*, guarded the prisoners on the ground floor.

The authority assigned Tong, a distant relative of Grandpa Kuy, to be the leader of Seng's group. He himself was a new person but the authority in his village trusted him for his hard work.

Seng continues: 'I did not know Tong initially, but he would look at me and give me a knowing smile. Whenever there was hard labour and during the night-time, he would exclude me from the group to work that shift.

'Every day, they gave us watery rice porridge, with many worms mixed in the rice grain. One day, I fell ill and asked for permission to stay on the prison grounds. I noticed, as the cooks poured rice grain into the large pot, legions of worms went along with the rice into the pot. They cooked without first washing the rice.

'The authority permitted me to stay away from work because I fell ill, but the authority reduced my rice allotment to half a bowl. We never had enough to eat.

'Before we were allowed to sleep, every night without fail, they made us each recount to our group our good works of the day. Of course, each person just repeated what the other person had said because the work did not vary much and everyone knew to talk the party line. You can imagine the repetitiveness and monotony. I nodded off many times from pure exhaustion.

'When I needed to use the toilet at night, I had to yell out, "My name is Seng. I am heading down to relieve myself." After I finished, I had to yell out again, "This is Seng. I am now back."

'A few men were killed because they didn't yell out their mission.

The authority believed these men escaped. Angkar effectively instilled fear in us.

'Once a week, they made us recite our biography, written out on paper. Initially, everyone wrote down truthfully. But after a few weeks of working in the fields and as we began to understand the mentality of the authority a little bit, everyone in the end disclaimed higher education. From then on, I was an ice cream seller.

'I don't know what they did with these scraps of paper. Most likely they threw them away. It was also unlikely that these Khmer Rouge men knew how to read. And oftentimes, they didn't remember what you told them.'

Uncle Seng stayed in this re-education camp for three months, the average length of stay for students in his position. Angkar had other camps for women, for teachers and for former soldiers. These groups of people moved from one *wat*, pagoda, or school to another, wherever the authority found space to place them.

Seng and Peng's sister Choulie Hok wanted to join her brothers believing they were really being given schooling. However, the authority denied her the trip to the 're-education camp' because she was in her third trimester of pregnancy.

Seng continues: 'We stayed in the last location the longest. By that time, everyone had lost so much hair. Just by moving my head, lice dropped by the dozens. We would go for days without washing our bodies.'

Aunt Renee chimes in: 'As we pushed our cart into the village, one older lady pulled Grandma Hao aside and whispered, "Don't let it be known that your children are educated, or else they will be taken to do hard labour." Our family came to the village after Bong Seng's family. So people prepared us with the news.'

Aunt Ry adds: 'Pu Thei also warned us. But we weren't supposed to feign complete ignorance either because then they'd send us to school to learn the alphabets. I remember a few women who had to be sent to school to learn A-B-Cs, only the alphabet for one hour each day, during the middle of their work days in the fields.'

The Seng family attempted a smooth transition into the new social and political structure. From November 1975 to the middle of the next year, they lived in the house of Grandma Hao's father, Ta Yi, across the dirt pathway from the Hok family. Already in this house resided his son Mei and Mok, and their children, one of them named Lei.

Then and now, among Cambodians, it is not uncommon for married couples to set up home in either parent's house for reasons of financial necessity or filial piety.

The three Seng sisters had the most difficult time adjusting. They had grown up in towns and cities, existing most of their years as full-time students, having had little responsibility outside of schoolwork. Hard labour had been designated to a maid or servant.

Aunt Renee recalls: 'Initially, it took two of us to carry a bucket of water from the well. À Lo saw this and sent us to be re-educated, *kaw'sang*. He rhetorically snorted, "Each of you is built like an elephant, *damrei*, and it takes two of you to carry a bucket of water?"'

It was true that my aunts, in comparison to the very slight build of most rural village women, were meatier, even at that time.

Upon seeing the struggle of his granddaughters, Ta Yi offered his assistance. '*Ch'uy srei*, Granddaughters, you should not be carrying heavy water after a long day working in the field. Let me fetch the water for you.'

Off he went to the well and would return, bobbing up and down from the weight of balancing on his shoulder a bamboo shoot with two big gasoline containers full of water, one dangling on each end of the stick. Like his daughter, Hao, Ta Yi possessed a strong build, strength built up over the years from the work imposed by rural poverty.

He had long ears. Born in China, Canton province, he emigrated to Cambodia as a young child in 1900 with his mother and younger brother Lam. They came to seek a better life and business opportunities. Later, Yi married a peasant, Nga, who was also ethnically Chinese, possibly with a bit of Vietnamese blood, already living in Cambodia.

Great Uncle Ân recalls his parents: 'Ta Yi only drank hot tea; he liked to smoke. He contrasted your grandfather Ta Kuy, in that he was very gentle and just. My daughter Vanna (Huot) reminds me of my mother, Yay Nga, in appearance and personality – very short and petite, economical and not one to waste words in her speaking.'

Everyone knew him as a great conversationalist, especially when he was with his buddy, Ta Khut.

Seng recalls: 'At dawn, I would pass Ta Khut's house and see the two of them talking. When I'd return at dusk, I would see them in the same position, very much animated in their conversation.'

Soon after arriving in Prey Roka, Grandpa Kuy convulsed in apoplexy. The stroke immobilised half his body and took away his speech. Without help, he could only inch along and only on level ground, dragging his foot while his arm listlessly hung by his side. After that, Grandma Hao picked up the slack of her daughters and that of her husband.

Despite his paralysed state, the authority assigned him to watch over two cows, making certain that they were fed and given water. If he did not have work, he would not receive any food ration. Many times the cows dragged him into the ground; he could not keep up with them.

At one point, Lei, his own nephew, threatened to beat him. Lei hissed, 'Your living has only depleted the food of Angkar. We get no return from your paralysed condition.'

To which, Seng's younger brother, Tith Hok, responded, 'Lei, he is your uncle, *oum.*'

À Lei shot back, 'Not my uncle. He's *khmang*, enemy, who leeches off Angkar!'

With the start of the monsoon season, in 1976, Prey Roka also began to eat communally, later than other zones. The Seng family continued their scrutinised existence in Ta Yi's house, under the watchful eyes of Mok and her children.

One day, in the middle of 1976, my mother and Mardi paid a visit to Prey Roka. She had secretly prepared food, *noum um'saum chaet*, for her father. *Noum um'saum chaet* is a popular Cambodian delicacy, where a whole peeled banana is rolled in rice, wrapped in banana leaves and securely tied in segments. The finished product is then steamed until done to taste.

My mother knew the dire circumstances and the family politics that existed in Prey Roka. Although the edict for communal dining had been enforced, my paternal grandfather had secretly withheld several sacks of rice grain. It was from this secret abundance that my mother made the sweet rice cakes.

Maman and Mardi arrived to a house empty of all Maman's relations. Everyone was at work except for Mok and her children. Grandpa Kuy watched over his two cows. Grandma Hao looked after the village children. Their three daughters worked in the fields among the other workers. Mei, Maman's uncle, had left for *kang chalot*, a travelling labour camp. And Maman's 80-something-year-old grandfather, Ta Yi, had left to gather firewood.

Maman chided her very young cousin, Lei, 'It's already past two o'clock in the afternoon. Your grandfather has yet to have lunch. He is very old and should not have to work this hard. Why don't you help to look for firewood, so he may rest and break for lunch?'

Immediately, À Lei went to his mother, Mok, to tattletale. Upon hearing this, Mok flew into an apoplectic rage. She, in turn, went to À Lo. He ordered Mok to whip my mother.

Mok huffed back from Lo's place, the stem of a wounded palm branch in hand. Upon seeing her antagonist, she lurched forward and swung, with all the fury of a woman's scorn, the root end of the palm stem at Maman. Hell could brew no comparable rage.

Again and again, she swung, as expletives poured from her mouth. 'How dare you ***** tell my son what to do? You are only a niece, ***** *khmang*! Both young and old do *padevat*!'

Powerless against the frenzy of a woman gone mad, Maman accepted the blows. She raised both hands in an attempt to protect her head and face. The stem cut into her skin and blood dripped from her arms. Mardi tried to intervene but was struck and shouted down. Finally, Ta Yi successfully intervened and the maelstrom subsided.

Maman and Mardi wanted to return to Chensa immediately. However, À Lo arrested them, declaring that Maman had illegally come to Prey Roka without first procuring a travel permit. Mardi managed to sneak away from the crowd and ran back to Chensa to tell Grandpa Duch of the emergency. Ta Duch reasoned that it would be useless to ask his village chief, Eam. Instead, he went directly to *k'nak srok*, the authority overseeing many villages at the district level.

Back in Prey Roka, later that night, À Lo called everyone in the household, save his aunt's family, for re-education, *kaw'sang*. My mother, along with everyone, sat there mute, as the village chief lectured them on egalitarianism and communalism. 'No matter how old you 'are, everyone works for the revolution, *t'ver padevat*.'

The next day, the intervention of *k'nak srok* released my mother from À Lo's authority. She returned to Chensa. That would be her last time in Prey Roka.*

---

* In February 2002, I extended my training visits in Svay Rieng by a couple of days in order to visit my relatives in Chensa. After surprising my family with my presence, I asked to meet Mok. It was uncertain whether the sedan that transported me to Chensa would be able to manoeuvre the craters and jagged dirt path to Prey Roka, but the owner willingly accommodated my request. Fifteen minutes

From that time on, the Seng family were given an abandoned one-room thatched hut by the river and moved out of Ta Yi's house. The structure barely had any roof left. The first few nights the Sengs could look through the roof and see the host of sparkling stars. But more often the sky opened up and poured torrential rain on them.

Knowing she could not rely on her Pollyanna-esque daughters and paralysed husband, Grandma took palm branches she had gathered, tucked in her sarong, climbed onto the roof and sewed the branches tightly together to form a sealed, protective covering.

Grandma Hao adopted the work ethics of her industrious, strong father, Ta Yi. During the period the family lived with Ta Yi, the authority assigned Grandma to look after the village children. She considered the workload to be light and the position ideal before Angkar regimented everyone's food. Then, the position gave her no time nor opportunity to steal or look for food to supplement their meagre diet.

Subsequently, she requested to be re-assigned to tending the village vegetable gardens when the family moved to the new house. The work required a man's strength and up until then mainly older

---

later, we arrived in Prey Roka and parked outside Mei and Mok's fenced-in wooden house. We found both of them resting underneath their house. I respectfully greeted my great uncle, Grandma Hao's younger brother, and barely acknowledged Mok. She felt the slight. It was my first time seeing her since Khmer Rouge years, but she amazingly appeared to be exactly as I pictured her in my mind, in appearance and demeanour: mousy, stout and short (she comes up to my ears in height), and perpetually unhappy (the kind of person where it is impossible to imagine a genuine smile or kind thought ever crossing that person's face). In my conversation with mainly my great uncle, I would steal glances at Mok, and periodically was forced to engage her in conversation when she interjected. We talked about superficial and present-day matters; I did not think it beneficial to raise issues of old. I had brought over left over candies, a gesture in hindsight more offending to them than if I had not brought anything at all. I did not intend to be offensive, but clothes, durable foodstuffs and other items had already been given away to relatives in Chensa. If I did feel badly, it did not last long. Another 15 minutes later, I left. As I walked side-by-side with my great uncle, Mok and her daughter attempted to repay the slight by whispering non-sensical comments about me.

men had been assigned the task. The authority had no problem with someone wanting to take on a heavier and grittier workload.

Before she joined the group, the men had been transporting water from the river, a considerable distance uphill to the gardens, to water the rows of fruits and vegetables. Grandma Hao was to *raet'tuk*, transport the buckets of water, 50 to 60 times each day during the dry season. The hump on her shoulders would attest to the gruelling weight and repetitiveness of her task.

But at the time of her transfer, the rainy season had started. Little need existed for the transporting of water. The gardens needed fertiliser. The fertiliser came from human faeces in the village outhouses. Grandma's task involved drawing human waste from these pits. Sometimes, it required that she slip into the hole of faeces and urine in order to mix and draw the amount needed.

This position in the village gardens, however, allowed her to steal fruits and vegetables to supplement the scant portion of food dished out to the villagers. She hid these stolen goods under the basket of grass she gathered to feed her paralysed husband's cows.

Moreover, Grandma took advantage of the Khmer Rouge leaders' habit of chain smoking. They would chop down a bush and pick off all the big leaves they used to roll their cigarettes. Grandma would water and nurture the chopped stems. These stems in turn would produce little leaves that she later plucked, dried and stored in a vase.

During the harvest season, she would secretly exchange them for sugar cane and palm juice. The aunts gained weight during a time when everyone else withered to skin and bone. This situation puzzled the authority and only added fuel to their animosity of the Seng family.

≈ ≈ ≈

Born into a poor peasant family, Yi Hao grew up in Kampong Také, a rural village in Svay Rieng. Through sheer determination and hard labour, her parents Yi and Nga made a life for their growing family of eight sons and three daughters. Nga gave birth to their third child and oldest daughter, Hao, sometime between 1913 and 20. Ân became their eighth child.* According to their village standards, Yi and Nga were considered well-off. They had numerous servants, numerous hectares of land, hundreds of cows and water buffaloes. They owned several boats to transport materials for buying and selling all the way to Vietnam. All the children helped with the family trade and received no education beyond the third grade, the highest education level offered in the village, save the second oldest son Bah who went on to further his education in Prey Nokor (Saigon) and, later, Ta Ân who went to live with Grandma Hao in order to further his studies. The little education available was only true for the boys; the girls, including Yi Hao received literally no education.

At the age 15 or 16, Hao married Kuy Seng, a very harsh man. The ceremony took place in her birth village and the couple moved to his poverty-stricken village of Kampong Marek, also in Svay Rieng province. There they had three children while living in a one-room hut: An, my mother Eat and Eng. Their home of clay

---

* I asked Great Uncle Ân about his siblings during his visit to the US in June 2005. Ta Ân cannot remember the name of his oldest brother, the first born to Ta Yi and Nga, nor remember whether he has other siblings following his younger brother Mei. The names of his siblings familiar to him are only nicknames called at home and not official ones. Ta Ân explains the lack of information in this regard: 'In our household, as in other Chinese households in our region of that time, children were to be seen and not heard, and little questions were asked regarding members of the family, especially of the parents; in the Chinese tradition, as practiced in Cambodia, the oldest child is not termed the first child, but the second; the first place is saved for the parents.' Of his siblings, Ta Ân remembers Bah (a brother who went on to Saigon to further his studies and then joined the French Army which greatly upset his mother Nga to the point of great illness; she bribed the French military authority with several kilograms of gold, packed in a couple of coconut shells in exchange for her son Bah's freedom); Hao (my grandmother); Nam (brother); Khung (sister); Khun (brother); Heo (sister); Kai (my great uncle Seng Chen Ân's nickname); Mei (brother still living in Prey Roka). Their mother, Nga, died of cancer in 1966.

mixed with straw sat indistinguishable from the other dwellings of the other villagers.

In the Chinese community, every family wanted a son. Grandpa Kuy would light many lanterns to brighten the whole house whenever a son was born to them. But whenever a daughter was announced, he would blow out whatever lantern was alight and head to bed for an early night's rest.

A big celebration followed the birth of An, Kuy and Hao's first child and first son. The happy father lit enough lanterns to make the poor village of Kampong Marek aglow. In 1942 or 1943, darkness greeted the birth of their second child, my mother. In 1945, immediately after the birth of the third child, Eng, Hao resumed her long work hours of early mornings and late nights. She traded and sold rice grain and various other knick-knacks from a rented stall in the local central market to support the growing family. In the meantime, her difficult husband leisured away the hours either with other women, gambling or carousing with his best friend, my paternal grandfather Duch.

Initially, the family had a neighbourhood girl look after the three children. This arrangement quickly ended when one day, the babysitter in anger tied the three children in a rice sack. After that, five-year-old Eat cared for her baby brother Eng. When he cried for feeding, she would take him from hut to hut in search of a woman who could give him breast milk. His siblings would come to attribute Eng's large frame to the fact that as a baby he had sufficient breast milk. He came to be known as the 'little monster sucking breast milk', *kaun yak bauy tuk duh*.*

---

* Cambodians are very descriptive in finding nicknames for people. For example, for the longest time I knew a distant relative only as *Mieng Aicht* or, literally translated, Auntie Manure. I have no idea how she acquired this name, definitely not because of her personality as she possesses one of pure gold and generosity, despite her talkative nature. I'm certain she cannot have been pleased with this nickname, but what could she do; she dared not correct older relatives? Moreover, they meant no harm by it as they used it lovingly.

In the 1947–8, the family moved from Kampong Marek to Kampong Chhauk, also in Svay Rieng. The move marked the family's ascent towards the middle class. They lived in a concrete building with more spacious accommodation to house their daughter and two sons. In addition, by this time, Ta Kuy had taken a second wife and had a son with her. They too lived with Grandma Hao's family; Hao gave this son an education and cared for him like a nephew.

Hao again rented a stall in the local market in town to sell meat, cloths, salt, pepper, rice and various other miscellaneous items. Her husband occupied his time idly trading and selling livestock. He did quite well, for in a short time he had many pigs, chickens, cows and water buffaloes roaming their spacious ground. He also contributed to the family income by operating a little casino shop in their backyard.

While here, in 1951, Hao's younger brother Ân came to live with them in order to pursue an education; no school existed where he was living in Kampong Také. Kuy and Hao registered him at school as their firstborn and most likely reduced his age as was the common practice in order that he might start in the appropriate class. Under Hao's care, Ta Ân did well in school and continued his education in central Svay Rieng, followed by high school and university in Phnom Penh. When Ta Ân graduated from high school in 1958, he was one of only 200 graduates in the whole of Cambodia. While in Phnom Penh, he received a scholarship to study in Paris.

The young Eat attended the privately-run Chinese school in central Svay Rieng.

Also while in Kampong Chhauk, the couple gave birth to four more children: Ani, Eap (Peat), Ry and Rey. During one of the pregnancies, Hao almost lost her life as a result of a blood clot and internal bleeding, *sabone*, and had to be hospitalised in the provincial hospital in central Svay Rieng.

After school, the children helped out their mother at the market stall.

Seizures struck each of the children before school-going age, at least two to three times annually. Each seizure lasted 15 minutes. 'The child is entangled by his placenta,' the neighbours explained to my grandparents. In reality, the seizures resulted from the unsanitised scissors used to cut the umbilical cord.

To stop the seizures, Ta Kuy mixed different herbs with water and spat the mixture, spraying the medicinal potion onto the seizure-stricken child.

The measles also posed serious health risks in an age and society that knew nothing of immunisation. Hao and Kuy concocted their own cure, informed by the traditions and customs of their era. They made their sick child drink coconut juice. But it was no ordinary coconut juice. In the juice, the parents mixed in egg whites. Then, they secretly dropped ten worms to swim in the mixture for a period of time. Afterwards, they took out the worms and added a drop of red dye into the liquid. The ailing child was then forced to drink the concoction. Oftentimes, the child drank the homemade medicine with his eyes tightly closed, desperately wrestling his parents as they pinched open his mouth.

An almost died from the measles. The disease reduced him to skin and bone. The family lost all hope of his recovery and braced themselves for his death. But he miraculously recovered. However, he lost the vision in one eye and developed 'rice disease' in the other.

Many neighbourhood children were not so fortunate as the Seng children and succumbed to death.

Chicken pox blinded many others.

At one point, cholera hit the whole town. One household lost all the daughters to the epidemic. At the peak of the infection, every house hung clay pots that had been painted white to dispel the evil spirit. Death struck everywhere. A dead silence encased the whole town. Families hired many local medicine men to come over to the house to chant away the evil spirits but to no avail.

One day, my mother's younger brother Eng broke his wrist. Ta Kuy grabbed hold of the wrist and twisted it into place. To form a cast around the broken wrist, he took a baby chick and ground it whole with lemon grass and a stick of bamboo shoots. This crude method straightened out the wrist and healed it one month later.

Ta Kuy possessed a very harsh personality and was a strict disciplinarian. His wife and children greatly feared him. Absolutely no backtalk or arguments were permitted. He prohibited conversation or sound of any kind around the dinner table at meal times. He permitted speech only after everyone had finished the meal. The children had to procure his permission first to leave the table. Corporal punishment met the child who broke the rules. He did not believe in sparing the rod, even with his wife.

All the children did their homework at the kitchen table. Ta Kuy watched with a hawk's eye and a whipping rod in hand for those children who dared to nod off during this time.

One day the two older boys went fishing. A catfish cut into An's skin and he bled noticeably. He went home crying, as blood dripped from the cut. Ta Kuy was in the middle of his usual afternoon nap and did not appreciate the interruption. Instead of sympathy, An received a whipping from his father for waking him from his nap, an additional salt to his injury.

In 1959, from Kampong Chhauk, the family moved west to the province of Kampong Speu, situated in central Cambodia, west of Phnom Penh. Again, Hao rented a stall in the market in town, selling and trading more expensive merchandise. The family bought a four-door silver Fiat. Ta Kuy crashed the car into a palm tree, totalling it.* The family replaced it with a four-door blue Renault.

---

* Uncle An reasoned that had it not been for this car accident, the children would never have been given an opportunity to learn how to drive.

They lived here until late 1970, when warfare forced them to join their children in Phnom Penh.

By everyone's standards, Yi Hao exemplified the perfect Khmer woman, *mae krousar krup daup*, perfect-ten head of household.

Grandma Hao was instrumental in overseeing that both her sons and daughters received quality education. Save my mother and one aunt, Eap, whose education ended at a junior high level, all of her children went on to finish high school and pursued a university degree. This was no easy feat when one considers that many parents at the time had neither the wherewithal nor the wisdom to send their children to the local public elementary schools.

Each of the three boys and their sisters, Ry and Rey, went to Phnom Penh for high school at Lycée Sisowath. It was a public school and did not charge tuition. Nonetheless, only children with recognised family names gained entry to this most prestigious of institutions. The Seng family fortunately had a family friend, Bun Nara, teaching there. He claimed the Seng children as his relatives and this connection gained them admission into the coveted Lycee Sisowath.

Even though tuition was free, Phnom Penh living was not. The dutiful parents paid for the living expenses and books of their children. The boys rented rooms in a dormitory run by the French priest Père François Ponchaud. The girls rented a nearby flat. Their older sister Eap, affectionately called Peat, also moved to Phnom Penh to live with them, but not as a student for the family considered her to be slow mentally. The homely Mieng Peat accepted this pronouncement without much questioning and contented herself to be the maid to the outgoing, more popular younger sisters.

Aunt Ry recollects: 'When we have to study for a major exam or entrance test, Ta Kuy would come to Phnom Penh for a few weeks before the exam day to watch over our studying. "If you don't pass, I don't want to see you at home," he warned us. But if we needed a tutor, he would immediately hire one to come to our apartment to teach us. For the more important exams, spanning normally a three-day period, we did hire tutors.'

An became a very good student. When he placed first in the national exam, the media hounded him for interviews. He tutored many children from well-known families.

Moreover, Grandma managed to save enough money from her pleasure-loving husband to send three sons and her younger brother to the United States and France to further their studies.

Grandma Hao possessed an indomitable spirit. The terror of the Khmer Rouge could not tame it. She suffered the killing of two daughters, the stroke of her husband and other unspeakable indignities. Grandma Hao worked in cesspools that were waist deep. To keep peace and earn mercy, Grandma would finish her shift early in order to help with her daughters' workload. She was to dig her own grave and face death with unflinching stoicism. But God was to have other plans for her then.

≈ ≈ ≈

Each aunt laboured in work brigades, *kang chalot*, separate from each other and from the men. Only the old, disabled or children lived in the villages. The authority sectioned off the rest of the population into travelling labour camps. Single women of several villages comprised one camp; single men made up another. Married men were also grouped together for *kang chalot*; if the wives did not have a new baby or toddler to care for, then they too were grouped into *kang chalot*, but possibly closer to their village home. In turn, the authority further divided the workers into groups of ten, composing a melange of base and new people. A person's absence was noticed. Angkar generally named a base person to be the group leader; the leader reported directly to the village chief.

The amount and type of work determined the length of time the labourers stayed in one location before moving on to a different work site. For most of the year they worked kilometres away from their villages, constantly on the move. During the spring season, people succumbed to death quickest, out of exhaustion from carrying out their task of digging dirt and never having enough to eat. When exhaustion set in, people became more prone to lose their temper, complain and make fatal statements against Angkar.

Aunt Renee recalls: 'When I went to *kang chalot*, I had to wake up at two o'clock in the morning to begin work. This occurred more often during the rice-planting season. We had to pull old rice stems to make room for the planting of new rice. Not only was it back-breaking, but we had to beat the bundles against ourselves to loosen the dirt from them.

'Our group worked, ate, slept and travelled together. We returned home to our village only when a communal meeting or celebration was called, usually after two or three months away.

'One time, I saw Bong Eat in prison because our *kang chalot* worked nearby, in Bung Rei.

'The group leader assigned me the task of carrying pots and pans and a sack of rice whenever we had to move from one work site to another. For fear of theft, the new people were not assigned to cook food.

'During the hottest hour of the day, all the base people napped. As they rested, the new people had to carry water, find firewood or run other errands; they made us continually busy.

'One time, I fell deathly sick. I lost all my hair. The authority transferred me from *kang chalot* to our village home to look after chickens.'

Villagers, then and now, tell time by the number of times the roosters crow in the morning and the position of the sun during the day.

Grandma Hao picked leaves and herbs from a nearby hill, brought them to a boil in three cups of water. She then ordered her daughter Rey to drink the concentrated one cup. She repeated this ritual whenever Rey ran a high fever.

Aunt Ry adds: 'While in *kang chalot*, death struck frequently and rapidly. Death became part of life. I pretended to be sick often, by refusing to eat my rice portion. The group leader reasoned that only a person who is gravely ill would repeatedly turn down food. Soon after, the leader sent me home to the village.'

Seng remembers: 'One week after my three months in prison, the authority ordered me to *kang chalot*. We were the front-line workers; we picked up and moved wherever work existed.

Seng and Veng, both men later to marry my aunts, worked in the same labour camps even though they came from different villages. The men worked in more strenuous projects. When the base people took their mid-afternoon nap, the new people continued on with work.

I enquire: 'Where did you sleep?'

Seng continues: 'Anywhere and everywhere. There were no blankets or pillows, or a change of clothes. We slept directly on the earth. It didn't matter, though, because we were always so exhausted that we could sleep anywhere.

'During the rainy season, I went to tear a piece of palm leaf to cover my face so the rain would not get into my nose. I slept like a baby each night through as the torrential rain poured down. I didn't even have a *krama*.

'Whenever I declared I was sick, without fail the group leader would come to lecture me, calling me all manners of names – anything from a royalist to a useless academic.

'I remember one À Nur who would pull the rice sack or *krama* over his head and exaggerate his illness, by quivering and making loud shivering noises, as the leader spewed out his tirades. But as soon as the leader disappeared out of earshot, he would stop his pretending and cussed out the leader, "Asshole!"

'He really liked me. He would share whatever treats he had with me. One time we stayed in an abandoned house. A chicken straddled in. À Nur prepared to catch it. I told him not to do it because everyone would be killed if the authority were to catch him.

'I told him, "I am just satisfied licking my lips at the thought of having it. It could be that it is a trick that Angkar released the chicken into the courtyard purposefully to test us. Don't do it."

'He thought it over and replied, "*Bong*, you're right. Better to lick our lips and dream of having had the chicken to eat."

'One morning, I woke up to find three new people in my group disappear. Of course, I didn't see the actual killing, but everyone knew their fate. No one dared speak or enquire.'

In the muted silence of human fear a sixth sense developed. News and rumours seeped out in bits and pieces as people were 'taken to be done away with'.

Seng adds: 'I don't know why in particular those men were singled out. I really don't believe there was rhyme or reason to the disappearances. The authority acted purely on their caprice.

'Around three o'clock every afternoon, everyone braced himself for a person from security, *nek santisok*, to call him "to carry the bed of Angkar", a euphemism to meet one's maker.* The sight of a black-clad man riding his bike in our direction at this time of day instilled paralysing anxiety in the labourers.

'We would all regain our consciousness and heave a collective sigh of relief if he rode past us. But if he stopped and called the group leader to whisper something into his ear, our hearts again throbbed uncontrollably.

'I remember one Saturday in particular when À Lo rode his bike

---

* It could be any pretext, to call people away. Seng remembered in particular hearing this phrase used.

from the direction of Kr'pong Chrouk towards us. I almost fainted from fear. I tried to be as inconspicuous as possible.

'When À Lo talks to you, he would not look at you in the face, but would look at either the ceiling or the sky. And when he talks, he would grunt his words and grind his teeth.'

Seng recounts another story involving À Lo: 'We had an old woman living near to us, very advanced in years with a hunched back, so much so that her head nearly touched the ground when she walked. She could be found always walking around looking for food.

'One clear night, when we had long days and clear, bright sky, À Lo passed her house and growled at her, "Why are you still living? Die! So we can use your ashes to plant palm trees! Your living is a burden to Angkar."'

It was customary for Angkar to plant palm trees in places of mass graves, using the human remains as fertiliser.

One day, while picking *ka'bah* from the cotton tree, Seng and Choulie's mother saw an arm on a pile of dirt. As most graves contained countless bodies and were thinly covered, the night killers failed to hide this one piece of limb.

Malnutrition took Ta Yi's life in early 1977; he had lived to his early eighties. By that time, the Seng family had already moved out of his house into the thatched hut by the river. His granddaughter Ry is adamant that had there been enough food, he would have lived longer.

When the authority wrapped him in a mat to bury him, he had yet to breathe his last breath. Hunger and age had slowed down his breathing. Grandma Hao felt his warm body and pleaded with the authority to let him stay until he was no longer breathing.

They sharply rebuked her, 'If we don't bury him now, why, would you like to bury him yourself?'

*

In the middle of rice-planting season, 25 July 1977, Angkar conducted its first communal wedding ceremony. Thirty-seven couples from the various surrounding villages gathered in my village of Chensa for the mass, collective marriage rite.

Many people decided to get married to avoid going to *kang chalot*, away from the village. Even though the rice ration in the village did not satisfy the hunger pains, the situation was still preferable to slaving away in the travelling labour camp. The first, middle and last thoughts in people's mind went to assuaging the acute painful cravings of continually not having enough to eat.

Grandma only wanted two daughters, if any, married in the mass ceremony. She reasoned that in light of the difficulty of the present situation, it was better not to bring children into the world and expose them only to a hard life. She echoed Solomon's wisdom, that better than both the living and the dying is he who has not yet been born, who has not seen the evil that is under the sun. In particular, she did not want her youngest daughter, Rey, yet hardly over her teenage years, to wed and had to creatively dismiss several suitors.

The authority had chosen Rey to marry a 'pure Chinese' man, the village idiot. If À Lo had been the village chief, he would have forced the arrangement. However, by this time the nice Pu Eam*
from Chensa had been transferred from my village to be the chief of Prey Roka. In exchange, À Lo came to rule my village.

Aunt Renee amusingly recalls: 'Whenever I saw a suitor heading towards our home, I would run to hide under the rice sack that was our blanket. This happened a couple of times.

'This was yet a time when Angkar permitted some freedom to choose who one marries. Later, they arbitrarily forced a woman and

---

* Many Cambodian survivors experience the Stockholm syndrome, whereby they feel an immense gratitude towards Khmer Rouge leadership who showed any sign of kindness towards them. Choulie Hok searched out village chief Eam who is now working in Phnom Penh when she visited Cambodia from the United States. My relatives also have given gifts to members of Mok's family who refrained from being cruel to them during the Khmer Rouge era.

a man to marry each other; Angkar was the final arbiter. The individual had no say in the choice of his or her spouse.'

Aunt Ry married Seng Hok, the oldest son of the only other new family alive in their village. His learned and cultured background, balanced with his quiet maturity, won over my grandma's confidence. She was, fortunately, the only arbiter in their union. He plays several stringed instruments by ear and, similarly to my mother's educational background, Pou Seng grew up learning several languages and attended a Chinese private school in Svay Rieng. But unlike my mother, he continued with his formal education. In junior high school, he had my father as his teacher.

Five years stood between them.

I enquire: 'Did you know each other before the ceremony?'

Seng laughs: 'We knew each other, but only modestly.'

Aunt Ry chimes in: 'We worked together at times.'

Seng adds, amused: 'Before, we regularly talked with each other. But when we found out we would be married to each other, we completely ignored each other.'

Aunt Eap (Mieng Peat) married Mok Vem, nicknamed Veng because he stood a head taller than his peers. Pou Veng won admiration from all who knew him. Initially, people were drawn to his striking features. 'He was very handsome, like a Chinese film star,' Aunt Renee recalls. His cheerful personality sustained the admiration.

All the couples arrived in my village of Chensa. A base person could not marry a new person. This prohibition did not stop many base women, *neary padevat* (women of the revolution), from secretly falling in love with men of the new people because of their fair skin and pampered former life.

Aunt Ry recalls one exception: 'There was one *Aye*, of the new people, who married a base woman. He came to our village by himself. The authority allowed for it because he was a very hard and able worker.'

Only the parents of the people to be married could attend the ceremony. Grandpa Kuy could not attend because of his paralysed state. The authority refused permission for Rey to attend even though two of her sisters were in the ceremony. She worked in the fields. Because the ceremony took place in our village, my mother managed to observe the ceremony.

À Lo presided over the ceremony in Chensa as its village chief.

Seng recalls his wedding day: 'It drizzled all morning that day. I had to borrow a black shirt from *nek moulitharn*, a base person. It had just been washed, so it was still damped. But it mattered little because the drizzling rain made us more wet. I also had to borrow a pair of flip-flop sandals.'

Everyone had to dress in mandatory black, with a red-white chequered *krama*, and wear sandals, fashioned from car tires, the only kind available.

The ceremony started around 9 a.m. Each couple sat next to each other in rows on the bench, facing the front, in my village dining hall, a former school. The respective leaders of each village chanted through a microphone their recognition of each couple as husband and wife and exhorted them to serve Angkar with genuineness and loyalty.

Then, the authority played a tape of wedding music, an altered Khmer Rouge arrangement.

My mother, at the sound of the soulful music, broke down in tears, sobbing profusely as sweet memories of an era long past flooded her. The tearful wailing carried with it infinite sadness. Memories swept her back to that glorious time of young love and perfumed existence.

She was weeping for her marrying sisters, for the tattered, vapid ceremony. Her memories of the extravagant pomp and circumstance surrounding her own wedding led her to shed tears at the surreal contrast of the present ritual.

She was weeping for herself, for the ecstasy of that first night with her husband and the painful reminder of what would never again be, her lover's embrace.

She was weeping for her lover, her husband. She yearned for him. *When will he come to her?* She was weeping because she already knew the answer.

She was weeping for the future of her children – À Kdee, À Sina, À Nong, À Srei, À Vuth. *How will this all end?*

She was weeping for her people. The dead, the dying, and the executioners.

The sharp pain of remembrance and desire overwhelmed her. Tears flowed and flowed for she had many reasons to weep.

The four noble truths of Theravada Buddhism teach that there can be no existence without suffering; the cause of suffering is desire; to extinguish suffering one must extinguish desire, by journeying on the noble eightfold path. Desire overwhelmed her at that moment and confirmed her humanness – she desired no such path, because her lamentations resembled the kind of sadness that does not desire consolation.

As when we mourn a love lost – any thought of him, be it painful, is better than no thought at all. In a perverse way, we relish the pain because this pain keeps alive his memory, and suspends in our mind what in reality is no longer. How wise are they who tell us that we do not know what we have until it is lost.

The elegiac wailing of my mother rose and fell to the rhythm of the wedding ululation, the two sounds accompanying each other in the bittersweet ceremony.

Towards the end, À Lo asked all the couples to stand en masse and to shake each other's hands. Angkar handed each of the newlyweds a new red-white chequered, all-purpose scarf, *krama*. The ceremony finished. It had lasted two hours.

The drizzling stopped. The sun shone at the end of the occasion.

The couples returned to their respective villages where a banquet has been prepared for them. About eight couples from Prey Roka participated in the collective wedding. That day, they enjoyed a feast of pork, beef and buffalo meat. My relatives conjecture that the authority determined the date of future wedding ceremonies – conducted only village by village rather than a combination of villages – based on their whim to provide an occasion to eat well.

Grandma Hao stole several chicken heads from the banquet in their village dining hall to take home for sacrifice offerings to the gods.

At home, she sat in front of her secret makeshift shrine of idols, her upper body deeply bowed, her legs crossed to one side and the palms of her hands pressed together, *som peh*. Grandma Hao murmured the Buddhist sutras she had learnt under more benign conditions. Her eyes, layered with films of suffering, flashed with intense sharpness and concentration. Her prayers softly whispered, she fervently petitioned the gods to her aid, to the aid of her husband, to the aid of her grandchildren in Chensa and to the aid of her children, in particular the newlyweds.

> *May peace exist in the marriage.*
> *If they should bear children, may peace greet these*
>   *little ones.*
> *May peace come to the land.*

Time and again, she repeated the refrains. She ended her petition by steeply bowing up and down three times, each time separating her pressed palms and prostrating her body and hands to the floor. Amen. *Sa thouk! Sa thouk! Sa thouk!*

Aunt Ry and Seng Hok spent their honeymoon period in the close-quartered, one-room raised thatched hut, shared by other

above left: Maman, undated

above right: Papa, probably before his marriage to
  Maman, undated

below: Maman holding Daravuth, with me, Sina, Lundi,
  Mardi, Phnom Penh, 1974

above: Maman's parents, Kuy Seng and Hao Yi, with her younger sister Ry between them, and me on the far right, probably 1972

below: Wat Koh home in Phnom Penh, 1974: (from left to right) Me, Mardi, Aunt Peat (Maman's sister who was killed one month after her wedding), Lundi (in front of her), Maman with Daravuth holding onto her leg, Sina and Aunt Ry

above: Khao-I-Dang, 1980: (back row) Uncle Seng, Ta An, Aunt Ry and
   Grandma Hao; (middle row) Mardi, Mara Seng (relative now in Paris), her
   brother Heang (behind topless boy) and Lundi; (sitting down) Daravuth,
   Vannak Seng (cousin now in Paris) and me

below: I was the lead ballerina at the Khao-I-Dang refugee camp (second from
   left), cousin Vanna Seng is second right, early 1980

above: Showing off our new clothes and shoes sent from Uncle
Eng in the USA: Sina, Daravuth, Me, Lundi and Mardi, 1980

below: The Seng family's official exit photo at Chonberi Transit
Centre, 1980: (back row) Grandma Hao, Aunt Rey (Renee),
Mardi, Sina and Grandpa Kuy; (front row) Lundi, me and
Daravuth

above: Maman's parents reunited with their son, Uncle Eng, our sponsor to the US, with church members looking on, Kent County International Airport, Michigan, 23 December 1980

below: Lundi, Mardi, me, Daravuth (front and centre), Aunt Rey (Renee) (far right), all greeted by sponsor Uncle Eng, Millbrook Christian Reform Church memebers, Aunt Ry holding newborn Donald and her husband Seng holding daughter Visal (Aunt Ry and Uncle Seng arrived a month or two before us), 23 December 1980

above: After our favourite outing to Burger King: (left to right) Sina, Mardi, cousin Sabrina (visiting from Toulouse), cousin Visal, her brother Donald, cousin Jeanette, Lundi and me, 1980

left: First week in the US spent admiring Christmas decorations at the local shopping mall in Grand Rapids, MI: (back row) Aunt Ry, Aunt Renee, me (in striped jacket), Grandpa Kuy, Grandma Hao, Sina and Uncle Seng; (front row) Visal, Daravuth, Lundi and Mardi, 1980

below: Wedding of Aunt Renee and Vibol Ung, string-tying ceremony to symbolise unity, Sina and Ta An looking on, Southern California, August 1986

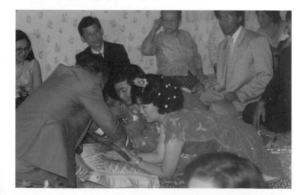

above: Ricefield behind Chensa, 1995

right: Chensa Village (my home under the Khmer Rouge) in the moonlight, frozen in time

below: Nephew Samuel and his mother Jennifer, amidst their new relatives (Papa's siblings, nieces and nephews) in Chensa Village, Svay Rieng Province, summer 2003

left: Me, posing in front of Khmer Rouge leader (Brother No. 2) Ieng Sary's plush villa in the heart of Phnom Penh, January 2002 (photo: Tom Fawthrop)

below: Visal and Abraham Chuang's wedding at the Nixon Presidential Library, Yorba Linda, CA, 26 June 2005: (back row, left to right) Lundi and wife Nita; cousins and bridesmaids Jeanette Seng and Rosanna Seng, Jennifer Ung; Bruce Farrell next to his daughter Jennifer (Farrell) Seng and her husband Mardi, their son Samuel (in front of her); Aunt Renee and her husband Vibol Ung; newlyweds Abraham and Visal; bridesmaid Vanessa Hok and her brother/groomsman Donald; groomsman Andrew Ung, maid of honour Theary; cousin from Toulouse and bridesmaid Sabrina Seng; cousin Samantha Seng; and brother Sina and his wife Nancy; (front row, left to right) relative from Oregon; Nan and Ân Chen Seng from Paris; bride's parents Ry and Seng Hok; uncle from Toulouse, Dr. An Seng; Lan and Eng Seng, my nephews Gabriel and Jared in front of them; and niece and junior bridesmaid Chantal Seng at the end

family members. The other members could accommodate the newly-weds only so far.

One month later, the Seng family grieved over the death of the other newlywed sister and daughter, Peat.

While Seng Hok moved in to live with his wife's family, Mieng Peat moved immediately following the ceremony to Pou Veng's village, O Sagum, about an hour's walk east of Prey Roka. The couples could decide to live with the family of their own choice.

The arrangement suited Peat's family because Grandma wanted her daughter to be away from Prey Roka, from the intense cruelty and suffering. According to her siblings, prior to the war Mieng Peat possessed a quiet disposition, just happy to observe life with a calm, content smile. Grandma Hao suspected that the authority made trouble for close-knit families, especially hers. The Khmer Rouge peasants, it appeared, were unleashing their pent-up indignities felt over the years from the snobbishness and arrogance of city dwellers, which until now were powerless to do anything about. In their mind's eye, my relatives represented all that they envied and hated of the bourgeois class. Also, Pou Veng possessed a buoyant person-ality and earned good standing with the authority in his village.

The Hong* family lived in the village O Sagum. The father was a nephew of Grandpa Kuy. People knew him as one of the richest men in Svay Rieng province prior to the Khmer Rouge era, 'who had a beautiful wife and beautiful children'. Hong adopted Veng as a little boy from his real father who lived in Phum Svay Thom.

After the wedding ceremony, Mieng Peat periodically and secret-ly wandered from her fieldwork to visit her family in Prey Roka. Pou Veng worked in *kang chalot* with Pou Seng.

---

* In January 2005, my visiting aunt and uncle from California and I went to vacation in Ho Chi Minh City in Vietnam with my Phnom Penh uncle, Sam Heang, and his family. The tour guide, who is a Khmer immigrant living in Saigon since 1975 and retired French teacher, knew the Hong family well. The discovery of this wonderful fact made me pause in amazement at how pieces of information have unexpect-edly unfolded, especially in the adventure of putting this memoir together.

Seng recalls: '*Nek moulitharn* loved Veng. He worked hard. They did not like me so I was afraid to wander far. But Veng would wander and climb palm trees. He would always bring back palm juice for me. At other times, he would hide a fish he had caught and fried to give to me.'

However, one month later, my maternal family received news of a tragedy. A few days earlier, a melee broke out between a group of new people and one of the Khmer Rouge leaders of the village O Sagum. A person of Chinese descent, known as À Ming, wounded but failed to kill this leader.

Seng remembers: 'À Ming had been in *kang chalot* with me. Earlier he had promised himself that if the authority ever come for him or his family, he would kill them first.'

While sharpening an axe one day, a Khmer Rouge leader approached him. He swung the axe at the caustic leader, who ducked down in time to save his life but not his ear.

Consequently, the one-eared leader unleashed his vengeance not only on the few instigators but the rest of the new people. The authority exempted Pou Veng from the mass annihilation out of affection for him. He told them he could not bear the thought of living without his wife. Instead of freeing her, the authority granted the husband's wish to die with my aunt in his arms.

'To preserve you is no gain, to destroy you is no loss,' I can almost hear the authority's response to my uncle.

Seng continues: 'That day Veng was working in *kang chalot* with me. We just harvested the rice. At this point, we were carrying dirt in Wat Laguern, a temple south of Prey Roka. The authority came to call Veng back to the village. They told him that he was needed to "help carry the bed of Angkar".

'Veng, knowing that he was taken to be killed, handed me his hammock. I told him that he should keep it so that wherever

Angkar takes him, he has a hammock to sleep in. We both knew of death's presence, but no one dared to express the obvious.'

The newlyweds, Mieng Peat and Pou Veng, were executed as they were tied to a stake hugging each other, along with all the new people in that village.

The authority carried out the mass execution in Phum Svay Thom.

Life is but a breath.

Over 300 years later, Thomas Hobbes' words continue to find resonance. 'In such condition [in time of war], there is ... worst of all, continual fear, and danger of violent death; and the life of man, solitary, poor, nasty, brutish, and short.'*

In Prey Roka lived ten-year-old Pout Ti and his large ethnically Chinese family. One day, À Lo sent Pout Ti away from Prey Roka by himself. In his absence, the authority destroyed all his family members.

'Where did my parents go?' choked Pout Ti asking no one in particular upon his return.

Amidst his convulsion, voices of his parents repeating, *Pout Ti, mom and dad are right here* haunted and beckoned him.

It broke Choulie Hok's heart not to be able to comfort the boy and tell him the fate of his family. However, Choulie knew, as certain as breath is to life, if the authority were to catch her in conversation with him, she would be accused of feeding him information and herself face death. Hence, it was better to avoid his eyes, his questions and his person altogether.

The next day, Pout Ti himself disappeared, to join the fate of his family members.

Towards the end of 1977, the shadow of death hovered over my maternal relatives, the Seng family.

* Thomas Hobbes, *Leviathan*, 1651.

Grandma Hao, newlywed Seng and Ry, and Rey had dug their own grave the day before. On the day, the village chief held a big feast with roast pig on their behalf. It was customary for the victims to eat well the last meal before an execution.

All this was to be changed that night. In the afternoon, several guards encircled their bamboo shack, each carrying ropes, guns and bamboo sticks. They squatted and smoked, waiting for night to descend.

One of the guards enquired facetiously the reasons the family was not attending the feast. My grandparents kept a solemn and strong face; Pou Seng assumed the same phlegmatic expression. Death's chilling edge ran down the spines of my two aunts as they wept and quivered feverishly through the day.

At the eleventh hour, as the sky darkened into night, the guards neared to bind them. In a distance, the silhouette of a young man on a bicycle pedalled furiously in their direction, 'Stop the killing! Stop the killing!'

Fortune smiled on them that night.

Vietnamese soldiers had advanced against the Khmer Rouge soldiers. The villagers had to be temporarily uprooted.

My relatives had received a last minute reprieve from death. Had À Lo still been their village chief, he would have carried out the original arrangement and had them killed.

During this period of late 1977, Choulie Hok also stood face-to-face with death and survived. In April 1975, one week before Phnom Penh fell to communism, Choulie visited her parents and siblings in the city. The Khmer Rouge had already gained control of central Svay Rieng where she had been living with her husband. But now she was entering her third trimester of pregnancy with a second daughter, and with her husband called away on military duties she wanted to be near family amidst the growing warfare.

Barely dodging bombs 'like sandstorm' and explosions, pregnant Choulie and her two-and-a-half-year-old daughter Mome arrived safely to join Seng and other Hok family members in Phnom Penh. One week later, the Hok family left in the mass exodus in the direction of Svay Rieng province. The Khmer Rouge herded them from one village to another, until the family was forced to settle in Prey Roka in May 1975. The following month, Choulie gave birth to daughter Touch.

Now in late 1977, the Khmer Rouge targeted widows of military men. Early one morning, the Khmer Rouge leader knocked on the Hok family's hut. He ordered Choulie and her daughters to go 'to a meeting of all military wives' of the three neighbouring villages.

Fear struck the heart of each family member. They knew the 'meeting' was with death.

The Khmer Rouge leader came back again to gather Choulie and her daughters. Two-and-a-half-year-old Touch sensed the danger. She pretended to be disabled and refused to walk. Choulie carried her to comply with the leader's order to keep apace. They had no choice but to follow him and join other military wives and children three kilometres south of Prey Roka.

About 275 wives and children of two villages gathered there. Paralysed with fear, the mothers and children helplessly waited for the people from the third village to join them in death. As they waited, out of thin air from the pristine Khmer sky, the Khmer Rouge leader called out the name of Choulie, the only name then uttered.

'Go back!' the authority ordered them.

She and her two daughters were free to go home. Mother and children magically floated back, as if 'walking on air'. Toddler Touch, who a couple of hours earlier lacked strength to walk, ran home, fuelled by the energy of life.

The gods did not shower the same favour on the other women and children. The ensuing days, Choulie saw their clothes worn by other base women and children.

Choulie reflects: 'Pou Eam was our village chief. If Lo had stayed, certainly he would have ordered our death.'

Parenthetically, À Lo is an interesting character study. For a couple of months, while ruling as village chief, he turned himself in to be imprisoned. As in the case of my grandfather Duch, the authority imprisoned base people, *nek moulitharn*, as well as new people. The only difference between the imprisonment of a base person and a new person lies in their fate. Ankgar usually released *nek moulitharn* whereas they killed the new people.

Aunt Ry recalls an example: 'One time, as I was digging dirt close to the main road, a security officer, *nek santisok*, came on his bicycle and called on Theem, a base person with relatively high standing. The security officer tied him up in the form of a hawk's wings and made him run in front of the bicycle as he was taken away. Theem had committed adultery with an older woman. The authority took him to prison but later released him.'

Immediately after the Khmer Rouge era, Pou Seng returned to Chensa from Phnom Penh as a government official. À Lo pointed Pou Seng out to his friends and neighbours and boasted, 'I presided over his marriage ceremony.'

Aunt Renee shivers and comments, over two decades later: 'Talking about the Khmer Rouge ... I am going to have nightmares again.' She picks up her cup of Starbucks coffee and heads out her nice front door into her nice upper-middle class neighbourhood of Cypress in Southern California.

Beginning in December 1977, Vietnam increasingly gained strength in Cambodia. While China supported the Khmer Rouge comrades, the Soviet Union supported its Vietnamese satellite. As their failure in establishing a pure, agrarian society dawned on them, the Khmer Rouge turned to within their rank-and-file to find scapegoats. During this time of internecine fighting, a faction of the Khmer Rouge soldiers defected to Vietnam out of fear of being purged next. These defectors joined their strength to the Vietnamese soldiers in defeating their former 'brothers'.

Vietnamese incursions into our part of Svay Rieng uprooted the villagers three times. The first times the Vietnamese soldiers advanced into the villages occurred towards the end of 1977 or the beginning of 1978. It gave my maternal relatives a reprieve from death. However, this same period marked the death sentence for my family in Chensa.

Aunt Ry hypothesises: 'I believe the three days the Khmer Rouge soldiers had Ta Duch arrested, they enquired into Bong Eat's family background – that she was of Chinese descent, her husband was in the Lon Nol military, etcetera. Why else would they take him for three days and then return him to the village?'

I enquire: 'How did you hear news of our arrest?'

Ry continues: 'We heard news of the arrest from a person in Chensa who said that everyone in the village saw the seven of you walking, escorted by guards. They walked you across Chensa. There's only one main road to Bung Rei.'

Half a year later, the wife of Eam, Chensa's former village chief transferred to Prey Roka, motioned for Aunt Ry to come towards her as Ry passed by her house. She whispered, 'Today, they released your relatives from prison.'

Her husband had been called away for a meeting of all the village chiefs. After the meeting and when it was safe to do so, Ry went back to the house to receive further news. It happened that the authority released my grandfather Duch from prison and made him speak in front of the gathering of village chiefs. The authority prodded him to ask for amends and to promise always to be loyal to Angkar. He assented.

Ry asked, 'Did you ask your husband whether my sister and children were with their grandfather?'

The chief's wife responded, 'No. I didn't dare ask him about your sister and her children. My husband only saw Ta Duch.'

The wife did not enquire further because she did not want to raise suspicion that she was close to any of the new people.

A week after Aunt Ry's conversation with the chief's wife, the five of us returned to Chensa from Bung Rei prison. We feared to come to see our relatives in Prey Roka. By this time, the Seng family had moved to the haunted house in Phum So, northwest of my village. One day, Mardi steered his ox-cart past the new house.

Aunt Ry recalls: 'I saw him from the house. We did not say anything to each other. He did not stop, but he threw several fish into the gate of our house. I had already given birth to Visal.'

The second Vietnamese incursion occurred in the middle of 1978. Once again, it uprooted the villagers, who had to live in open fields or find shelter in another villager's house. During this period, wholesale massacres of cadres and soldiers occurred in the eastern zone, where we lived. My relatives in Prey Roka had to leave their village for three to four days.

Aunt Renee remembers: 'We took my father to the dining hall so he could ride on the ox-pulled cart where they stored all the kitchenware. Initially, the authority refused; they wanted him to walk. Of course, he could not walk in his paralysed state. Finally, they consented and allowed him to ride with all the earthen pots and pans. By the end of the journey, he had charcoal smeared all over him.

'One time, we had a hard time keeping up with his cart; we were separated from him. When we caught up with him one day later, he beamed with immense happiness and relief upon seeing us. He thought he was separated from us for good.'

Aunt Ry muses: 'These incursions provided us with some of our happiest moments, because we had plenty to eat. We could eat as much of whatever we found. The cacophony of the situation did not permit the authority to control the food ration.'

Seng recalls: 'Everyone had left the village. We were the only four people left – Mom, Ry, Rey and myself. Rey complained that the two baskets she had to *raet* off the bamboo pole were so heavy. We peaked inside and discovered many silver pots, pans, and expensive plates and bowls Mom had taken with her from Phnom Penh. She had hidden them at the bottom of the river. At the news of the Vietnamese incursion, she quickly dug them up. Initially, we were angry with Mom for making Rey carry these chicken nests. Little did we know until then that Mom had hidden treasures in them.'

During these incursions, the authority feared that people would defect to the Vietnamese. Suspicion ran high against people who lingered behind and did not keep up with the other villagers. Living less than 15 miles west of the Vietnamese border, escape was conceivable. Instead of retreating, some villagers hid in their huts and waited for the advancing soldiers. Often, upon the discovery of these villagers, the soldiers would force them at gunpoint to join the other villagers. However, others managed to leave with the Vietnamese soldiers once they retreated.

Aunt Renee explains: 'It was easier for an individual to escape to Vietnam, but we were a big family. Yet, it would have been possible for us to escape if we knew the region well. But during that period, the scope of our perspective was limited to the immediate village and the sites of *kang chalot*, the work brigade.'

On the fourth day, the villagers returned to their huts. My relatives did not arrive home until 11 p.m. that night. Half an hour later, a *nek moulitharn* named À Voung came looking for my uncle

Seng. This Voung came from *santisok*, the Khmer Rouge security division. The people feared him for his fierce and vicious demeanour. Countless deaths resulted from his hands.

He grunted, 'Seng, Angkar needs you to work tonight. We're all meeting at the dining hall.'

Everyone in the hut quivered. Seng found his voice, '*Bong*, what is the work?'

The Khmer Rouge apparatchik replied, 'It's confidential.'

With Angkar, everything was *lak' ka*, confidential.

Seng looked around the hut at his in-laws. He looked into the glistening eyes of his young pregnant wife, Ry. Fear filled them. He tried to be strong for all of them and left quietly with Voung into the night.

After they disappeared into the night, Grandma Hao left immediately for the house of their village chief, Eam.

'*Pou*, where are you taking my son?' Grandma enquired.

He reassured her, 'It's okay. We needed him to do some work.'

Grandma returned home. Everyone in the hut awaited her arrival. Their eyes asked her for answers amidst the dead silence.

'Pou Eam said he was needed to do work,' Grandma answered.

It was now past midnight. An hour has passed since Seng left. Still no sign of him. They waited some more. Amidst the waiting, their senses acquired an added sensitivity. Each person could hear the breathing of the others, read each other's thoughts, and feel the particles of the oppressive tropical air and the agony of having time suspended.

Two hours later, Seng returned. The authority really did need a group of men to dig a hole to hide bags of rice, salt and other goods should the Vietnamese soldiers once again advance on them. The Vietnamese soldiers had previously emptied their stockpile of goods when they retreated.

After the second Vietnamese incursion, the authority called back all the people from *kang chalot* to work in the village. The authority wanted tighter control over the people and reasoned that it would be possible only if everyone was concentrated in one location. It lessened people's chances of running away with the invading Vietnamese soldiers.

From October 1978, famine swept through the land. Across Cambodia, peasants abandoned rice cultivation. Malaria devastated the concentrated populations.

A few months before the third and final Vietnamese invasion, the authority ordered the Seng family to a deserted cemetery of Wat So, situated one mile north of Prey Roka. My relatives moved from their hut by the river to an isolated, haunted, two-storied house made of bamboo shoots. Wat So was a former temple that had been turned into a vegetable garden. Here, some people witnessed spirits, ghosts and flames of fire in the middle of the night. Others heard weeping and wailing coming from that direction.

(These stories of ghosts and goblins kept surfacing. Sina encountered a host of dark spirits chasing him across the fields in Chensa. Other survivors experienced similar haunting spooks and phantoms; they described scenes that could have been taken from a Stephen King novel or Milton's *Paradise Lost*. Evil unleashed its fury and its children ran amok in the God-forsaken *srok Khmer*, Cambodia. During these four years of hell on earth, these evil spirits roamed the killing fields and haunted the living.)

One week before Angkar asked my relatives to move, someone found a woman, the former resident, hung from the ceiling of her house. She left a baby behind. Her relatives came and took the baby away.

Aunt Ry recalls the move: 'I was in the eighth month of my pregnancy with Visal. The authority ordered us to move into a haunted house to punish us, reasoning that we would kill ourselves like the woman before us, or that we would be visited by the ghosts, goblins, and other evil spirits that moved among the fiery flames in that place.

'We could not take time off from our regular work schedule to move our hut. We had to move all our belongings during our sleeping time, at night. From our old thatched hut to the new house measured a good mile, at least.

'Only the five of us lived in this house, out in the middle of nowhere, amidst a haunted cemetery. We were afraid but very happy for the move because there was food there. At night, Mom would go steal sweet potatoes, huge ones, because the base people, *nek moulitharn*, were afraid to come near there. Also, she would steal bananas, a whole stem at a time, and would hide them at home until they were ripened. However, she had to be more careful with bananas because the authority would count them. Other times, Mom sneaked out chicken heads from the dining hall to take home to offer as food sacrifice.'

Seng adds: 'I find it baffling that these people were so afraid. They spoke of evil spirits and fiery flames flickering at night. We didn't see anything. We didn't have to work at night after we moved to this new place; the authority was too afraid of the ghosts to make the trip to call us to work.'

On 30 October 1978, Ry went into labour. Her husband went into the night, walking across the haunted yard into the vast open fields towards the main village to call his mother and the village midwife, Vann.

A melange of emotions flooded the soon-to-be father as he traversed the dark landscape into the beautiful balmy night. The effulgence of the vast Khmer sky animated the thoughts of the philosophical Seng. Flashing beams of intense joy sliced through the thick, pervading interior of fear and pain of his present life. However, these heightened sensations of reverie were quickly clouded.

Will there be hope for this unborn child, struggling to enter into the dying, hopeless world that is the present situation? Why rejoice at life when the grave awaits life's coming?

In the meantime, Grandma Hao sliced a bamboo stick ever so thinly and made scissors out of it to cut off the umbilical cord. Having had seven children in poverty, she recalled how seizures struck all of them as young children because the scissors the midwives used were rusted and not sterilised. She had learnt her lesson.

That night, Aunt Ry gave birth to a baby daughter, Visal.

Aunt Ry recalls: 'I had Visal during the cool season. Mom went to ask the authority for a blanket for her newborn grandchild, hoping out of pity they would grant this one request. They retorted, "You have been used to blankets; now try the rice sack." It got really cold at night, especially for a newborn baby.'

Grandma Hao took the gritty rice sack, cut the seam, and washed it in the pond water. She used the sack as a blanket to wrap the newborn granddaughter.*

Seng reflects: 'In hindsight, I don't know how we ever survived the regime ... truly a miracle.

'They profoundly maltreated us, inflicting unspeakable suffering, *t'ver bahb*. We didn't know them beforehand and we didn't do anything to provoke the situation. It will take countless future generations before their sins will be atoned for. They will be forever cursed, *bahb*, as a result of the depth of their depravity. It escapes my comprehension the intensity of their anger and hatred towards us. They glared at us as if they wanted to bite us then and there.'

Cambodian Buddhists believe in *kahm*, that acts committed in a previous life affect the present life and acts committed in the present life will affect a future life. The consequences of bad action lead to human suffering. In the end, most Cambodians are resigned to

---

* In the summer of 2005, Visal obtained her doctorate degree in pharmacy at the University of Illinois at Chicago and married her love, Abraham Chuang, a dedicated Christian and patent attorney. They live and work in Irvine, southern California.

accepting collective responsibility for their suffering, *kahm*. *'T'ver bon ban bon, t'ver bahb ban bahb.'* 'If you sow good, you'll get good; if you sow bad, you'll get bad.'

Less than two months after the birth of Visal, the third and final Vietnamese incursion again forced the villagers to retreat from their homes. It posed the most difficulty for everyone, especially for the parents of a newborn baby. Unlike the other incursions when the villagers were uprooted for only a few days and a short distance, the last incursion pushed my maternal relatives inwards, away from the Cambodian-Vietnamese border. They almost reached Neak Loung, the Mekong River-crossing transit town, situated between central Svay Rieng and Phnom Penh.

At one point, they traversed over ten kilometres of clearing devoid of trees and vegetation for shade. Dehydration almost killed them. Fortunately, in one place they found *rama* leaves. They pounded them, squeezed droplets of juice into their parched mouths and poured some on their faces for moisture.

At another point, they encountered a splinter group of Khmer Rouge soldiers who gave them the whole chicken they were in the process of skinning and cooking.

Seng recalls: 'They gave us everything, the whole chicken. Even the axe they used to chop the chicken.'

Again, the family became separated from Ta Kuy. They had failed to catch up with his wagon. Their thoughts went to him. He must be so scared and uncomfortable, all alone in his wagon of kitchenware. They prayed to *preah*, god, to safeguard him from all harm, from all the asininity that warfare produced – intentional or accidental.

The family rested in each village they encountered along the way. The villages were emptied of residents. The family scrounged around for food and collected any valuable and practical items they found.

The undernourished, not-yet-two-month-old baby Visal cried. Her toothless little mouth opened to release her infantile angst. Her helpless parents tried to comfort her as best as they could, as the maelstrom swirled around them.

'My daughter, *kaun srei*, it's all right. Everything will be all right,' they promised her and desperately tried to believe it themselves. Aunt Ry gave her breast milk and sang lullabies. The lullabies provided greater comfort to the adults than baby Visal.

The family continued on. They had been on the run for several days now.

They found rest on the road, huddled together among the other thousands of weary travellers. The next morning, they woke up to a world on fire. People rushed by, beset by fatigue and bewilderment. Explosions sounded off near and far. The sky billowed with smoke. The horizon crimsoned with flames and more explosions. The planes above hummed and rattled.

Confusion ruled the streets and chaos gripped the atmosphere. With a two-month baby in tow, the family could not catch up with the mass migration ahead of them. These people were urged forward in the direction of Neak Loung by the rolling tanks behind them. The rumbling tanks crushed some who hesitated or failed to clear the way.

Seng remembers: 'The Khmer Rouge soldiers stood on one side and the Vietnamese soldiers on the other side. The mass of civilians stood trapped in the middle. Everyone converged in Neak Loung. We viewed all this from a mile back.

'The stronger ones who managed to escape the pandemonium in Neak Loung told us not to proceed further. People died in the stampede and the rolling tanks crushed them.'

Ry adds: 'Hundreds of civilians were killed during the first few days of this "liberation" Stories reached us about the Vietnamese soldiers driving their tanks over fleeing Cambodian villagers.'

Loud speakers blared announcements of liberation and victory. Flyers of Vietnamese liberation propaganda littered the streets and fields. On them appeared the names of Heng Samrin, Chea Sim, and Pen Sovann,* all former Khmer Rouge soldiers who escaped to Vietnam out of fear of being the next purged.

The Seng family decided to return to their village of Prey Roka, but they were afraid. Ry voiced their concerns, 'The authority is going to accuse us of defecting to the Vietnamese.'

My aunt's sentiments captured what would have been an inevitability during prior incursions – that the authority would have them killed for having mingled with Vietnamese soldiers. However, the Vietnamese soldiers had no intention of retreating this time around.

On Christmas Day 1978, the final Vietnamese blitzkrieg successfully consolidated its hold on its western neighbour, Cambodia, an act viewed at the time as liberating – and in hindsight as the lesser of two evils. Fuelled by Vietnam's paranoid fear of Chinese 'encirclement' of the region, the invasion led to a prolonged foreign occupation of Cambodia. Not until Gorbachev cut off foreign aid to Vietnam and the United Nations forced the Vietnamese troops out over a decade later did Cambodia regain its sovereignty.

---

* Politics and principles certainly make strange bedfellows. Twenty years later, Pen Sovann toured with the pro-democracy leader Sam Rainsy and stayed a couple of nights at Mardi's house in Sudbury, MA, sleeping in the bed of my nephew Samuel.

Chapter Six

Reprieve from Death: Vietnamese Invasion
(December 1978)

The beginning of 1979 witnessed the ending of the Khmer Rouge reign of terror. The Cambodian people gained liberation through invasion by a bellicose foreign power, Vietnam. It would simply be naïve to believe this invasion stemmed from humanitarian design. Nonetheless, as my family would readily acknowledge – echoing the sentiments of many Cambodians, politics aside – if it had not been for the Vietnamese presence, we would not have survived.

When my maternal relatives received information advising them against proceeding on to Neak Loung, the family heeded the warning and decided to return to their village of Prey Roka. Grandma wanted to retrieve her hidden valuables and other day-to-day belongings the family had left behind. Her thoughts also went to the fate of her five grandchildren in Chensa. Additionally, the family needed to find Grandpa Kuy, who became separated from the rest of the family amidst the confusion of the evacuation.

However later that morning, as they proceeded to return to Prey Roka, the wagon carrying Ta Kuy retreated from Neak Loung and found them. Ta Kuy felt indescribable elation upon seeing his family. Despite his increased separation anxiety, he finally agreed to continue his ride back to Prey Roka in the wagon carrying the kitchenware.

The relatives found an abandoned cart to wheel their possessions and headed back to their village.

During this period, Uncle Seng's relatives, the Hoks, did not return to the village. They survived the genocide, the only other family of the new people of Chinese descendants besides that of my maternal relations to do so. Unlike my relatives, the Hoks were a family of many men who managed to carry all the necessary belongings with them when they left the village and took advantage of the open grain storage along the way.

As people returned to their villages, suppressed animosity and simmering hatred emerged in a new balance-of-power game. Old grudges found new wounds. Those who felt cheated in having their rice ration skimmed off under the old Khmer Rouge era took revenge on those who measured unfairly. In at least one instance, they chopped off the fingers of the nemesis.

The few surviving new people engaged in vengeance against the Khmer Rouge apparatchiks and a lot of the vengeful retaliation occurred among the base people themselves. Many, my family included, were too exhausted and just too happy to have survived to engage in revenge, but they witnessed much.

V.S. Naipaul said we should hate oppression, but fear the oppressed. 'Fear the oppressed' basically summed up what occurred during the Khmer Rouge as well as the months after.

Someone chopped up the body of the chief of the *sangkat*,* Saroeun, into three segments. The person finished off the wife and children as well.

There lived a man next to my relatives who engaged in metal work. One day, Pou Seng saw him furiously sharpening a long knife. Seng inquired, '*Bong*, where are you going with that?'

He surreptitiously answered, 'I'm going to hunt animals. Stay inside the house with your family.'

---

* Many villages form a *sangkat*.

In reality, he went searching for the Khmer Rouge leaders and village chiefs who had wronged him. They all, in turn, went into hiding. The village chief of Prey Roka, Eam, survived the retaliatory purge because he did not mistreat people under his rule – relatively speaking. Although I do not know whether he is still alive today, Lo went into hiding and survived the chaotic transitional period as well.* It could be that he successfully eradicated most of his enemies, so that the few who survived had neither the spirit nor the energy to seek him out for destruction.

Overnight, the viciousness and cruelty of most of those who had had power transformed into obsequiousness and feigned camaraderie.

Seng recalls: 'After we returned from Neak Loung, I ran into one *Ta*, older man, who had been in charge of the vegetable gardens. He had guarded the place with an iron hand. But when I asked him for a melon, *trasok*, he became profusely obsequious and generously offered me as many as I desired, for he was "no longer the supervisor".

'Another time, a group of workers liberally gave me sacks of rice grain. I didn't even ask. I had only stood there watching them.'

Immediately after their arrival, Grandma travelled to Chensa to look after the welfare of her five orphaned grandchildren. After the usual pleasantries, she informed my paternal grandparents that she would be taking the five of us to live with her. 'We're planning to move back to Phnom Penh. These kids need to go to school.'

---

* According to my relatives in the States, Á Lo is no longer living. They believe he defected when Vietnam invaded Cambodia. His insecurity among the Vietnamese troops made him again change his mind. But before he could defect back to the Khmer Rouge, the Vietnamese soldiers killed him. However, a relative in Cambodia said Lo is still alive, living in Svay Rieng. In January 2005, another relative, Ta Mei, echoed this fact – Lo is still alive and holds a political post at the district level as member of the royalist party.

My father's parents protested. 'There is no food in the city. Here, you take the three younger children with you. We'll keep À Kdee and À Sina.'

I had been fidgeting uncomfortably, partly from the ants crawling on my feet as I tried to squish or brush them off with my other foot, and partly from listening to the heated discussion over our future. However, upon hearing of the separation, I cried out, 'No! No! I don't want to be separated from Bong Dee and Bong Na!'

Prior to my outburst, the children had been listening in sombre silence, glancing uncomfortably here, there and back again to the dirt floor. Our future stood on a delicate balance. As a seven-year-old, stripped of mother and father, I did not possess a strong loyalty towards either side of the family. I did not know my maternal grandmother well enough to prefer living with her because we parted ways immediately upon our arrival in her village of Prey Roka. I was hardly four years old and so much had occurred since our separation. Neither did I hold strong loyalty towards my paternal grandparents despite the fact that I had been living with them for two-and-a-half years. Well, I may have had an inkling of preference for them because they formed the more current memory in my mind.

However I knew whatever happened I wanted all of us to stay together. I needed consistency and my brothers had been the only source of consistency in my life. Moreover, we shared a common tragic experience, a bond that would forever tie us together despite growing pains.

Grandma Hao refused the Solomonic arrangement. 'No. These children need to stay together.'

My paternal grandmother retorted, 'The two boys are too old to attend school. We need them to help around the farm.' They would have wanted to keep Lundi as well, but he had seriously wounded himself the day before, playing with hand grenades out in the fields.

Grandma Hao pleaded, 'Please allow me to take these children with me. Why don't we let the boys decide?'

We all look at each other and once again directed our gaze downwards, intently studying the dirt floor and the ants scurrying about on it.

Grandma Hao started to lead away with her the three young ones. Mardi followed. By the time the group reached the gate, Sina ran after us, pulling his water buffalo after him. We dared not look back, in fear of catching the hurt expression of my father's parents.

Upon reaching Prey Roka, Grandma Hao immediately took Lundi to the nearest post of Vietnamese soldiers. A grenade had exploded and shrapnel had hit Lundi, deeply wounding him. He needed immediate hospitalisation.

Grandmother and seriously injured grandson walked through fields strewn with mines and various other shards of warfare in search of the new authority. Believing a medical centre to be nearby, Grandma did not bring an extra change of clothes or food with her. She only had the necessary currency of gold, until then valueless, that she hid in her bra. Writhing from excruciating pain, Lundi tried to hold on. Once they reached the nearest soldiers post, bad news awaited them. No medical facility existed in the area. The soldiers directed them to another location.

A day trip turned into a month-long expedition and stay.

For the next few days, Grandma and Lundi walked from one location to another following the instructions given them in Vietnamese. Finally, they ended up in the provincial capital of Svay Rieng where Lundi was treated for his injury, among a sea of other war patients.

Grandma Hao's infinite compassion contrasted starkly with the compassion fatigue of the general population.

Back in Wat So, my brothers helped the maternal relatives to ground rice grain for storage. Tong, a distant relative, came with a wagon and transported the grain to Ang Ka'bah, a town situated midway to the provincial capital of Svay Rieng. This marked the start of our plan to move back to Phnom Penh.

One month later, Grandma and Lundi returned to us from their visit to the hospital in central Svay Rieng. Now that we had everyone, the family set out for Ang Ka'bah, a midway point to Svay Rieng town and then Phnom Penh where we had relatives.

We walked amidst the mass migrating population, carrying whatever belongings each individual could hold.

As the group neared Ang Ka'bah, I got into a shouting match with Aunt Rey. I threatened to run away, to go back to my grandparents' farm in Chensa.

'Go! See if I or anyone else care!' came the retort.

I will make them sorry, I vowed to myself. My head throbbed. Intense hatred and rage consumed me. Streams of tears blinded my eyes. But I was not quite resolved to go all the way back to Chensa. We had been travelling for a couple of days and I feared being lost in the chaotic crowd.

I have to go through with my threat, my wilful spirit whispered in me. *My will is stronger than hers and anyone else. They will be sorry if anything happens to me.*

Rage fuelled my steps into a run. I periodically looked back to see whether anyone was sorry yet and following to call me back. I saw no familiar face. So I continued on, dodging the tired and listless crowd of migrants. My legs ached. I stepped on something sharp, which stung my bare foot. But I was still too angry to give much notice to this pain. The throbbing in my heart and head hurt more.

I tilted my head up and squinted into the bright sun to gauge the time of day. *How long have I been on the run?* It must have been a few hours, possibly half a day. The fact that no one followed me to apologise only hardened my resolve not to turn back, despite my fear and loneliness at this stage. I looked around at the weary population, their hustling and bustling, going to and fro, in all different directions.

Up until that point, consuming rage had erased all thoughts of exhaustion. Now, exhaustion steeply set in. I found shade under a tree and plopped myself against it. I began to fear the coming of night. *What will I do? I cannot go back. My pride will not let me. Yet, I do not think I can find my way to my paternal grandparents' house in Chensa. I hope someone kidnaps me, then they will be forever sorry. Oh! How I hate all of them!*

Papa, Maman, where are you? Everyone is so mean to me. Where are you? Come defend me. You would take my side. I know you would.

My heart blackened with intense hatred for the relatives, for the world before me. My rib cage protruded and rubbed against my dirtied, tattered shirt – soiled from the dust storm and the heavy flowing snot and mucus I had wiped on it. *I am so light, yet I feel so heavy, as if crushed with the weight of hatred and anger of the last four years.* Twinned to the burning hatred, self-pity also found a welcome home in my seven-year-old body.

Several groups huddled nearby, also finding rest that late afternoon. Some stopped temporarily to eat. I had missed lunch. I ran away before the family stopped to eat. I wished someone in the group would see me and give me something to eat. Hunger temporarily overshadowed my anger.

I sat there, oblivious to the chaotic world – on the verge of dying, on the verge of rebirth, it could not make up its mind.

I wish my head would stop throbbing. A fresh stream of tears choked its way out of my body, to moisten once again the crusted snot glued to my face. The people before me blurred under the cascading veil of tears. Self-pity became an ever-present friend, a comfortable blanket that was always within reach to wrap around me.

Among the apparitions, I detected a familiar figure on a bike. It was Aunt Ry. The others calculated that she would be the most appeasing person to call me back. Inwardly, my heart rejoiced at the sight of her, a way out of the debacle. Outwardly, I knew I had to continue with my posture of rage. They were in the wrong and I would make them feel remorse.

I pretended not to see my aunt as she neared, her eyes roaming the crowd. Amazingly, she spotted me amidst the human mass; she screwed her eyes to confirm her find. Exasperation, not the hoped-for elation, spread across her countenance.

She jumped off her bike and huffed towards me. 'Stupid! Very stupid! You are very fortunate not to have been kidnapped! Do you know we wasted a day of travelling because of you? You are now a young lady; act like one. I don't have time for this. Do you know I have a newborn baby to care for? Just wait until we get back. Mieng Rey will beat the crap out of you!'

I did feel a little badly that Aunt Ry, who had recently given birth, came to look for me. However, I quickly rationalised that this would not need to have happened if everyone had been nice to me. On the ride back on the back of Aunt Ry's bike, I braced myself for the storm ahead.

The whipping came. My wrists in an inescapable hold, I writhed at the lashes' sting. Not a surprising response, but certainly not the one I felt I deserved. Of course, everyone took Aunt Rey's side and berated me for being an uncontrollable little monster.

'This is for your own good. She would not have disciplined you if she didn't love you,' another adult tried to comfort me later on, as my chest still heaved up and down.

I wish she would love me less next time.

On reaching Ang Ka'bah, Uncle Seng and Tong continued on to Phnom Penh. The rest of the family would move to Phnom Penh a couple of months later.

While in Ang Ka'bah, Grandma Hao and Sina travelled to

Vietnam. Travelling into Vietnam was most difficult, especially if a person could not speak Vietnamese. (Grandma Hao spoke fluent Vietnamese.)

From Ang Ka'bah, they went to the provincial capital. From there, they initially took a taxi and then rode on the city bus to Prey Nokor (Saigon), Vietnam. They passed miles and miles of rubber plantations.

While in the town of Tay Ninh in Vietnam (but also claimed by Cambodia, situated northeast of Svay Rieng's capital), they accidentally discovered that Grandma Hao's distant cousin, Hieu, ran the province as its governor. They stayed with him. Hieu, a cousin and best of friend of Grandma Hao's older brother Bah, had left Cambodia in the 1950s and fought for the Viet Cong, which explained his high position as governor. Grandma wanted to move the family from Cambodia to Vietnam because we already lived very near to the border. But Hieu dissuaded her from doing so because the people living in Vietnam fared not much better. Here, Sina learnt to ride a bicycle.

Through this fortuitous encounter, Grandma gained other contacts and information of other relatives in Vietnam and the addresses of her sons in the West. She sent a letter to her oldest son An in Toulouse, France, informing him who had died and who survived. In turn, he informed the other brothers, Ani also in Toulouse and Eng in Michigan.

≈ ≈ ≈

During this period, across many cultures and several languages, Uncle Eng had bought a modest one-story, three-bedroom house on Chamberlain Street in Grand Rapids, Michigan. Next door to him lived an elder, Dave Bosscher, of Millbrook Christian Reformed Church. Through neighbourly interactions, Dave came to hear of Eng's personal and family background.

When he first arrived on the US grant to train Cambodian Air Force officers, Uncle Eng took a language test with Lackland Air Force in Texas. They then sent him to flight training school at Fort Rucker, Alabama. During his stay, the Khmer Rouge consolidated their power, culminating in the capture of Phnom Penh.

Uncle Eng had two options: stay in a refugee camp in Pennsylvania or get someone to sponsor him to become a permanent resident. He opted for the second alternative and found a major named Russ Wicker to sponsor him. He left the air force base in June 1975 when his grant ran out.

Now a holder of the green card, Eng had to find work to support himself. Someone offered him a job working on the railroad. He refused and found work in the Alabama cotton mill. The gruelling, menial work not only put food on the table but, by keeping Eng preoccupied, assuaged the deep loneliness that comes with the permanent loss of country and everything familiar and the terrorising fear of loss of family.

During this time, Eng received news of waves of refugees landing on the shores of Florida. Twice, he hitched a ride to Florida to search for his family, wishfully believing that by chance his relations had managed to escape Cambodia. Both times, his hopes were shattered.

Loneliness once again embalmed his life. But all was not lost. While scanning the crowd for his family in Florida, he laid eyes upon a sweet feminine form with waist-length silky hair, Lan, a Vietnamese refugee. The two lonely souls felt an instant attraction and have become inseparable since that time. She moved to Alabama with him.

Eng received news from a friend, Poun, living in the refugee camp in Pennsylvania. Upon hearing of work in Alabama, Poun moved down to join his friend Eng. While in Alabama, Poun received a letter from his friend Cuong who left the same refugee camp in

Pennsylvania and found work in a 'soap company' in Grand Rapids, Michigan, internationally known as the Amway Company. Cuong invited Eng and Poun to move to Michigan.

In January 1976, Eng, Lan and Poun moved up to Michigan and joined three others in a rented apartment in central Grand Rapids. The group rented the apartment from Cuong. At that time, Amway's founder, Richard De Vos, took Cuong, his wife and two children into his home.

In early 1979, Eng rejoiced over news about his family. Having had his hopes diminished through weeks and agonising months, then extinguished after four years, Eng had to digest and re-digest the information.

≈ ≈ ≈

After a couple of months living in the town of Ang Ka'bah in Svay Rieng province, the family moved to Phnom Penh. During this period, the population across Cambodia had awakened from the stupor of death under the Khmer Rouge and began migrating in every direction – to towns, cities, or another country of safety. Along the way, the testosterone-filled Vietnamese soldiers taunted the migrating pedestrian population, *'Voulez-vous coucher avec moi?'*

'What are they saying?' I curiously wondered out loud.

'It's none of your business,' tartly replied an adult. I detected not anger but an edge of embarrassment in the answer.

'Bong sro'lagn aun. I love you.' When their French failed to elicit a favourable response, they shouted in Cambodian from the rumbling tanks to the Cambodian female population travelling on foot.

CHAPTER SEVEN

Phnom Penh Reunions
(1979)

By the time we arrived in Phnom Penh, half of the capital had been brought back to life after its comatose four years. All those 'persons leftover from death', as that was what we were, the remainders of a genocide or 'survivors', streamed daily into this city. The former Khmer Rouge soldiers who Vietnam propped up to hold power in the new transitional administration had the first pick of all the empty villas and key positions. The rest of the population claimed ownership of the other available residences.

The Phnom Penh air was drenched in political cabals.

Uncle Seng and Tong had found work in the Ministry of Education. They moved into a spacious two-storied villa in Phnom Penh's choicest real estate of Bung Kang Kong, less than a five-minute walk to the Independence Monument, *Vimean Ackareach*. When the rest of the family moved from Ang Ka'bah to join them, we settled into this villa. Among other trees and vegetation, a huge mango tree provided shade in the courtyard as well as ripe juicy fruits. (Currently, it houses a foreign embassy.)

Many evenings, the children walked to the *Vimean Ackareach* to play hide-and-seek. Prominently situated in the middle of a rotary of boulevards and public gardens lined by palatial villas, the

Independence Monument stood out as an island of strength, its tiers of spires pointing heavenwards to inspire hope and promise to the weary population. It did not provide many hiding places, but we had fun chasing each other up and down and around the layers of steps encircling the tower.

We met long-separated relatives and family members who had either arrived before or soon after us in Phnom Penh. Some of them moved in with us while others settled into other available villas in the same neighbourhood.

Grandma Hao's younger brother, Ân Seng, whom she adopted and raised as a son, moved into our villa with his wife, Nan. Later, they were joined by their three daughters Vannak, Vanna (Huot), Mara (Mau) and their son Soraun (Heang).

≈ ≈ ≈

In September 1974, Ân Seng had gone to study in Paris on a scholarship. His wife joined him in Paris one month later, leaving their four children in Phnom Penh with Nan's mother and siblings, including brother Tien. They remained separated when Phnom Penh fell in April 1975 and throughout the Khmer Rouge years. In 1979, they found their children again amidst the chaos of Phnom Penh under Vietnamese rule.

While in Paris, Ân and Nan closely followed the news regarding the communist takeover of the country. The welfare of their children inside the country consumed their waking hours. Then-foreign minister Ieng Sary issued a statement, through his official at the Cambodian embassy in Paris, directing all interested persons with children in Cambodia to return; however, they must promise to work as farmers.

Both weighed their decision to return against the news of killings and the mass evacuation of city people. Ân reasoned,

'Cambodia is a Buddhist country; we do not kill in cold blood as reported.' In May 1975, they submitted their application to the Khmer Rouge authority in Paris, specifying the reasons for the return. Like all the other responses, they wanted to return to Cambodia to help develop the country after the war and to be reunited with family. Ân and Nan waited restlessly from one month to the next, especially anxious for news of their four children. At that time, their youngest daughter Mau was only 21 months old. Their only news was a letter from Nan's mother, dated one week before Khmer Rouge took over Phnom Penh, informing them that she has been hospitalised for high blood pressure.

At this time, the Khmer Rouge representative in Paris was known as the Khmer National Union. Waiting one day felt like one month, a month like a year. Ân and Nan wondered when Angkar would permit them to go back to Cambodia. Was the waiting because Angkar had not yet located their children? In the application, Angkar asked them to specify the address they had in Phnom Penh and their birth village.

The absence of information of the welfare of their children caused such great anxiety, that Nan fell ill and had to be hospitalised for more than one month. After her release, Ân and Nan decided to live in Toulouse in order to be closer to family, my uncles An and Ani.

Around September 1975, Angkar called Ân and Nan for an interview. They received the call with great elation, thinking that Angkar had found their family and wanted to inform them of this. At the interview, the questions remained the same: Why do you want to return to Cambodia? Do you not know our country is still very poor, the result of recent warfare?

Ân and Nan responded as before, to help develop the country and be with family again.

In their hearts, they reasoned, 'It's only normal for a country that only recently endured a war to face shortages. It will not take more than a year before our country will see prosperity again. The rice grown in Battambang alone can feed the whole nation. How much more now when everyone is put to farming? In one year, we will undoubtedly be in abundance. Also, we cannot go on living separated from our children.'

Around December 1975, Ân and Nan procured their travel documents from the Cambodian embassy. They paid for Nan's ticket; the French government paid for Ân's because his scholarship included a return ticket. Of the 1,000 individuals who responded to Ieng Sary's announcement, about 700 to 800 left from France – Cambodians around the world who wanted to return had to go to France in order to receive the authorisation from Angkar. Moreover, there existed only one flight to Phnom Penh, from Paris via Beijing.

On 31 December 1975, Ân and Nan left for Phnom Penh with 100 others. They comprised only the second flight of returnees. By this time, King Sihanouk had already returned to Cambodia, and his presence helped soothe the anxieties of these returnees. Ân and Nan had never encountered political turmoil when the king was present in Cambodia, so thought the country must be experiencing genuine peace.

They took one suitcase; among the packed items were medicine for personal use, black clothing, four mosquito nets and candies for their children.

They stayed in Beijing for nine days awaiting the next flight to Phnom Penh. On 10 January 1976, they left for Cambodia. As the plane landed in Pochentong Airport, everyone clapped with happiness upon arriving in their beloved land. Young Khmer Rouge men and women came to greet them at the airport. Each wore a white shirt; the girls had on black skirts and the boys black pants.

As they deplaned, Ân said, 'Look, there's Mardi's mother.' Upon hearing this news, Nan numb with excitement followed her husband's pointing finger, looking for Eat. Dejectedly she replied, 'No, that's not her.'

Dead calm greeted them along the way from the airport. They saw no one; but they already knew of the mass exodus to the countryside. The Khmer Rouge stripped them of all belongings, except for the essentials. They obeyed passively and remained silent. Their single wish now was to stay alive in order to find their family.

The Khmer Rouge split the returnees into various groups. Each group lived and worked together; Angkar prohibited them from interacting and communicating with local Khmers. Ân and Nan joined 200 others at Stung Meanchey, outside of Phnom Penh.* Several months later, Angkar moved them to Dai Kr'hom (Red Dirt) in Kampong Cham, where a group of 300 to 400 returnees worked.

Towards the end of 1978, possibly October or November, the Khmer Rouge gathered all Cambodian returnees from the various campsites and relocated them back to Phnom Penh, in Bung Trabaek, called 'F-30'; the 'F' stood for 'foreigners'.** In December, Ieng Sary visited Bung Trabaek to convene a meeting of all the returnees. He told the group, 'I want to gather all of you from overseas to see how many of you are left. There have been traitors who put to death people from among you.'

Ân and Nan had witnessed the disappearances of many returnees throughout this period, but until the Ieng Sary meeting, they did not know that killings occurred. Ân and Nan had believed the

---

* Now the sight of mound after mound of garbage. In September 1995, CANDO volunteers toured the area in an air conditioned van. We saw children rummaging through the mounds. I wanted to talk with some of them and opened the door of the sealed van. A strong poisonous stench assaulted me in those initial seconds. I almost fainted and had to enter the van immediately and shut the door.

** Or it could be translated from Khmer as 'O-30', the O for 'overseas'.

Khmer Rouge's explanation that these individuals were needed to help out in another region as they were transported in a truck to their death. They looked around at everyone at the meeting and noticed only about 200 people; the Khmer Rouge had killed the other 800 – 80 per cent of the original returnees.

On 1 January 1979, during a season of abundant fish, Ân and Nan, after dinner, made fish paste. Around 10 p.m., while in the middle of this activity, Angkar suddenly announced an emergency and ordered them to prepare themselves for a trip; the organisation did not elaborate as to the destination. A military vehicle transported the group to a railway station. There was only had one rail carriage which quickly became full. Angkar transported the rest back to Bung Trabaek, including Ân and Nan. It was around midnight.

Ân and Nan tried to sleep, but lingering uneasiness prevented them from rest. They quietly discussed with each other the reasons for such emergency, that they should leave piles and piles of fish to rot.

Around 3 a.m., Angkar announced another emergency and ordered them quickly to get into the military truck. During these days, they were divided into groups of ten people, with one presiding leader. Once in the truck, everyone waited anxiously for the leader of one group to look for his missing tenth person; he was found still untying his mosquito net.

The truck again unloaded them at the same railway station. Everyone climbed into the one carriage. The younger men found space on the rooftop. Around 5 a.m., at the breaking of dawn, the train left the station. When they arrived at Pochentong Airport, the young men on the roof heard gunfire; they turned to look in the direction of Phnom Penh. The sky filled with spectacular lights, like fireworks. They whispered to each other, 'There's fighting in Phnom Penh.'

They arrived in a district somewhere in Kampong Chhnang province. The train halted and they descended. Ân and Nan saw many wounded Khmer Rouge soldiers. Their painful wailing and moaning chilled the witnesses to the core. The Khmer Rouge authority carried these black-clad wounded ones into the train and left for an unknown location.

As for the group of returnees, the Khmer Rouge soldiers led their respective groups from one village to another while looking for their commanders, who had hidden along the Thai border. The soldier leading Ân and Nan's group had a radio; he turned it on. It blared within earshot of the group that Vietnamese soldiers had advanced into Phnom Penh, controlling almost everything. At this news, the soldier immediately turned off the radio.

The soldiers led the returnees to a work camp where they worked alongside the local Khmer population, cutting rice grain. The local people asked Ân and Nan, 'Where do you come from, that you should have so many surviving men?'

Nan enquired, 'Why do you ask such questions?'

The people replied, 'Where we were, they took away males, some not yet 15 years old – all of them.'

'Where were they taken?'

'To be killed,' came the chilling response.

The news jolted Ân and Nan to the core.

Ân and Nan quietly discussed with a few trusted friends the idea of journeying west with the hope of crossing into Thailand.

When they reached a village in Pursat province, the soldiers suddenly went into hiding; Vietnamese soldiers, each with a gun in tow, were all over the village. Fear seized Ân and Nan upon seeing Vietnamese soldiers; they recalled how Khmers believed they had swallowed Khmer land, mistreated their people and took their heads to boil tea.

Amidst the chaos of invasion, the groups of returnees dispersed and went their separate ways, dodging bullets, gunfire and explosions from the fighting between the Khmer Rouge and the invading

Vietnamese soldiers. Again, Ân, Nan and five trusted friends discussed ways to cross the Thai border.

Upon reaching Battambang province, northwest of Pursat, Ân and Nan followed an irrigation ditch that had been made by Khmer Rouge soldiers, known as 'the canal of 17 April', the day Phnom Penh fell. They walked and walked. They rested for one week in Koh Kralaw village. Ân and Nan slept in a chicken coop with two other friends, one male, one female.

While in this village they met a Chinese man who used to live in Phnom Penh. He approached Ân and Nan and commented that, based on their demeanour and complexion, they were once residents of Phnom Penh. He went on to detail the sufferings encountered in the village: people went without food for so long that they ate cadavers to fight off death. If people noticed a dying person, they would volunteer to bury the dead in order that they may slice the leg meat of the cadaver to fry for food. In Koh Kralaw the Khmer Rouge soldiers had starved the people to skin and bone – meat could only be found in the leg area.

One morning around 4 a.m., Nan went to a nearby bush to relieve herself. Suddenly bullets and gunfire lit up the sky. She alternatively ran and crawled, desperately dodging the red flashing lights whizzing by, to find her husband in the chicken cage. He was the only one there, waiting for her. Everyone else had deserted the area.

Vietnamese soldiers who knew several Khmer phrases went around the region, pointing their guns at and interrogating people, searching for Khmer Rouge soldiers, 'Pol Pot? Pol Pot?' Without fail the people answered, 'No, I'm only a commoner.'

Ân and Nan had known no greater fear. Simultaneously running and whispering prayers, Nan chanted, 'My mother's breast milk is very expensive; please help me to survive in this time.' According to Khmer tradition, those experiencing great fear whispered such prayers. Nan constantly prayed, 'I've never committed a sin against anyone; please may my children only meet people full of loving-kindness.'

For the next two months, Ân and Nan criss-crossed this mountainous region, amidst clusters of people who went to and fro. They knew no one. Periodically, they asked someone the whereabouts of their family. Nothing. After the repeated negative answers, they were resigned to the idea that everyone in their family had perished.

Ân and Nan each carried a sack; inside were two plastic sheets to protect them from the drizzling rain (one to serve as a mat, the other a blanket), three changes of clothes, the mosquito nets and candies, saved for their children, despite their extinguished hopes of ever finding them. They discarded everything else to lighten their load. This sack they carried on their back. They made another smaller, narrower, one-metre-long sack that they filled with rice grain; they each wore this across their body.

Along the way, they survived on tree leaves and potatoes thrown away by local people. They slept wherever they found themselves when night descended – along the rice paddies, along the road, in an abandoned hut. At times, they stayed at a vacated village two to three days to grind rice grain left in haste, piles after piles, and fill their sacks.

Rarely did they taste meat; they ate mainly boiled leaves with salt, which they carried everywhere. At other times, at a rest stop, Ân prepared the rice while Nan went in search for a person driving an ox-cart. She would run to him and plead, 'My husband is very sick; may I please have a piece of *prahok** or meat for him?'

Some took pity on her and gave Nan whatever they had; others refused. A person driving an ox-cart had meat or *prahok* because,

---

* A very potent and odorous mixture of minced fish, definitely an acquired taste. Known as Cambodian 'cheese', the potency and feeling remind me of eating French Roquefort cheese. It is one of my favourite Khmer dishes. If I wasn't practicing law, I would make it my ambition to export Khmer *prahok* and introduce the world to it.

during this period, even the cows, pigs, chickens and ducks ran away in every direction. Those who owned an ox-cart had the mobility to catch these animals, and they would kill, marinate and cook them along the way. Sometimes, Nan traded two or three sewing needles she had saved for the meat; other times, she exchanged four or five pieces of candies from her one-kilogram stash. When pure exhaustion struck, they sparingly took a piece of candy for themselves. They had some medicines left that had very much passed the expiration date. They kept them because to have was better than not to have anything.

After walking to and fro, they arrived back in Pursat province. At some places, they saw dead bodies, very bloated, in the middle of the road. When they reached Svay Daun Keo village in Pursat province, the sound of gunfire had been silenced; the Khmer Rouge soldiers had retreated along the Thai-Cambodia border and the Vietnamese soldiers had gained control over most of Cambodia.

At Svay Daun Keo, Ân and Nan slept in a Buddhist pagoda. Near it flowed a river with fish in abundance. Every morning Ân and a friend took a mosquito net, dragging it to catch fish. After an hour of casting nets, they caught about five kilograms of fish. Sometimes, they had no use for the net; the Vietnamese soldiers threw grenades into the river and many fish floated to the top. The soldiers only took the big fish, leaving behind the smaller ones for the Khmer runaways. Nan dried the fish and prepared them for their continuing journey. They stayed in this pagoda for ten days.

Imagining the journey to be long, Ân and another friend gathered pieces of wood and made a wheeled cart to transport belongings they no longer had strength to carry. When it was finished they continued their journey. In their group, they had seven adults and five children, all returnees from France. The adults took turn pushing the cart along the national route in the direction of Battambang. Everywhere they encountered Vietnamese soldiers in large numbers, their vehicles driving back and forth without stopping. All the Khmer Rouge soldiers had gone into hiding.

By this time, several markets had sprouted up. Rice and gold were the only acceptable currency. At that time, Ân still had his Rolex watch. He wanted to sell it but not mindlessly, as it had value. They spread the words, seeking a buyer. One day, a Chinese man came forward. In the course of their conversation, they learnt that the man came from the same village as Nan's mother, Prey Sandaik. He mentioned that one of Nan's aunts was still alive. He took them to meet the aunt. In turn, Nan met other family members.

Ân and Nan informed them of their desire to escape the country to the West, through Thailand. Everyone wanted to go with them: six adults and seven children (Nan's uncle Thei, her cousin Dain, her uncle Theng and his five children, Theng's son-in-law Nim and his seven-month-old baby). Along the way, they ran into a friend who brought along his family and his aged mother, Yay Kim, and another friend, Sin.

In order to reach the Thai border they had to cross Kop Nimut village. They found a trader who conducted business between Thailand and Cambodia to be their guide. Once again they rested for the night wherever darkness found them. They did not fear because they were among many other migrants. They arrived into Kop Nimut at night-time and rested at the house of the guide's relatives. The guide demanded three *dumlung* of gold from each person. The 70-year-old Yay Kim, who had asked Nim and Sin to carry her, paid for everyone in the group, as no one else could afford it. The journey into Thailand was full of danger; at times the guides plundered their clients; other times, Thai thieves committed the crimes.

The group started their escape with 17 people, including children. At certain points, the group crossed remote jungle hamlets with no one else in sight. Their guide, like others in his business, carried a sword or machete. Four hours into their journey from Kop Nimut, their guide stopped in the middle of the track. He complained about the hardships and the insufficient amount given him for the trip. He demanded more gold. The group swore to him that they had given all they had.

'I don't believe you,' he menacingly barked at them. 'I want all the women to strip naked so I can inspect.'

At these words, everyone shirked back in fear. The aged Yay Kim spit out a diamond she had been carrying in her mouth to give him. Nan handed over her gold necklace.

Upon receiving these, the guide once again spoke nicely to the group, 'We're almost near Thailand. From here, we only need to cross two more rivers.' He pointed and explained to the group the path ahead. 'Now, go on ahead; I'll follow you from behind.'

The group did as the guide suggested. About 200 metres later, they turned around only to find their guide had disappeared. The group then realised they had been abandoned, but they remembered his directions – to walk straight ahead and cross two rivers.

After one hour of walking, the group saw children riding on water buffaloes. Ân and Nan asked the children, 'Little ones, what is the name of this village?'

The children shook their heads in confusion. It dawned on the group that these were Thai children; they had entered into Thailand. They walked another kilometre when Thai soldiers accosted them. 'Stop! Sit down! Whoever has gold must now produce it!' They threatened the group in Khmer, as many soldiers along the border spoke Khmer. Everyone remained silent and they did not inspect them. 'Khmer or Yuon (Vietnamese)?'

'Khmer,' the group promptly replied in unison.

'If Khmer, go there!' The group followed the pointing finger of the Thai soldier. About another kilometre away, they met more Cambodians living under flimsy tarpaulin tents that they had tied together themselves. They had reached Nong Chan camp. Ân and Nan felt reborn, finally free of fear and danger, in Thailand and among other escapees.

At Nong Chan, Thai merchants sold everything imaginable. Those who had hidden gold traded it for money and bought everyone rice. The act of buying with money sent a surge of happiness into Ân and Nan – it was the first time in almost four years they had used it.

The United Nations went into the camp daily, asking the refugees whether they had relatives living overseas. In which country? What is the relationship? The UN gave immediate assistance to those who had spouses in a third country. Ân and Nan wrote a letter to my uncles An and Ani in France. Nan had committed their address to memory, fearing to keep it in writing.

Early in the morning of their ninth day at Nong Chan, around 6 a.m., about 20 trucks rumbled into the camp. Announcements blared from an intercom for the Cham* people to get into the trucks. Elation spread across the faces of the Chams. They ascended the trucks with jubilation, believing they have been called to Malaysia. They waved farewell to the remaining Khmer population. The truck drivers were all Thai.

That evening, Ân and Nan listened to a Voice of America broadcast in the Khmer language. They heard that Thai soldiers dumped the Chams of that morning at the top of Dang Rek Mountains and forced them to descend into the heavily mine-laden fields into Cambodia. Many Chams died.

Ân, Nan and the remaining Khmers in Nong Chan went into an emotional, desperate uproar. They were trapped; they could not retreat as they feared Thai thieves, and they could not go on further. No one slept that night. They waited for the arrival of dawn, with just enough light so they could begin their escape somewhere,

* Cham is the Muslim population in Cambodia.

anywhere. Around 5 a.m., Ân, Nan, their group and others scurried into a nearby pagoda, about half a kilometre away. They reasoned and prayed that the Thai soldiers would not mistreat them inside a temple, out of respect for the monks and Buddhism.

As they had predicted, many trucks rumbled into the camp again at 6 a.m. that morning, parked in rows. Thai soldiers, each holding a baton, came for them in the temple and ordered the group into the trucks. Those who refused they kicked into obedience. Ân and Nan's faces despaired of life as they climbed into the truck. No one breathed a word, too exhausted from life to make a sound.

Four soldiers guarded each truckload, each soldier armed with a machine gun. Two sat on guard in the back and two watched in the front of the truck. Along the way, the trucks stopped for the captives to relieve themselves; the guards followed and closely watched them, treating them like hardcore criminals. At one point, the convoys stopped at a village alongside the road and the Thai villagers rushed forward to hand the Khmer captives bags of rice through the windows. Their expression mirrored the despair of those inside the trucks, as if they knew the danger and fate waiting ahead. It could be that the Thai soldiers ordered the villagers to prepare these meals because at another village the Thai people again had rice already prepared to hand over to other Khmer captives who had not received any the first time around.

Around 7 p.m., the vehicles stopped at the top of Dang Rek mountain, on Thailand's side. On the other side of the mountain lay Cambodian soil. The soldiers ordered the Khmers to get out of the trucks. They did and sat listlessly on top of the mountain as the guards circled around the group to prevent an escape. The soldiers did not order the people to descend the mountain to Cambodian soil, as night had fully set in.

Since morning, the only meal the group received came in that rice bag handed out by the sympathetic Thai villagers. The families in the group had rice, a cooking pot and salt with them. However, they had no water. Hunger gnawed at them; the children cried painfully for food. The moaning of the sick added to the turmoil inside Ân and Nan. No one slept a wink as they anxiously awaited their fate. Their hopes dashed to pieces, they wondered what cruelty awaited them tomorrow.

Nan tried to toughen her spirit; she knew her relatives looked to her and Ân for guidance. Moreover, she told herself, she must survive for her children.

At dawn the next morning, around 5 a.m., the soldiers ordered everyone to walk forward along the mountain ridges. Like a gang of criminals, the soldiers led them. Two kilometres later, on the top of Preah Vihear, the earth flattened, making the walking less difficult. Here, everyone stopped; the soldiers pointed downwards and east, and ordered them to walk, adding, 'That's Khmer land.'

Ân and Nan could not see bottom, as Preah Vihear slopes steeply, but could hear mines exploding. The Chams who left a day before certainly must have stepped on the landmines. The Khmers pleaded with the Thai soldiers, 'We are not protesting a return to Cambodia. But this way, there are too many mines. Please, sirs, drop us off at Poipet and we will take the national route into Cambodia.'

One Thai soldier, who spoke Cambodian most fluently, climbed onto a large rock and proclaimed, 'All of you, gather all the money you have with you and give it to us. We will take this to the Thai government for consideration.'

Immediately a man in the group picked up a water pail and went around to collect money from everyone. Half an hour later, he collected a pail full of Thai bahts. He handed it to the soldiers. Chaos and fear filled the air. Ân, Nan, her relatives, Sin and Yay Kim huddled together. Mines frequently exploded, raising the hair on the skin of the Khmers. The Khmer Rouge had planted millions of them along the border.

An hour later, the soldiers returned and ominously screamed, 'Even the Thai gods cannot help you now! You must descend. Now!'

Ân, Nan and the rest of the Khmers prostrated themselves before the soldiers, like sinners before angry gods, pleading for mercy. The soldiers spurned their pleas. They pulled out their guns and shot into the air past the heads of their captives and into small tree branches, downing them onto the supplicating Khmers.

Five metres away from the main group sat a family of five adults, with a mother nursing her eight-month-old baby. The baby's father spoke, 'I'm willing to die on Thai soil; we fear to descend on Khmer soil; we fear the landmines.'

One Thai soldier retorted sarcastically, 'You're really willing to die on Thai soil, is that right?' He then drew his gun and shot the man who spoke. Everyone in that small group rose to run, but the soldier shot them one at a time. The mother, embracing the baby in her arms, had moved just one step forward when the fatal shot hit her; her arms loosened and the baby dropped to the ground, screaming. A soldier swung the baby by one arm towards the stunned Khmer woman closest to him, ordering her, 'Take this child!'

She replied, 'Sir, I can hardly carry myself. How can I carry this baby?'

The soldier threatened, 'If you don't take the baby, I will shoot you!' The woman obeyed and took the baby.

After witnessing such cruelty, everyone began the descent from the steep mountain of Preah Vihear in the direction of Cambodia. As soon as she was out of the soldiers' field of vision, the woman left the baby in the nearby brush.

The soldiers sprayed bullets in their direction, levelling those straggling, especially the elderly who moved haggardly behind.

They also kicked down smaller boulders and rocks, hitting people in the back.

(During this period, Yann Ker, who had been with the Khmer department of Voice of America in Washington, DC, went to work for the US Embassy in Thailand; he handled refugee assistance along the border.* He interviewed refugee witnesses of the Dang Rek Mountain atrocities. From the very beginning, Voice of America extensively covered the Dang Rek stories. The United Nations High Commissioner for Refugees also put pressure on the Thai government to end its atrocious policy of forced returns into mine-laden fields. Tens of thousands of lives later, the Thai soldiers stopped this forced repatriation under the weight of international pressure.)

Descending since early that morning until nightfall, the group had not reached the bottom of the mountain. Darkness forced them to rest. They sat in a line, each person resting his head on his knees. No one dared to leave the line, fearing danger. They had gone without sleep for the last 48 hours, and food and water for the last 24. That night, the three children of Nan's brother-in-law Thei, ranging from age four to ten, complained of extreme thirst and cried for water. The father Thei forced himself to urinate into a can. He then distributed the urine to his children, each receiving a spoonful, just enough to wet their dry throats.**

At the break of dawn the next morning, when visibility arrived, the group again began their descent. They hoped to reach the bottom soon and that there would be water there. Families carried members who had been wounded from gunfire, inching forward excruciatingly. Some died along the way.

Around 3 p.m. that afternoon, the group reached Khmer soil. They saw many dead Chams, victims of landmines. Still in a line,

---

* Mr. Yann Ker still works for Voice of America, based in Washington, DC. He came to the United States in 1962 on a Fulbright scholarship to study at Georgetown University.
** They currently live in Houston, Texas.

the group walked over the dead bodies. They reasoned this to be the safest path, as the dead bodies had already detonated and born the brunt of the landmines.

Two hours later, still gingerly avoiding landmines, they ran into four Vietnamese soldiers walking towards them. Everyone in the group clapped in elation, as if receiving gods who had just descended from the heavens for their salvation.

The Vietnamese soldiers told the group, 'People, please, rest here for now. Do not go further; we have yet to de-mine the other landmines. Around here, you can move around for about five metres, as we have already de-mined the area.'

Nan's relatives and Yay Kim walked to a grassy area that had been trampled on and spread their plastic sheets. They plopped their weary bodies on the sheets. Ân and Nan rested under two small trees nearby. Directly above them, someone had tied a *krama*, the Khmer all-purpose scarf, to make a small hammock; in it laid a baby, freshly dead, as the body had not yet bloated. They immediately fell asleep from pure exhaustion.

Around 2 a.m., a piercing moan came from Nim, 'Oaoy! Oaoy!' It woke up Nan; the rest continued in their deep slumber. Nan got up and felt his temperature. He felt like burning coals and shook furiously.

Nim muttered, '*Bong*, my chest hurts and feels like it's going to burst.'

Nan reached over to Nim's wife and shook her to wake her up to care for her husband. Without opening her eyes, she mumbled, 'I cannot wake up.'

Angrily, Nan lectured her, 'Listen to the painful moaning of your husband, and yet you care not to look after him?' Nan pinched and slapped her to arouse her; she still could not. Everyone slept like a dead corpse, without making a sound or movement.

Nan tried to support Nim as she helped him sit up. She sat

behind him and rubbed his chest. Nim moaned and cried for water. Nan soothingly told him to hold on for another two or three hours, for daybreak, when they could resume the journey and would certainly find water.

Nim mumbled his gratitude, 'You're like my mother; I would never forget your kindness.'

A little later, some youths courageously went further down and found water. They sold a bowl for one *chi* of gold, about $40 to $50. Everyone rushed to buy it.

Nan reflected, 'Why this intense suffering? Under the Khmer Rouge era, even though we may not have had enough to eat, at least we had plenty of water. Now we have no rice, no water for the last two days.' She dreamt of all her favourite food while living in France. Even if she wanted to cry, she had no tears left. Thoughts of her children kept up her spirits.

Around 5 a.m., family members shook the others to wake them up to continue the journey. Nim's wife carried her child. Nim, still with a high fever, carried their belongings. Nan's sister Nain carried her four-year-old son, who had been reduced to skin and bone. Again, everyone walked in a single file line, never veering into the mine-infested side brushes. Some who deviated to relieve themselves stepped on mines and were blown to pieces. At certain nooks and crannies, they found *chamrong*, traps made of sharp bamboo poles, planted in the vegetation by the Khmer Rouge for unsuspecting victims. In particular, the Khmer Rouge soldiers set up these deadly bamboo traps to hinder the Thais from entering their territory and cutting down their forest.

Three long hours later, the group landed at the foot of the mountain. Here they no longer feared landmines. Ân, Nan and their group took a much needed rest. A ribbon of water flowed near them. The water quickly turned cloudy, made so by the heavy traffic of people jumping in to draw water and refresh themselves.

Nim filled a pail full to cook rice; the group had missed the last five meals. He also dipped himself in the stream, bringing down his temperature considerably. Everyone had gone without food for so long that their stomachs no longer hungered, the feeling replaced by a new sensation of airiness. No one wanted dried rice; they made rice porridge instead. Nan took one spoonful of the porridge and quickly her stomach churned and threw it out; it could not accept this foreign element, food, as it had gone so long without it.

Four Vietnamese soldiers came forward and told the weary travellers, 'People, after two more kilometres of walking, you will meet the national route. There will be soldiers waiting to distribute rations to you.'

The news injected new energy to the Khmer population. All of Nan's prejudices about the Vietnamese – their mistreatment of Cambodians, their aggression and annexation of Cambodian land throughout history – quickly softened at the kindness shown by these soldiers; her perception changed from one of distrust to gratitude. She thought, 'If a Vietnamese soldier were to give me a gun to shoot a Thai soldier, I would not hesitate for a moment.' The Thai soldiers' cruelty of the last couple days was forever etched in her memory.

Two kilometres later, Ân, Nan and their group found Vietnamese soldiers waiting for them under a tent as they had been told. The soldiers greeted them and handed out rice rations to each person: one can for an adult, half a can for a child. There would be another distribution centre in another ten kilometres, the soldiers informed them.

After some calculating, Ân, Nan, and the group decided that they could not make this distance in a day; they had too many children and the aged Yay Kim. They must make the rice grain last; again they made watery rice porridge. Even though it was plain rice porridge eaten only with salt, the group felt renewed. At other locations, Vietnamese soldiers would hand out out powder or cotton, *samlay*, grain.

The uprooted Khmer population crowded the road. The wife of Nan's uncle Theng *raet* (balanced a pole on her shoulder) – her child on one side, hanging from the pole, their ration/belongings on the other. Her husband, Theng, walked empty-handed, barely able to carry himself along. The group slept wherever they found themselves when darkness descended.

My great uncle, Ân, commented, 'I would have died from pity, had our children been with us, to suffer like this.' Unlike his wife's stout-heartedness, Ân's soft heart weakened his spirit and he easily fell into hopelessness.

The group had been walking for the three days. They did not recognise the villages and communes they passed; the surrounding terrain and environment appeared unfamiliar to all of them. They only knew they were in Preah Vihear province.

They continued on amidst other migrating groups of people. One week later, they arrived at a village with some people living in it. Those who no longer had energy stayed and lived with the local villagers. Ân, Nan, and their group decided to rest momentarily, to ease their exhaustion. It had been ten days since they last had meat to eat.

Nan had two sarongs left. She entered the village to trade these sarongs for meat. Every appearance spoke to the extreme poverty of the villagers, their squalid environment and their tiny flimsy huts. These villagers eyed the sarong with longing, especially after having had to wear black for the last four years. However, they answered Nan, 'We have nothing to trade you, only the barking dog.'

Growing up Nan detested the idea of eating dog meat. However, at that moment, hunger for meat consumed any other sentiments, and she traded one sarong for that one barking dog.

Sin prepared the dog meat. Everyone partook of the feast and savoured the delicious treat, like eating beef, thought Nan. The group prepared the leftover meat for future meals on the road. Nain, sister of Nan and wife of Thei, carried her withered son Thavit, or the skin on bones that he had become.

At one point along their journey, he hoarsely begged his mother, 'Please, Mom, may I have some dog meat the size of my palm? If I have some, I can walk on my own. You will not need to carry me anymore.' Nain did as her son requested and prepared a slice of dog meat with a bowl of rice for four-year-old Thavit. The image of little Thavit enjoying the food burned into his aunt Nan's heart.

The times that Vietnamese soldiers handed out flour, the group mixed it with water to make bread.

Half way across Preah Vihear province, in the direction of Kampong Thom, the group encountered a body of water they had to cross by boat. In this region, dense forests of bamboo shoots cover the earth. The group dug up and cooked young bamboo shoots to eat with rice, a culinary treat as welcome as meat. With grateful hearts everyone ate these young bamboo shoots, common in Khmer cooking, even if only flavoured with salt.

At this location, the Vietnamese soldiers divided the population into two groups: Khmer on one side; Chinese on the other. The soldiers allowed Khmers with aged people and young children to cross first. Ân, Nan and their close-knit group of relatives and friends crossed on the second day. News later reached Ân and Nan that the Vietnamese soldiers kept the Chinese group in the bamboo forest for another two weeks before permitting them to cross; many died while waiting in the May monsoon downpour.

Upon landing on the other side, the group had another 70 kilometres of walking before reaching their destination of Kampong Thom province, the midway point to Phnom Penh and a familiar reference point. Groups without children and aged adults could

make the distance in one week's time on foot. Ân and Nan knew
their group would not be able to make this time because of the
many children, the aged Yay Kim and the sick.

Many trucks carrying Vietnamese soldiers rumbled back and
forth. No one knew where they were going or coming from.

It was now May. Since January, Ân and Nan had been on the
run, living on the sides of roads, under scorching sun, bracing
against whipping winds and shielding themselves from blustering
monsoon rain. The sky composed their roof, the dirt their bed.
Once in a while, they slept in abandoned huts. Besides fighting
against the elements, Nan daily struggled against despair and
hopelessness; she coughed and coughed, a symptom of hunger,
exhaustion and everything else whirling in Cambodia in those
periods. 'Walk on, walk on,' she meditatively chanted to herself,
refusing to moan or reveal her weaknesses to anyone, for she knew
everyone was looking to her for guidance and strength.

However, she did whisper to her husband, '*Bong*, I can hardly
walk anymore. When we reach Kampong Thom, if there is a medical
clinic, I would like to rest there for two or three days.' That was all.

Ân and Nan leaned on each other for strength. Yay Kim could no
longer walk. Her son went into the road and flagged down one of the
countless passing trucks; the Vietnamese soldiers stopped and gave
Yay Kim a ride upon seeing her quivering and shaking from old age
and exhaustion. Kampong Thom was still another 20 kilometres away.

Upon reaching Kampong Thom province, the group encountered countless groups of wearied families sprawled on the sides of
the national route, spreading their plastic mats every which way,
their bodies hugging the earth for rest, as trucks whizzed by dangerously and others of the migrating population moved onwards.
Those who had gold traded it for food and clothing. Ân accompanied his wife to the medical clinic, 500 metres more from where
their group had stopped to rest.

They found Yay Kim at the clinic, dropped off by the Vietnamese soldiers. She had temporarily lost her mind and did not recognise Ân and Nan. She mumbled how she would not rest in Kampong Thom, but will continue on to her ancestral province of Kampong Cham.

While a medical personnel was attending Nan, a woman slapped my great uncle Ân on the back and asked, 'Ân, isn't it?' Ân turned around and confirmed, 'Yes, that's me.' After a few seconds getting his bearings, he recognised her as the 'mother of Ti' who lived near my relatives and me by Wat Koh in Phnom Penh. Ân and Nan knew her well.

Ti's mother confessed, 'I hesitated to approach you, knowing that you had left for France in 1974. Why are you back in Cambodia?'

Ân and Nan once again recounted bits and pieces of their ordeal. Ti's mother added, 'Ta Kuy, Yay Hao, Ry and Rey are still alive. I even met the five children.' The five children of course was a reference to my siblings and me. She related Grandpa Kuy's paralysed condition and his lost of speech, and our orphaned status.

Ti's mother gave Ân and Nan our address in Phnom Penh. No medicine could be more potent in curing Nan's ailments; she no longer needed to be hospitalised as all her diseases seemed to disappear miraculously from her body. The news of our survival and whereabouts jolted Ân and Nan out of stupor and hopelessness. They walked back to their group of relatives and friends with the unexpected news. 'Wait here for us; we're going to Phnom Penh to find these relatives.'

They waited for transport with Vietnamese soldiers. After a bit of wrangling and one *chi* of gold (about $40) later, the soldiers agreed to give them a ride. Along the way, they saw Yay Kim's family, and shouted to them from the moving truck, 'Yay Kim is resting at Kampong Thom hospital!' The pedestrians yelled back, 'Thank you, we're on our way to Kampong Cham to find family!'

The Vietnamese soldiers dropped off Ân and Nan at Prey Kdam around 5 p.m. They had just missed the last ferry. They walked back and forth looking for shelter for the night, and ran into a man from Prey Sandaik, who used to live next door to Nan's mother. They asked him for shelter for the night. He refused, possibly fearing that Ân and Nan might steal from him as he was a seller of rice grain. But he did allow them to stay along the side of his house; immediately he closed the door tight and locked it.

It drizzled that night; the two could not sleep, vigorously shaking away the cold and the splattering sound of the raindrops. They earnestly prayed for morning to come quickly so they might continue on their journey to find all of us in Phnom Penh.

The next morning, Nan inquired of their distrusting host, 'Have you been back to Prey Sandaik?'

He replied, 'Yes. Your mother is still alive.'

'And my children?' Nan excitedly pursued.

'I don't know. I remember seeing one woman who's fair and looked *barang*. Maybe your younger sister?'

Nan beamed with joy and hoped, 'No. Not my sister. It must be my oldest daughter Vannak.' This piece of information acted like a magical cure and once again Ân and Nan were rejuvenated.

They caught the 5 a.m. ferry which dropped them off on the other side of the body of water. Anticipation fluttered through their weary bodies, knowing that Phnom Penh was only another 20 kilometres away. They walked most of the way, once catching a ride on two bicycles with friendly strangers for about five kilometres of the journey.

At 6 p.m., they arrived at a location known as Kilometre 6 and encountered a barricade into Phnom Penh. They walked up to an armed Vietnamese soldier, guarding the gate. Ân and Nan pleaded with him for entry to no avail, and received the firm response, 'No more people can enter. Must wait until tomorrow morning.'

Being so close to finding us after all these years and experiences, Ân and Nan could not wait until the next morning. They retreated a bit and surreptitiously walked along the edges of houses and, when opportunity presented itself, crawled under the barricade into Phnom Penh. They walked for another hour and found all of us at that spacious two-storied house, south of Independence Monument, given to Uncle Seng for his work in the Ministry of Education.

Everyone embraced and cried tears of joy and incredulity, that we should find each other after separation since 1974 and having had all hope extinguished again and again. Ta Ân and Nan came to us around May 1979. Ân embraced Ta Kuy, both his brother-in-law and adopted father. The sight of Ta Kuy dragging one foot while his one arm fell listlessly by the side struck sharp pangs into Ân. Ta Kuy tried to speak; only incoherent groans came out as he cried and clung onto Ân, for the longest time refusing to let go.

Grandma Hao's absence was immediately noticeable to Ân and Nan, but she had once more journeyed to Vietnam to send letters to her sons in France and the United States. Cambodia did not have a postal system.

Ân and Nan only stayed with us for two days, very much anxious to make the 80-kilometre trip to Prey Sandaik to find their family. They borrowed Aunt Ry's bike. Usually the trip takes a day on a bike, but not when rode by two people. Nan pedalled four to five kilometres; Ân pedalled the rest of the way, stopping to rest many times.

At nightfall, they entered the nearest village. No one gave them shelter. Khmer Rouge atrocities and fears still left fresh imprints on the population's shattered minds. The villagers directed the two travellers to the pagoda further ahead. Ân biked Nan there and found an imposing temple, vacated of any life. Spooked by the eerie silence of the temple, they biked back to the village and again pleaded with the people for shelter. The owner of one hut pointed to a bamboo bed in his courtyard, under a large mango tree, and there Ân and Nan found rest for their aching bodies and souls.

Around 2 a.m., they were rudely awakened by thunderous noises and flashes of lightning, which jolted them out of sleep into fear. But it was just that, lightning, and pounding raindrops then struck at them. They were after all in the monsoon season. The couple ran to huddle with the cattle under the main hut. The rooster crowed at 3.30 a.m. and the rain stopped. They returned to lie under the mango tree and waited until dawn, around 5.30, when they once again continued their journey.

They arrived into Prey Sandaik around 9.30 that morning. Nothing was recognisable to Nan; all the houses Nan knew from before 1970 looked different. Ta Ân continued pedalling when a voice echoed Nan's name into the open sky, 'À Nan! You just passed your own house!'

From that second on, Nan's name echoed from one hut to the next. Her younger sister, Lim, upon hearing this name ran out to embrace the couple, soon joined by other siblings, Tien and Vuth, and their children, Vannak, Vanna (Huot) and Soraun (Heang).

Their youngest daughter Mau (Mara), ran in the opposite direction, joyfully proclaiming to the curious gathering neighbours, 'Look! The parents of Bong Nak, Bong Huot and Bong Heang are reunited with their children! They're just crying and embracing!'

When Ân and Nan separated from their children, Mara was a little over one year old. Now, this six-year-old could not make the connection that these parents of Vannak, Huot and Heang were also her parents.

Nan embraced her aged mother, who had shaven her head. When she heard that many Cambodians had returned from overseas, she went to a fortune-teller to enquire about the fate of Ân and Nan. The fortune-teller told her that her children returned to

Cambodia and at that moment were facing intense suffering, but alive. All this took place when Ân and Nan underwent their ordeal in the Dang Rek mountains. Nan's mother now beamed with indescribable joy to hear that her second child, Nain, was still alive, presently waiting for Ân and Nan in Kampong Thom province.

That evening, Ta Ân came down with a fever, shaking furiously. They had run out of medicine (and the candies for their children). He moaned in pain throughout the night, his body as hot as fire. The next morning, they took him to the village medical clinic; the medical personnel gave him a shot from a syringe left over from who knows when, reasoning that anything was better than his present condition. The syringe did reduce his temperature by a little; Nan hired a man to pedal her husband back to Phnom Penh where better facilities and medicines were available, or so she hoped. Having only been reunited with her children for two days, she could not accompany her husband.

During this period, the occupying Vietnamese forces made their presence known everywhere in the village. Someone told Nan that she overheard these soldiers saying they had come to help Cambodians for the next 25 years. Upon hearing this, Nan's age-old mistrust of Vietnamese – their mistreatment of Cambodians, their plundering and swallowing of Cambodian territory – surfaced anew. She thought, 'Now the whole of Cambodia will be another Kampuchea Krom. I must get my children out of this country.' Kampuchea Krom (Lower Cambodia), which contains sizeable Khmer minorities, used to be what was known as Cochin China under French protectorate and is now the southern provinces of Vietnam.

Ta Ân arrived in Phnom Penh two days later and Aunt Rey took him to Calmette Hospital.

≈ ≈ ≈

The new leaders – pawns as they were of the true power brokers, the Vietnamese – ardently recruited any surviving persons with higher education to help run the various newly-created ministries in the transitional government. Uncle Seng and Tong had found work in the Ministry of Education. Seng worked in the enviable position as personal secretary to the minister of education, Chan Vann.* The minister lived in an elephantine villa on Norodom Boulevard, directly across from our house.

My aunts taught elementary school. Every morning the children would catch a ride on one of the overloaded convoy trucks travelling in the direction of the school to attend classes. We hung off the railings or sat on the transported materials, forming the mounded roof of the truck. We learnt the Vietnamese language in one class and sang many Vietnamese songs. The adults were not too happy to hear the Vietnamese tunes sung at home; it only confirmed their suspicions of their neighbour's expansionist design, and fuelled their resolve to escape an occupied Cambodia.

Other times, we walked when we could not find a place to hang onto a truck. One day on the way to school, Sina ran into Pou Poun, the man who used to look after us when Papa was away on military duties, as we were a family of women and children, before the reign of the Khmer Rouge. He had served in Papa's battalion. He became part of the group of Khmer Rouge soldiers who defected to Vietnam.

Upon arriving into Phnom Penh in January 1979, the Vietnamese soldiers transported to Vietnam countless truckloads of goods left by the businesses and residents of Phnom Penh when they exited in April 1975. The Khmer Rouge soldiers cared very little for the television sets, refrigerators, factory machines and products, gold and silver of the palace or any other valuables. In certain instances, the Khmer Rouge soldiers had consolidated the

* As of 2005, the vice president of the National Assembly.

appliances into piles of refrigerators, stereos, etc, easing the work of the looters. By the time we arrived into Phnom Penh, most of the valuable items had already been looted and plundered, although we did find a couple of intricate silver and gold plates that we pounded into easier carrying form.

We heard rumours that the residents of one villa had hidden a bag of diamonds, gold and other precious metal in the sewage system of their house when Phnom Penh fell under communist control. My relatives asked Pou Poun to act as their bodyguard and accompany them to this house. They lied to the new residents that they used to live in that house prior to the war and wanted to inspect it. They searched the sewage system but did not find anything.

Like a tadpole trapped at the bottom of a deep well so the Cambodians lived under the Khmer Rouge, as slaves who had limited freedom and little perspective outside of the narrow stream of light of their present circumstance. However, the piercing of Cambodia's sovereignty allowed outside news and information to seep into the country. This prospect of receiving untampered news kept the ears of many Cambodians attuned to all sources of information to balance against the heavy Vietnamese propaganda infiltrating the country.

The new government blamed the genocide on one criminal, Pol Pot, acting on Chinese orders. It successfully shifted the focus of the blame from 'communism' in general to that of a single Chinese puppet. This is evidenced in the way Cambodians have come to place responsibility for the horror: 'Contemptible (À) Pot killed my parents.' In explaining history in this context, the Vietnamese-backed, Leninist-Marxist government adeptly exonerated the philosophy of its political fathers yet succeeded in excoriating Vietnam's historical nemesis, China.

*

Sometime later, Nan returned to Phnom Penh to look after her husband, leaving her four children with her mother in Prey Sandaik. She went to visit Ân, still hospitalised at Calmette Hospital. During those days, only very important people were admitted for treatment at Calmette. But Aunt Rey had befriended Dr. Song Tan,* the deputy director of (and most senior physician in) the hospital, who forged a certificate for Ân Seng asserting him as a man of high position.

Grandma Hao returned from Vietnam with news that enlightened the adults of the social and political conditions; Cousin Hieu (then governor of Tay Ninh) informed them that at all cost, they must leave Cambodia because the whole of Cambodia would be another Kampuchea Krom, annexation inevitable.

Nan informed everyone that she would not stay in Cambodia. She did not expressly invite the others to escape with her, fearing blame should they encounter cruelty like her Dang Rek experience. But as for her immediate family, she was determined that they would find a way to escape this country of genocide, this country of occupation, this country drenched in blood and suffering, with no future. Grandma Hao did not need an invitation as the thought of escape had also been percolating in her head.

Dr. Song Tan had also been listening to the radio and gleaning information from the various news media for ways to escape. He had little trust in the new regime, an intuition developed from his interaction with his patients. Reciprocally, he sensed that they did not trust him.

Several incidents confirmed his suspicion. During this period, animosity towards Chinese people ran especially deep because China was fighting Cambodia and Vietnam. Everyone with the last name of 'Bai' quickly changed it. As a person of visible Chinese ancestry, Dr.

---

* Currently, a very successful paediatrician with his own private practice in Southern California. He did his residency at the University of Hawaii and became the first Cambodian-American paediatrician in the United States.

Tan had reason to fear. One incident involving a junior member of staff furthered his fear. This man had less education than Dr. Tan but the authority called him into politics and overlooked the doctor.

'Shit. They do not trust me.' The thought resonated through Dr. Tan's head.

Another time, he was summoned to be the doctor of President Chea Sim's son. Upon his prescription of medicine, they first made him try out the medication. 'Song, why don't you have a little bit first?'

Other times, the Vietnamese nurses played spies and reported the goings-on of the doctors and hospital staff to their superiors.

'They're all Khmer Rouge, communist at the core. These people disguised themselves. And they don't trust me. I will next be killed if I don't get out of here,' thought Dr. Tan.

The precarious and chaotic state of affairs strengthened Dr. Tan's resolve to escape the country. He had heard news of the atrocity inflicted by the Thai soldiers on Cambodian civilians in Dang Rek Mountains along the northwestern border of Cambodia and Thailand. The killings rivalled the Khmer Rouge brutality, if not exceeded it. The Thai soldiers looked upon the Cambodians with condescension, from a sense of superiority towards that of a third world country.

However, he also heard radio reports that the United Nations would soon open up refugee camps along the Thai-Cambodian border. Despite the reports of mass killings, Dr. Tan reasoned that at the propitious time, he would attempt an escape towards the border.

'The Thais cannot possibly kill everybody,' he calculated. 'Moreover, anything is better than the current situation.'

(Warfare is weird in this inverted sense – to make people prefer the unfamiliar to the familiar.)

He would employ people whose business it was to guide people across the border – riding on *trak*, as this underground railroad system was known.

After admitting Ta Ân to the hospital, the two quickly struck a friendship and gained each other's trust. They exchanged information and news regarding their backgrounds and the political and social climate.

Ta Ân's condition and temperature fluctuated from day to day; he went in and out of consciousness. Sometime in June, after a month of hospitalisation, he came back home to us when the syringe shots reduced his temperature a bit, only to return two days later when the fever returned with greater force. Dr. Tan found the virus that caused the fever in Ta Ân's blood, a strand of malaria commonly found in the jungles of Preah Vihear where Ân and Nan had been during their Dang Rek ordeal. He knew the medicine needed to treat the virus but no such medicine existed in Calmette Hospital. Even under the competent care of Dr. Tan, without appropriate medicine Ân's fever could not be cured. The hospital only had medicine long expired.

In early July, when her husband's condition continued to show little sign of improvement, Nan asked Grandma Hao to make another trip to Vietnam with her. Grandma Hao agreed but questioned whether Nan could get past the border patrol as she did not speak Vietnamese. The two women first went to Svay Rieng province to procure a guide who knew the terrain into Vietnam. They rode with Vietnamese soldiers for a negotiated price of gold from Phnom Penh to Bavit town, bordering Vietnam, in Svay Rieng province.

In Bavit, they found a guide who charged each woman one *chi* of gold to get them to Prey Nokor, Cambodia's name for Saigon, normally a one-hour car ride. The guide would take them into Vietnam via a detoured back road because of Nan's inability to speak Vietnamese. Nan carried a sack ostensibly with a change of clothes and foodstuffs; at the bottom, she sewed a secret compartment and hid one *dumlung* (or ten *chi*) of gold. On her body she had another five *chi*. Certainly, Grandma Hao had similar secret holdings.

They would not be leaving until 10 p.m. that night, which would allow them to enter Vietnam before dawn. The guide told them to rest at his house; anxiety and anticipation prevented them from sleep. Sure enough, at 10 p.m., another man came to lead Grandma Hao and Nan into the pitch-black night. Walking along rice paddies, their vision was limited to the small cloud of sand made by their footsteps. Grandma Hao had already told Nan to be mute, to leave all answers upon interrogation to her to answer in Vietnamese.

They crossed into Vietnam around 1 a.m. and encountered only charred huts, eerily with no living souls. Nan whispered to their guide, 'Why is the village emptied of people?'

The guide explained, 'During the Khmer Rouge years, intense fighting between Khmer Rouge and Vietnamese soldiers took place in this region; now everyone fears to live here.'

Another hour later, they saw three Vietnamese women planting rice, who asked the travellers, 'Where are you going?'

'To plant rice in the field ahead,' promptly replied Grandma Hao in Vietnamese.

Through certain areas, the three delinquents waded through watered rice paddies, full from the monsoon rain. The water came up to the chests of the women; they shivered from the very cold water.

Around 3.30 a.m., they reached a Vietnamese village. The guide knocked on the door of one household and immediately the door flew open; most likely the hut served as a rest stop for such expeditions, a planned arrangement. All the Vietnamese villagers along the border knew Cambodian. The owners of this hut laid out a mat directly on the dirt floor for Grandma Hao and Nan to sleep on. They also boiled hot water for the women to drink, since they were visibly shivering from the cold. The women changed out of their wet clothes, drank the hot water and slept for about an hour. At

5.30, they bid the owners goodbye and rode on a motor-pulled cart to Tay Ninh, where Grandma Hao had visited on her prior trips. The terrain now appeared familiar to Grandma Hao.

Upon reaching Tay Ninh, Grandma Hao went to the house of the provincial governor, Hieu, who she had visited on her first trip with Sina. Grandma Hao introduced Nan as the 'wife of Kai' (meaning Ta Ân) to several other grandmotherly women, who appeared to know my grandma well. Now that the two women were deep past the border into Vietnam, they spoke Cambodian openly with one another and the others. Hieu told the women not to stay in Cambodia; they must find a way to leave for a foreign country. Grandma Hao and Nan tried to decipher what he meant by his warnings. They caught a taxi to Prey Nokor (Saigon) after having had lunch at his house.

At Prey Nokor, they looked for a nephew of Ta Kuy who had escaped Cambodia in 1975. Fearing for his security, he refused to let the two women stay with him for the night; he explained that whenever a new person enters the village, soldiers descend on the house to interrogate without fail. He directed them to another nephew, Kim Loung. He too refused to let the women stay. These two nephews possessed sufficient means and feared to risk their welfare.

Grandma Hao and Nan had one last hope in a third nephew of Ta Kuy, Huon. If he were also to reject them, they would be left stranded in a strange environment, as delinquents, without shelter for the night.

Huon proved to be different to the first two nephews. They found him living in extreme poverty, in a tiny leafed hut with walls dotted with holes. He possessed two bamboo beds, one for himself, the other for his three sons. He sold ice cream for a living. He apologised to Grandma Hao and Nan for his poverty, explaining, 'It's not that I'm hard-hearted, but as you can see, I literally have no space for you to stay.'

Grandma Hao understandingly replied, 'We are okay sleeping on a mat directly on the floor.'

That night, as with every other night, he woke up at 3.30 to make ice cream, which unintentionally woke everyone up along with him.

Without wasting time in the morning, Nan wrote a letter to Uncle An in France and Uncle Eng in the United States, asking them to start the paperwork for our sponsorship. Grandma Hao and Nan decided to change my last name from Kao to Seng, along with those of my four brothers, to match those of my sponsoring uncles. They also reduced our ages. Not knowing when the time for escape to the West would come, they did not want my oldest brother Mardi to pass school-going age. But in reducing Mardi's age, they had to reduce all our ages accordingly. Nan did the same to the ages of her children.

In the letter, they only asked An and Eng to sponsor two families, those of Grandma Hao (including my siblings and me) and of Nan's. (Aunt Ry and husband Seng expressed great ambivalence about an escape, especially with Seng's high post in government and their baby Visal still not yet one year old.)

The soldiers moved many of the Khmers who had escaped into Vietnam since 1975 to Wat Rainsey village, once belonging to Cambodia. The two women left for this village on a motor-driven cart; all the drivers appeared to know Wat Rainsey well. Besides desiring to learn more about the conditions in this region, Grandma Hao had a niece, Yao, living there since 1975.

The condition of Wat Rainsey village could not be distinguished from hell on earth. The women arrived to clusters of huts, each the size of a bed, built next to each other like the tightness of a bunch of unripe bananas. The air thickened with unbearable stench. The women walked through trampled mud, which reeked of faeces and urine, slipping periodically on the wet red silt, while searching for Yao's place. They found it, a leafed hut precariously balancing over an unsanitary lake again reeking of urine and faeces, off a teetering bamboo walkway.

Yao greeted her aunt and Nan with dry coughing fits, 'Keih! Keih!' No more than skin on withering bones, Yao suffered from *rabane*, tuberculosis. Amidst her coughing fits, she described to her visitors the hardships and sufferings of the Khmers who lived there: If you want to live outside Wat Rainsey village, you must bribe a Vietnamese soldier. (Keih! Keih!) Plus rent is very expensive outside of here; (Keih! Keih!) you have to spend at least $200 a month to survive. A family of five must spend $1,000 a month (Keih! Keih!).

Everywhere Hao and Nan turned, they saw heart-wrenching, bottomless hardship. Some had lived there five years and still had no prospect of moving on to a better place or a third country. Those with money had to pay Vietnamese soldiers $8,000 to $10,000 per person to submit the necessary paperwork requesting permission to go to a third country. Grandma Hao and Nan calculated that it would cost their families $2,000 to $2,500 a month to live in Vietnam while waiting indefinitely for a hopeless exit to a third country.

Despairing, Grandma Hao and Nan decided to return to Cambodia. Yao gave her visitors directions to the house of a family she knew living on the border should they decide to rest for the night along the way back. The two women reached the border around 3 p.m. that afternoon and found the house. Grandma Hao decided to continue on and cross the border; she told Nan to wait until night-time to reduce her chances of being caught. It was too dangerous for both to wait around and linger, so Grandma Hao went to catch a ride on a military truck of Vietnamese soldiers heading into Svay Rieng.

Nan asked the wife of the family whether she could stay the night and she consented. However, around 6 p.m. the husband arrived and told Nan her presence posed too great a risk. Instead, he volunteered his 15-year-old son to pedal Nan on a bike into Cambodia. Fearing an encounter with Vietnamese soldiers, the son pedalled Nan along rice paddies, about half a kilometre away par-alleling the national route.

All of a sudden, a shot shattered the pristine air; a Cambodian soldier had spotted them. He marched towards the travellers and asked, 'Where are you going?'

Nan replied, 'I came to buy macaronis for my children to eat; now, I'm on my way home to Bavit.'

Nan held her breath in fear as the soldier searched her travel sack. He found the macaronis and handed Nan back her sack. She took it, with great relief that he did not discover the gold sewn to the bottom of the sack. That night after the boy returned home, Nan sought shelter in one of the huts along the way, but all refused her. She spent the night sitting on a bamboo bed outside of one hut and prayed for morning to come quickly. The next morning she caught a ride with a Vietnamese car travelling west into Cambodia. She found Grandma Hao waiting for her at a relative's house with whom they stayed prior to entering Vietnam. The next day, Grandma Hao and Nan left for Phnom Penh.

When Grandma Hao and Nan arrived in Phnom Penh, Uncle Seng had received news that he had to move to a different house, located immediately next to the Independence Monument, *Vimean Ackareach*.* We did not mind the move. The old house had too much traffic. Frequently, Vietnamese officials stopped by the house to request Seng to do this or that. Moreover, the house's proximity to the minister's residence and the Ministry provided little privacy. Rumours also surfaced that the house would soon be turned into an embassy.

As the new house had an extra room, Nan decided to move her children from Prey Sandaik to Phnom Penh, fearing permanent

---

* I believe the present place of the Documentation Center of Cambodia.

separation should roads be made impassable in the future. She and the four children walked the seven kilometres from Prey Sandaik village to Takeo province to find the many military trucks rumbling to and from Phnom Penh. She explained to her children, 'I will not let you live in Cambodia. We must find a way to escape so that all of you may find an education in Paris.'

Nearing Pochentong Airport, on the outskirts of Phnom Penh, upon seeing concrete buildings, the youngest daughter Mara asked, 'Is this Paris?' The Khmer Rouge emptied Phnom Penh when Mara was a baby; she spent most of her six-year-old life living in a hut woven from dried leaves.

Nan enrolled them in school with us.

When we first arrived into Phnom Penh, Grandma Hao gathered numerous sacks of aromatic 'chan' flowers. With the children attending school, Grandma Hao caring for paralysed Ta Kuy and granddaughter Visal, Ta Ân convalescing in the hospital, and the other adults teaching and working, Nan took these flowers to trade at the various markets. One day while pedalling materials to sell at Chbar Empouv market, she spotted Sin who had experienced the Dang Rek atrocity with her, walking by himself at Chamkar Mon. She stopped and called to him.

'Have you heard about your sister Nain?' he asked. 'Two weeks after you left Kampong Thom, Vietnamese soldiers ordered everyone to move to this remote village, far from any medical centre or civilisation. She has died due to lack of medicine.' Nain had caught *krun santum*, where her fever burned her to unconsciousness. The news deeply saddened Nan, in particular, to have had her sister survive the Khmer Rouge only to succumb to death so quickly during a time of relative potential peace.

Sin went on, 'Families of Theng, Nim and Dain are currently living in Svay Sisophon in Battambang. Many Khmers are escaping to Thailand. I'm thinking of going as well.'

The new government did everything in its power to fan reports of killings and deaths of those who attempted to escape the country in order to dissuade the migration.

Nonetheless, a plan for escape circulated in the minds of the adults and Pou Song (Dr. Tan), fed by reports from Grandma Hao's trips to Vietnam, Nan's encounter with Sin and various other personal experiences. Ta Ân told Dr. Tan, 'When I regain my strength, I'm going to make another escape through Thailand.'

Pou Song replied, '*Bong*, if you go, I'm going with you.' Dr. Tan tended to Ta Ân with even greater care.

At the beginning of August, new medicine entered Cambodia. Pou Song elatedly told Ta Ân, 'We have the right medicine to treat you now. Certainly, you will regain full health by next week.' Dr. Tan's prediction came true; the new medicine cured Ta Ân and he came home to us healed the following week.

Nan decided to travel to the northwest province of Battambang again and assess the situation first-hand. During that period, social and political conditions changed so rapidly from day to day that she did not want her Dang Rek experience to be more than a cautionary tale and be a strike against an escape via Thailand. She rode up with Vietnamese soldiers, not knowing exactly what to do or whom to see upon arrival.

Upon reaching the town of Battambang, Nan walked around the main market, hoping to see any familiar face. She vaguely recognised a woman and asked to stay with her for the night. She enquired about the dangers of crossing into Thailand. 'Nowadays, many people make the trip. When they reach Svay Sisophon, they hire guides who know the terrain well. I am planning to leave myself.' The response gave Nan great affirmation and joy.

She decided to return to Phnom Penh immediately. Once again, she caught a ride with Vietnamese soldiers. The truck stopped at the midway town of Pursat. When the soldiers went into the market,

Nan did the same, still glowing from the wonderful news she had received in Battambang. She was so lost in thought that the truck of soldiers left without her. She took a motor-pulled cart to Kampong Chhnang province to catch a boat to Phnom Penh. She made arrangements to stay with the boat owner for the night before in order to leave early for Phnom Penh the next morning.

When Nan arrived to Phnom Penh, Ta Ân had found and begun work at the Ministry of Public Works, *Krasuong Satearanaka*, in the department that arranged transportation for people to return to their ancestral village. The government provided free transportation in convoy trucks for whoever wanted to return to their province because Phnom Penh did not have enough food to feed everyone. Moreover, the mass migration into the city resulted in chaos and filth and produced a breeding ground for marauders and plunderers.

Daily at work, a Vietnamese courier handed Uncle Seng two sets of *Agence France-Presse*. Seng kept a copy for himself and handed the minister the other copy. Ta Ân also did his own research by wandering around the city during his work hours and most evenings to gather news and information and to assess the state of affairs. The two men then convened at home in the backyard to discuss and exchange information they had picked up. *Agence France-Presse* daily covered the politics and fighting along the Thai-Cambodian border and the actions of Prince Sihanouk.

From then on, we all prepared ourselves for the right time and opportunity to escape Cambodia.

CHAPTER EIGHT

Escape via Thailand
(November 1979 – December 1980)

The moment for escape to Thailand came one week after Visal's first birthday, in the early part of November 1979. At his work with the Ministry of Public Works, Ta Ân registered all of us as having our ancestral village in Battambang.

The weekend before our scheduled departure from Phnom Penh, my paternal grandfather from Chensa serendipitously came to visit us. We told him of our plan to escape. On his return trip to Chensa, Grandpa Duch took with him all the furniture, the rugs, the statues of *preah* Buddha and other items in the house we planned to leave behind. We bid him a bittersweet farewell, knowing that that would be the last time we would ever see him again. And it was. He passed away in the mid-1980s.

At the last minute, Uncle Seng decided to make the escape with us. He asked for Monday and Tuesday off. He sent words to his office that he was not feeling well. This change of heart posed a problem as the family had originally decided to leave paralysed Grandpa Kuy with his daughter Ry and son-in-law Seng.

We had planned to convene on the outskirts of Phnom Penh, at Psah (Market) Dam Ko, staying over that Tuesday night at the house of a friend of Ta Ân's called Sart. We planned to ride on one of the many convoy trucks leaving from this busy market Wednesday morning in the direction of Battambang, the north-western province, bordering Thailand.

The group included: *nekru* (teacher) Mokla, Khan Seng and their two children; Ta Ân, Nan and their four children; Thei and his three children; Tien and his wife; Pou Song (Dr. Tan) and his wife; Aunt Ry, her husband Seng, one-year-old daughter Visal, and Seng's younger brother, Tith Hok; Grandma Hao and Aunt Rey; my four brothers and myself.

We left Grandpa Kuy temporarily behind with the family of his younger sister, who refused to risk the escape with us. Our family reasoned that Grandpa's paralysed, immobile condition would pose too great a risk on everyone in the group, especially through uncharted, mine-laden terrain. Plans for his escape would have to be made later once the family had reached the other side of the border into Thailand.

Grandpa Kuy burned with rage upon being abandoned. He cried profusely and broke everyone's heart with shame and pity. He believed the abandonment to be permanent despite the family's assurances to the contrary.

Late Tuesday afternoon, several hours before our departure, Pou Seng's boss, Minister Chan Vann, along with his Vietnamese entourage, unexpectedly dropped by our house for a visit, to enquire into the health of his personal secretary. We followed his glance around the house. Inevitably, he noticed the missing pieces of furniture and other items, but he did not pursue the subject. All the adults held their breath, hoping the visit would end quickly and smoothly. After the customary pleasantries, the minister and his entourage left.

Later on in the evening, Seng went out to buy the day's edition of *Agence France-Presse*. That evening, the families abandoned the villa in Phnom Penh and walked to Psah Dam Ko. Other relatives and friends joined us there. Except for the common currency of gold and other precious stones, we carried little else with us.

On the Wednesday we planned to leave Phnom Penh, the hospital scheduled for Pou Song to make a noon presentation because he was the most senior physician.

Pou Song recalls: 'I had the presentation prepared. But I knew I had to leave because there might not be another opportunity. I even had to drive past Calmette Hospital the Tuesday before to meet everyone at the pick-up point.'

Early in the morning, we smeared charcoal on our faces to darken our fair skin in order to fit in with the rest of the travellers. At sunrise, around 5 a.m., we walked to the market to receive the rice allotment of ten kilograms per person. When we arrived at the truck depot, soldiers directed the bustling, bewildered crowd in Vietnamese, '*Ve'nha di!* Go home!'

An atmosphere of fear and suspicion saturated the morning air as the travellers quickly wrangled for room inside one of the convoy trucks. By this time, everyone in our group had made his or her way inside one truck, lined among many other ones.

Eight-and-a-half years old, I squatted there with my other brothers in the middle of a convoy truck. 'Is it far, where we are going?' I whispered to the older brothers.

'Keep quiet,' responded Mardi.

I looked around at the crowd inside our truck, some huddling in smaller groups, some standing. Little Daravuth sat leaning against Sina, his gaze concentrated on an object next to him. Aunt Ry held Visal close to her. Her one-year-old daughter neither cried nor made a fuss. The other adults sat mute, each heart throbbing with simultaneous anxiety and expectation.

My eyes rested on the men in the back – Ân, Seng and Song – and I fell into a giggling fit. I poked Lundi and directed his gaze to the three men with charcoal-smeared faces. He found the sight amusing as well and joined in my giggling. These men held the most senior positions, possessed an intellectual air about them and would be the most missed. They disguised themselves darkly, wrapped *krama* around their heads and found space to hide in the very back of the *camion*, truck.

The other adults failed to see the amusement amidst the tension and glared at us. 'Stop that,' Grandma hissed and pitched a hawk-eye stare in my direction.

As we sat there waiting for the line of convoy trucks to move, someone from our group noticed in the distance Minister Chan Vann's official car, followed by his entourage on motorcycles. Words stealthily but quickly spread among the adults in our group. The children intuitively comprehended the danger. We collectively held our breath. Quickly, the three men covered their faces with their *krama* and pretended to sleep, crouched there in the back of the camion.

Life came to a standstill.

At that instant, the engine started and the truck began to inch forward. Chan Vann and his entourage circled the marketplace and cursorily glanced around. They must have left soon after when they could not find us.* We did not stay to find out because by that moment the caravan of convoy trucks revved and rattled. A few seconds later, the truck picked up speed, transporting us on National Route Five in the direction of Battambang, Cambodia's northwestern province. We had embarked on the first leg of our freedom trail.

The trip quickly took an uncomfortable turn. Once we passed the outskirts of Phnom Penh into the countryside, the truck rocked and swayed as it tried futilely to veer around or go through war-made craters in the jagged, decrepit road. Not infrequently, it slid

---

* When I met Chan Van during my first return trip to Cambodia, he understood our need to escape and reasoned what is past is past. My uncle Seng also conjectured that had his boss really wanted to find us that morning of our escape he would have persisted in the search.

off the main road onto side paths in the fields to bypass yawning gulfs across the road. Initially, I squatted and rolled myself into a bundle because of the tight quarters in the truck. However, over time, I learnt to shift and twist my body with the swaying motion of the truck, alleviating my tightened muscles.

At each checkpoint along the road everyone tried to be as inconspicuous as possible. Once again, Ân, Seng and Song covered their faces with their *krama* and pretended to be asleep as the Vietnamese soldiers attired in army fatigues jumped onto the back of the convoy truck and scanned the quiet, exhausted, huddled group. We had heard rumours that these soldiers killed many people along the way.

That afternoon, the convoy trucks stopped in the town of Pursat. A few adults from our group risked being found out and went out to buy the noodle soup sold in this provincial town.

Grandma had hidden gold and several $100 bills throughout the Pol Pot years. For the trip, Grandma pinned the dollar bills to the inside of her bra. Pou Song also had US dollars with him which he had saved from his student days prior to the genocide. In 1974, he joined the International Medical Student Association and was one of the members asked to attend a conference in Lagos, Nigeria. However, the Lon Nol government refused to let him go, but it did reimburse him for the trip. He had kept that US currency until now.

Other adults hid gold and silver, rolled up in tubes, in the cavities of their bodies. Completely valueless during the Khmer Rouge era, these items again found currency.

During this stop, when we had noodle soup to eat, we also took the opportunity to relieve ourselves in the fields. The adults signalled to each other to be extra careful about the precious stones they carried in their bodies.

We arrived in central Battambang around 6 p.m. that evening; here the truck dropped us off. We rested in the town for the night.

The next morning, our group rode on motor-pulled carts to Sisophon, the 'no man's land'; we arrived amidst a crowd of thousands of other nomads. We found rest at the house of Ta Ân and Nan's relative, Theng,* who had experienced the Dang Rek atrocities with them. Theng informed us of the social and political climate of the region. 'Merchants and hired guides take people across the border every day. And recently, the United Nations created a refugee camp called Khao-I-Dang. The trip is fraught with danger. Some merchant-guides are not to be trusted; they plunder people.'

The merchant-guide charged an average of two *chi* of gold per person. Because we were many people, we would make our guide a rich man.

Theng suggested that we wait for Nim, brother-in-law of Nan's brother Tien, who had also experienced Dang Rek with Ân and Nan, to come back from trading in Thailand to be our guide. He could be trusted.

Our group stayed with Theng for three days until Nim returned. He agreed to be our guide and refused to be paid for his service. He had not forgotten the kindness and care Nan had shown him when he fell deathly ill on the descent from Dang Rek Mountain earlier that year. After Nim rested for a day, we began the next leg of our journey to freedom, this time on foot. Nim told us we must make the distance across the dense jungle to the border camp in one day. Night must not catch us while in the thick of the jungle, prey to mines, robbers and Khmer Rouge soldiers!

From Sisophon, we walked to Site Two (also known as refugee camp No. 007), situated on the border of Thailand and Cambodia. The morning of our departure from Sisophon, the authority accosted Pou Song, suspicious of his white skin, believing

---

* At the time of writing, Theng, cousin of Nan's mother, lives in Prey Sandaik village.

him to be Vietnamese. His denial and non-accented fluency in Cambodian dissipated their fears.

Nim had an old bicycle he pushed on this trip in order to carry materials from Thailand for trade back in Cambodia. Alternatively, little Daravuth and his same-age second cousin Mara rode on it as Nim pushed the bike along. The ride was never long enough, as one or the other bickered to have his or her turn. At times, Nim pushed both of them on the bike at once. He could not bear to prolong their painful wailing of exhaustion.

Aunt Ry carried her one-year-old daughter Visal in a pouch she had made by tying a *krama* around her body, hung close to her stomach. Uncle Seng carried their belongings and periodically relieved Ry of Visal. Unusually for a baby, Visal cried rarely. Maybe, she developed a sixth sense and knew we were entering dangerous terrain and had at times to travel quietly.

I walked in the middle of the group, carrying my share of belongings.

Again, the adults signalled to each other as one of them ventured into a nearby bush to relieve himself. 'Be careful, *pr'yat.*'

At times, we were the only people traversing the well-beaten dirt trail inside the jungle. Periodically, traders passed us by in both directions, either on foot, bike or ox-cart. Everyone tried to stay close together and not to venture beyond the main jungle trail. We knew Khmer Rouge soldiers roamed those areas. We had to be careful also of common robbers and plunderers. Moreover, mines existed among the leaves of those trees.

Other times, we encountered sand spots that made it strenuously difficult for Nim to push the bike through. My heavy feet could hardly pull in and out of the sand.

At one point, Nim ominously warned us of a stretch of jungle thicket two kilometres ahead, where people were frequently plundered. He detailed how on a previous trip across the border he knew of a group that had been robbed and butchered to death. The bodies laid strewn behind the bushes amidst the leaves. 'Hence, we must pass through this stretch of forest and do so very quickly.'

The children groaned for rest, food and water. 'My feet hurt. Can we rest for just a little bit?'

'Just a little longer. When we break to eat,' replied an adult sympathetically.

'We cannot stop here. It is too dangerous,' whispered Ta Ân, echoing our guide's warning.

'I'm so thirsty, almost to the point of death,' I moaned.

As Sina reached for the water canteen, a voice chimed in, 'There's no more. I finished the few drops that were in there. Let's pray we'll run into a merchant selling water soon.'

The 'just a little bit longer' turned into another hour. Soon not only the children, but also some of the adults complained of aches in their body and initiated a rest period. In particular, upon reaching the danger zone, Aunt Ry suddenly turned deathly pale from sheer fatigue and with pained expressions, announced to the group, 'All of you go on ahead. Leave me behind. I cannot go on any longer.'

At that pronouncement, she collapsed against the trunk of a nearby tree. Anxiety spread across the adults' faces; sour expressions covered the children's. Nan interjected, 'We need to keep moving. Whoever can do so should make every effort to continue on. Remember Nim's warning. If danger were to come, at least it would not catch everyone.' As Nim was anxious and did not dispute the need to move on, the adults told Ry to rest and regain her strength; the group would wait for her up ahead.

We hurried on for another three kilometres and stopped to wait anxiously for Aunt Ry. Everyone welcomed the rest, even if laden with worries of Ry's condition. Half an hour later, she came to us.

Soon after we reconvened our journey, the group passed a person selling water for the outrageous price of 20 Thai baht for a cup. Grandma bought several cups of the unsanitary liquid and passed them among the group. I did not think I could ever again possess a desire as strong as the one I had for water at that moment.

The moment the water touched my lips, my tense body contracted and slowly relaxed. The formless liquid tingled down my throat, soothing my parched body and soul. I did not know nor care about the microbes that filtered into my system along with the H_2O. Undoubtedly, they found ready company with other microbes already in existence there.

Uncle Seng recalls a tender moment: 'By this time, everyone had almost wilted from thirst. I handed Visal the cup of water, sensing from her listless expression her longing for it. Without a moment's hesitation, she pushed the cup in my direction and as if to insist, "Papa, you drink first." She had just turned one year, a week prior to our departure from Phnom Penh.'

At some point, a discussion arose among the adults whether they should hire a wagon to carry the more vulnerable members in our group and lead us out of the jungle to our destination camp. The resounding complaint of exhaustion forced the decision-makers to a resolve: the group will hire the next man with an ox-pull cart.

Soon after, a man driving an ox-cart did come along. Aunt Ry, with baby Visal in her embrace, and some of the younger children, including me, took turns riding with the man driving the ox-cart. The pace of our group quickened. We caught up with another group, which had been ahead of us, and passed them.

Several times, the man driving the ox-cart attempted to persuade us to take alternative routes. The adults told him that we should stay on the main trail.

'I know this part of the jungle and traverse it daily,' he persisted.

His cajoling triggered strong suspicions among the adults. They wanted to stay on the main road, despite their uncertainty, because other people travelled back and forth on it. Moreover, we put more trust in our original guide than this new person. Around late afternoon, the man suggested that we stayed the night with him.

At this time, Sina had taken rest on the cart. He sat on something that triggered his curiosity. He pulled the covering to discover a machete. Quickly and quietly, he informed Ta Ân of his find.

Our fear increased. Calmly and without raising suspicion, Ta Ân paid and thanked the man for his service. He told him we would again be travelling on foot on our own.

A mixture of worry and tension wore on Nim's face as he informed the group, 'We're not going to make it to the camp No. 007 by nightfall; it looks like we will have to spend the night in the middle of the jungle. I fear the Khmer Rouge soldiers.'

His statements sent chills down our spine. Each merchant-guide carried a large sword or machete like the one Sina discovered earlier; Nim had one as well. It was already 7 p.m.; we still had a long distance to travel. We unwrapped the bag of rice that Theng's wife had prepared for us early that morning.

That night, we found rest in a clearing inside the forest. We went to bed on the surrounding marshes, some on their *kramas*, some directly on the earth. We had been walking almost non-stop for the last 12 hours, a journey filled with extreme apprehension, always in anticipation of high drama; we had found the limit of our exhaustion and slept like logs, not moving a muscle. A couple of groups of other weary sojourners later joined us and rested nearby.

But Nan could not sleep; her mind wandered to the days of Dang Rek mountains, when the Thai soldiers ordered them to descend into the mine-laden fields. She periodically opened her eyes to observe Nim; what was he doing? She noticed that he did not sleep but sat guarding all of us.

In the middle of the night, around 2 a.m., footsteps crunched on leaves. A group of Khmer Rouge soldiers descended upon our group; Nan discreetly opened her eyes halfway and noticed two males dressed in black, each with a machine gun strapped across his body. Flashlights criss-crossed the dark clearing in the woods, shining into the faces of the travellers, sprawled on the ground.

Suddenly, the glaring light rested on Pou Song. The Khmer Rouge cadres yelled for him to wake up and accused him, 'He's Vietnamese, *yuon*!'

'No. I'm Khmer,' Pou Song quickly responded in perfect Cambodian.

They turned to Nim, 'Where are you going?'

Nim answered them, 'To the camp to find rice. As you can see for yourself, *Bong*, there are many children here and they're starving from lack of rice.'

They continued, 'Today, did you encounter Thai robbers?'

After Nim answered in the negative, the soldiers left. Later, Nim explained, 'I have been trading across this border for a while now that these soldiers know my face.'

At dawn the next morning, the adults woke up each other and the children, and we continued on. Nim told Ta Ân and Nan that the husband of Nain (Nan's sister who died of a fever after Dang Rek experience) and their three children left for the border camp one week ago; we would meet them there that day.

That morning, what seemed like an eternity later, we emerged from the jungle into splattered clearings and followed a migrating crowd to our destination. Nim told Dr. Tan to wrap a *krama* (Khmer scarf) more tightly around his face; his complexion and build drew unwanted attention.

On 21 November 1979, we arrived at camp No. 007, the Son Sann*-controlled Site Two, to mass hysteria and squalor. From 200 metres away, we noticed people sitting idly in lines, waiting to be inspected by the soldiers to see whether there were any Vietnamese among them. Pou Song tried to sit inconspicuously, with his face lowered, refusing to look directly at the eyes of the soldiers.

Nim told the authority, 'Everyone here is my relative; they could not stay in Phnom Penh that is why they came here.' Without another word, the soldiers permitted us to enter the camp.

The presence and smell of human faeces and urine filtered through the air of dust storms generated from the uprootedness and commotion of the tens of thousands of skeletal, exhausted nomads. People relieved themselves anywhere and everywhere. The few out-houses that existed could not accommodate the streams of refugees seeking shelter in Site Two. That first day, everyone succumbed to one illness or another. The place also served as a hotbed for crime of all kinds.

Site Two had nothing, except the makeshift tent of the International Committee of the Red Cross. The foreign administrators

---

* Son Sann had served as prime minister several times prior to the Khmer Rouge takeover. I met him for the first time in September 1995 in Phnom Penh at the introduction of my uncle An who had been politically active in France with his resistance movement against the Vietnamese invasion of Cambodia. That weekend of my uncle's visit to Phnom Penh and my introduction to the patriarch, a grenade was lobbed into the Buddhist Liberal Democratic Party's annual congress, held at Son Sann's Phnom Penh villa. Shrapnel inflicted injury to his son, Soubert, a humanitarian before a politician. Uncle An and I had been on a riding tour of Phnom Penh the morning of the attack. We had had dinner with the family and several party members the evening before. Although I kept in touch with Soubert through his care of two orphanages he founded (while serving first as vice president of the National Assembly and currently as a member of the Constitutional Council), I did not see Son Sann again until almost five years later at his home in Paris. I had a layover in Europe on my return trip from South Africa that I extended to a month's stay with maternal relatives living in France. One of those weeks I spent with my uncle's family skiing at Son Sann's timeshare in the French Alps in Courchevel. (One of the other three weeks, my friend Lisa, who joined me in Paris, and I swapped broken-hearted sagas of love wonderfully tasted, confusedly experienced, ruefully abused and ultimately lost. Shopping provided temporary relief. But that's a different story, isn't it?) Son Sann passed away one year later.

recruited Pou Song to work as a translator for them because of his proficiency in English and medical background.

Here, we received further news about the recently-opened United Nations camp, called Khao-I-Dang, a site on the other side of the border in Thailand. In order to get to the coveted Khao-I-Dang, one must first go through Nong Samet, a post straddling the two countries. But the camp administrators restricted access to Nong Samet, only taking sick people. Son Sann's Khmer Serei, the resistance movement in charge of Site Two, did not want Cambodians to escape the country. They reasoned that the loss of manpower and strength to fight against the Vietnamese-installed government in Phnom Penh would work to the detriment of their cause.

Pou Song's work in the ICRC came to our rescue. The morning after our arrival, we took one-year-old Visal to the hospital to Dr. Tan. He told the hospital foreign staff that Visal could not be cured and needed hospitalisation in Khao-I-Dang.

Also, Pou Song recalls: 'One aid worker, probably a homosexual, gave me a rectal exam to see whether I was sick.'

Sick or not, Pou Song was marked sick and was given access to Nong Samet. He claimed all of us as his family, including family friend Long and his group who had recently joined us in Site Two.

We stayed in Site Two for only two days. Given the filth and scarcity of Site Two, we would have died if we had stayed any longer. Eventually, the opportunity to Khao-I-Dang opened up for everyone, but we did not know that.

As we prepared to hoist ourselves into the truck, one female soldier pointed a gun at our group and menacingly growled, 'You cannot enter the vehicle! All of you are disowning your country! Why are you not helping us to push back the Vietnamese?'

At hearing this, Dr. Tan stepped forward, pointing to Visal, and explained, 'This baby needs immediate medical attention in Khao-I-Dang.'

We wrangled our way through the crowd and climbed onto one of the convoy trucks transporting us across the Thai-Cambodian border to Khao-I-Dang.

A murmur arose in our family, 'Where's Mardi?'

Everyone anxiously looked around in the convoy truck. Everyone in our group was accounted for except for Mardi. Panic vibrated through the huddled group inside the convoy truck. There was no time to get off the truck to look for him.

We all scanned the massive crowd from our enviable location in the covered convoy truck, the sure ticket to freedom. No Mardi. The cacophony outside made it difficult to detect anybody. Everyone in the sea of faces appeared alike and non-descriptive: dust-ridden, attired in tattered sarongs or neutral-coloured clothes, apparitions with black hair and pleading, desperate faces.

Suddenly, a voice pierced through the dissonance of the impatient crowd, '*Chum! Chum!* Wait! Wait!' It was Mardi.

'Hey! It's Mardi!' I cried out in jubilation, and directed the gaze of the others with my pointing finger to a dancing 14-year-old boy, his arms flailing in the air and his body weaving through the noisy throng. Our eyes fixed on him as he wiggled himself to the end of our convoy truck, in front of the agitated crowd.

As he climbed in, the interrogation and caustic remarks poured forth. 'Where were you? Did you not know we were leaving? Crazy! Why, do you want to stay here for the rest of your life?'

It was my relatives' expression of their concern for him, showing through their exasperation and anxiety, how the thought of missing him exacted a great toll on them. Similar reactions occurred when they disciplined us. Especially as the whip snapped against my body, without fail, an explanation accompanied it, 'We wouldn't exert the energy to discipline you, if we didn't care.'

If only they would care less and save their energy.

As Mardi opened his mouth to explain his whereabouts, the engine roared to life. The truck first inched forward and then picked up speed and carried us to our last leg of the freedom trail.

Everyone glowed with uncontrolled elation. The heavy sighs quickly turned into beams of great expectation of safety and liberty.

I nudged Lundi, 'This is for real.'

'Ahh! We will have life!' The thought resonated through Pou Seng.

Hope flickered in our eyes. The grins on our faces refused to go away. Little conversation was exchanged; at that moment, we communicated more in our silence, as everyone revelled in his or her own thoughts, dreaming of the limitless possibilities awaiting us. The power of hope injected in us new strength and softened even the more acidic personalities in our group.

The Khmer Serei (Free Khmer), one of the many democratic factions fighting against the Vietnamese occupation, would turn vicious in their attempt to prevent people from crossing the border into Khao-I-Dang.

Pou Song remembers: 'I knew one man. He was a Khmer Serei, known for killing many people. He acted as the chief 'gatekeeper' to Khao-I-Dang. He would extract money from people in exchange for access to Khao-I-Dang. Of course, it was pure robbery because some who gave money never made it on the list.'

Co-existing with the deep compassion of the international aid workers lingered characters who robbed and plundered with amazing ease, taking advantage of the vulnerability of a desperate and exhausted mass of people. But despite their brutality, over time they could not contain the call of freedom for the tens of thousands of displaced Cambodians flooding into Thailand.

Twenty-one years later, at the introduction of a friend in New York City, I met an Italian surgeon ('the best dressed man'), who worked with the World Health Organization at Khao-I-Dang during that November 1979. He recalled the situation: 'The aid community had never seen anything like it before, to have over 100,000 refugees in one location. Now it's nothing to have several millions in a camp. These Cambodians appeared as apparitions in the dust: skeletal, gaunt, sickly, wearied from their journey.'

Several years after its establishment, towards the end of the camp's official closing, over 250,000 people had settled in Khao-I-Dang.

On 23 November 1979, our convoy truck halted in the open field, at the foot of a mountain, on the other side of the border from Cambodia, sweetly known to us as Khao-I-Dang. Khao-I-Dang was situated about ten to twenty kilometres away from the border. We knew we had passed into safety, that we would be protected by the international community.

Every imaginable non-governmental organisation had a presence in Khao-I-Dang – Medecins Sans Frontier, the International Rescue Committee, various UN subsidiaries and religious affiliations, to name but a few.

During this period, we lived in a state of liminality – that twilight zone of being neither what we were nor what we would become.

Upon our arrival, the international aid workers handed out to all the families a sheet of cloth, bamboo poles and rubber bands from which to build our makeshift tents.

That first night, everyone slept directly on the ground and quivered from the cold mountain weather. We woke up the next morning to find frost in the field. As the camp sat at the foot of a mountain and November fell in the cool season, the temperature dropped considerably below what our bodies had been accustomed to. Aunt Ry wrapped one-year-old Visal in the all-purpose *krama* and their family snuggled under the tarpaulin tent to shield the baby from the cold and wind.

I curled myself into a tiny ball on the grassy field under the flapping blue tent, desperately shivering away the cold mountain air.

In addition, the aid administrators gave us rice grain, canned fish, oil and gasoline. The United Nations wanted to give us more materials, but Thai officials blocked the idea because they did not want to turn the situation into a long-term arrangement. In particular, the United Nations High Commissioner for Refugees (UNHCR) objected to the forcible return of asylum seekers. Thailand, on the other hand, feared for its security.

The Cambodian crisis created a political dilemma of semantics for the parties concerned. Were these Cambodians 'displaced persons', soon to be returned to their homeland, or 'refugees', awaiting the green light to a third country?

According to the 1951 Convention Relating to the Status of Refugees, a 'refugee' is a person who 'owing to a well-founded fear of being persecuted for reasons of race, religion, nationality, membership in a particular social group, or political opinion, is outside the country of his nationality, and is unable to or, owing to such fear, is unwilling to avail himself of the protection of that country.'

It is arguable whether we fit this definition of a 'refugee'.

The plaque marking the refugee camp expressed the ambiguity: 'Khao-I-Dang: Holding Centre for Kampuchean Nationals'. For different reasons, the international community shared the Thai's reticence to call us 'refugees'. It feared opening a floodgate for Cambodians to escape a country that was on the brink of extinction, when the population should be retained to rebuild the country. Moreover, Cambodia needed to retain a maximum population to serve as a buffer zone between Vietnam and Thailand.

Pou Song joined in the letter-writing campaign to urge the international community to recognise Cambodians as refugees and to give us asylum in a third country.

That November 1979, First Lady Rosalyn Carter toured Khao-I-Dang.

Eventually, the international community struck a compromise. They would not recognise us as refugees but would give entry to people with relations in a third country. First, the priority went to people with spouses in the third country; second, to people with parents or children in the third country; and finally, to anyone with other relatives in the third country.

My relatives put in our application for both France and the United States.

We settled in our rows of makeshift tarpaulin blue tents; but not long after each family owned a little hut. Over time, each family added to their hut a tin roof, covered with branches, and grew a vegetable garden. Each hut was connected to each other and had little space, allowing for little privacy. Later in our stay, UNHCR also distributed dried fish, sugar and vegetables.

On the morning following our arrival into Khao-I-Dang, Pou Song immediately went to the camp's makeshift hospital. Countless bodies laid strewn and semi-conscious on rows of raised bamboo beds. Here he found work.

The rest of the adults found work to supplement the handouts among the various non-governmental organisations. Aunt Rey worked in an orphanage created by CARE with 14 other women. The bond of friendship among these women has lasted to this day. CARE paid each caregiver in cash (ten Thai baht per day) and in kind (food). CARE built a school behind the orphanage. A 'white woman' oversaw the school.

Aunt Renee reminisces: 'I remember one Japanese or Taiwanese woman who helped out in the orphanage as well. I had forgotten her until I saw a picture of her at Long's house the other day.'

Other schools went up, many of them created by Christian organisations, to teach the Cambodian and English languages.

Proselytising took place as well. Mardi converted to Christianity and became fervently religious and a pacifist. At one point, the brothers became involved in a brawl; someone egged on Mardi to fight, but he just walked away. Aunt Ry asked to be baptised.

A field separated the camp from a Thai village, which we could see from Khao-I-Dang. As we stood facing the village, the mountain loomed to our left and the main tarred road ran in the direction of the Thai village to our right.

Periodically, a group of older boys and men illegally crossed the field or travelled alongside the mountain to the village. They went to trade the UN-distributed items with the Thai villagers in exchange for various fruits and other knick-knacks.

Sina joined these excursions on three occasions. On his first trip, Sina traded the UN-distributed oil with these Thai villagers who received him and the other escapees benevolently.

If and when they detected a truckload of Thai soldiers on the main road heading in the direction of the village, the outlaws would make their escape alongside the mountain or across the field, knowing that the truck would not chase them there.

The second time Sina ventured to the Thai village, a truckload of soldiers descended upon them in the village. Sina found safety in the hut of a friendly Thai villager. The soldiers criss-crossed the village, chasing after the other outlaws. They caught some of them. Sina waited out the soldiers. When they finally left, he quickly made a run for the refugee camp.

During Sina's third time, he and some of the other escapees ran out of luck. The Thai soldiers tricked them by planting themselves in the field and alongside the mountain. Upon seeing the truck carrying the soldiers rumbling towards the village, Sina and another man near him scrambled towards the mountain. Halfway to Khao-I-Dang, a Thai soldier jumped out of nowhere and arrested them, pointing an AK-47 at them. Several other soldiers chased down the other escapees.

The soldier pushed along his two captives with the butt of the gun. Defeated, the boy and the young man marched in the direction of the camp with their hands raised behind their heads. Fear electrified Sina. He had heard horror stories about Thai soldiers' mistreatment of Cambodian refugees, killing some of them upon arrest.

Fortunately, this soldier released the two refugees at the camp without inflicting harm. That ended Sina's venture outside Khao-I-Dang.

To deter future excursions, the Thai authority built a barb-wired fence around Khao-I-Dang. Nonetheless, other Cambodians risked arrest and continued their trek to the Thai village. The Thai officials sectioned off the front of the refugee camp as the detention centre for those captured. They were made to sit under the humid sun for days. The detention centre never ran out of captives. After a while, this area provided an amusement site for the other bored refugees.

The camp administrators distributed food on a weekly basis. We had enough to eat. Moreover, we supplemented the food ration by our own purchase of noodles and other items from Thai merchants lining the other side of the barbwire fence enclosing our camp and restricting our movement. When we had our own little vegetable garden we grew bean sprouts; we sold some to others and kept some to make yellow Asian crepes, *baign choiw*.

Pou Song recalls: 'Oh, it was so good! But at that time, everything tasted good.'

During those first few weeks, our family found great contentment. We had fresh water from a well we had dug. We could send and receive mail via the ICRC. The international aid workers set up a tracing centre for the Cambodian refugees to find lost relatives.

Back in Michigan, the Bosschers invited Eng and Lan to attend their church. As an elder, Dave Bosscher raised the plight of Eng's family with the other church elders. Uncle Eng started to research the US refugee procedure. He commenced the necessary paperwork to get his family out of the Thai camps. He filed affidavits of his relationship to them.

On a regular basis, Uncle Eng sent money to us in the refugee camps.

In Khao-I-Dang, the men sat outside their makeshift blue tarpaulin tents, under the Thai evening sky, and exchanged war stories. They recounted experiences they had had or those they had heard. Some people had been on the run for months. At night they travelled, at times swimming the Tonle Mekong; during the day they hid.

Until finally, these people reached the Thai-Cambodian border. Along the way, they ate uncooked rice grain in order to survive.

Initially, the international community had a difficult time believing the accounts given by the Cambodian refugees. Particularly, many left-leaning writers refused to believe that a modern holocaust resulted from their ideology and had occurred before their very eyes. Additionally, these writers doubted the sincerity of the Cambodians because of the manner the refugees told their stories. Deeply shell-shocked from the horror of the last several years, Cambodians recounted their experiences in fantastical terms and in an aloof manner, many times, devoid of emotions.

Moreover, Cambodians generally avert their eyes when they spoke because they did not want to be confrontational, especially with someone they assumed to be in authority.

To these Westerners, untrained in Cambodian culture, psychology and sociology, the Cambodian stories were beyond belief. Unsurprisingly, it took reports by other Westerners who had ventured into Cambodia during this period to vindicate the veracity of the Cambodian refugees.

*

In Khao-I-Dang, around March 1980, our initial exhilaration of safety and liberty quickly changed to fear and uncertainty. We experienced intense suffering from the increased fighting nearby. The adults listened to broadcasts on Voice of America to get an understanding of the politics behind the bomb blasts, shelling and gunfire that daily rang in our ears.

Ngor Haing, Pou Song's colleague at the hospital, was given a position with the embassy in Bangkok, outside Khao-I-Dang and away from the fighting. The aid administrators retained Pou Song because his skills were more needed in the camp. He turned green with envy of his friend's transfer.

(This was the same Ngor Haing who won an academy award for his role playing Pran Dith in *The Killing Fields*.* He was later gunned down in Los Angeles. The motive for his death is still mired in intrigue and obscurity to this day.)

We envied the status of the foreign expatriates and aid workers as freemen. We viewed ourselves as prisoners. Fully engulfed in our survival mentality, we would do almost anything to stay alive.

As soon as we had arrived, Grandma and Ta Ân began researching ways to get Grandpa Kuy out of Phnom Penh. It took three attempts and cost the family several thousand US dollars before Grandpa Kuy finally joined us in Thailand. Through word of mouth, Grandma and Ta Ân procured a trader in the business of helping people escape Cambodia. The man asked for the total sum up front. Of course, Grandma refused his demand. She paid him several hundred dollars

---

* About 20 relatives and I went to see the movie when it first came out in Chicago. We found ourselves laughing more than crying, certainly confounding and irritating the other moviegoers in the theatre. We lived the four-plus years of horror; no two-hour film could adequately have captured our emotions, as well done as *The Killing Fields* was. Correlatively, the adult relatives knew some of the Cambodian actors in the film and were telling colourful anecdotes. Definitely, a surreal film embalmed all of us as we watched our collective life – as Cambodians – being told to the world by Hollywood. I'm certain there were a few 'We're so fortunate, *samnang m'en th'en!*' repeatedly whispered to no one in particular in the theatre that afternoon. A belated apology to the non-Cambodian watchers of the movie in that theatre at that time!

and promised the difference upon the arrival of Grandpa Kuy. The man ran away with the money and we never heard from him again.

In the second attempt, Grandma was again cheated out of several hundred dollars.

Although disheartened, Grandma and Ta Ân did not give up. The third time they hired two men, one called Gnat, who had close contacts and rapport with Thai soldiers. They asked for one *dum-lung* in gold, which the family dutifully gave in advance. Two weeks later, the men came back empty-handed. They went to Phnom Penh and found Ta Kuy gravely sick, his body full of blisters and sores, currently sleeping on the floor of the Chinese hospital on Monivong Boulevard. His condition was too severe for them to transport him, the family must give them more gold.* After some discussion, weighing the veracity of their account, the family gave the men the amount demanded and a hammock for them to carry Ta Kuy.

Some time later, Lundi, who had been visiting the announcement board without fail, informed us that the names of our three families were on the list of families called to relocate to Phanat Nikom/Chonberi, the site for refugees preparing to leave for a third country. We were to leave Khao-I-Dang on 12 July 1980.

The dawning of 11 July brought no news of the two men or Grandpa Kuy. Our family packed up our things in a state of great agitation; in particular, Grandma Hao went about packing in palpable anxiety. With much animation as they frequently checked the time, the adults conversed among themselves and with friends to discuss alternatives available to them. The sun set and the descending darkness extinguished all hopes of seeing Ta Kuy. That night, as we finished last minute preparations and waited to leave, the silhouettes of two men approached our shacks. They belonged to Gnat and his companion.

* Later, Maman's cousin Mieng Maly, who had been caring for Ta Kuy during that time, confirmed his very sickly state

'Where is Ta Kuy?' the questions angrily poured forth when it was obvious to our family he was not with them.

'He is near; we have transported him to the Thai border,'* replied the men. Then they began their narratives of the hardship of escaping through dangerous terrain, carrying a man, not only possessing a very difficult personality, but one requiring a lot of physical care and attention. They detailed the effects of Ta Kuy's stroke and illness and their burden and indignity of cleaning after him along the way. 'We would like more money.'

Grandma Hao and Ta Ân fumed at the extortion. They quietly discussed the situation between themselves and went back to the men. 'As you can see, we are leaving for Phanat Nikom. Not one penny more will we give you. However, if Ta Kuy is as near as you said, then get him to this camp, Khao-I-Dang, by tomorrow, and we will give you five times your requested amount.'

Ta Ân and Grandma Hao reasoned that if the men really did have Grandpa Kuy at the border, then they would get him to Khao-I-Dang in order to be paid the larger sum. But if their story was a ruse, then the family had prevented further loss.

Our three families left for Phanat Nikom/Chonberi the next morning, 12 July.

Sure enough. On the night of 12 July, the two men carried Ta Kuy to Khao-I-Dang. Before leaving, Ta Ân had arranged for Tien to settle the matter of payment. Grandma Hao and Aunt Rey asked

---

* Sam Heang, currently a parliamentarian representing Siem Reap, recalls hearing tales of a sickly, paralysed man who had been abandoned by his family in Phnom Penh and who was then being transported through Sisophon to find his family on the other side of the Cambodian border. Little did Sam Heang know that people were discussing his relative. Sam Heang, who had lost many of his immediate family during the Khmer Rouge era and who had been desperately searching for any surviving relatives, bemoans the fact that had he known that Ta Kuy was a relative he would have interceded with assistance as he was then living in Sisophon and in a position of authority to do so. Sam Heang and Grandma Hao are first cousins; his father, Ta Lam, immigrated to Cambodia from China with his brother Ta Yi, Grandma Hao's father.

their friends, Tann Chhan's family, to get Grandpa on a UNHCR's transport to meet us at Phanat Nikom/Chonberi.

By the time Grandpa Kuy reached us, the family had expended a total of $4,000. The gold and dollars my family had secured on their person when leaving Phnom Penh had long since run out. The money came from my three uncles in France and the United States who pooled together their resources. Uncle An mailed the money via Père François Ponchaud, the French Catholic priest, who the uncles had known from their university years in Phnom Penh and who travelled back and forth between France and the Thai refugee camps during this period. He also wrote *Cambodia: Year Zero*,* which brought the Cambodian genocide to the attention of the world.

The call to Chonberi brought us one giant step closer to our ultimate destination, the United States. However, failure to secure Grandpa Kuy's arrival offset our elation at moving there.

Chonberi had concrete structures: four rectangular buildings, sectioned off by four columns, formed in a square, with wall-less, stage-like fronts facing each other. Everyone knew the on-goings of everyone else in the block as the structures had no front or side covering. We had a corner area so we were exposed only to the family on our right.

A central courtyard connected the four rectangular structures. It also provided much needed open space.

We preferred this arrangement to the raised makeshift huts with taupaulin coverings of Khao-I-Dang, where we had to roll our mats directly on the dirt floor for sleeping. It was a messy and unsanitary condition, especially when the monsoon rain poured on the flimsy shelter and flooded our living and sleeping area. Here, we lived on raised concrete floor and had concrete roof to shelter us from the torrential downpour. Also, it was a lot more spacious.

* François Ponchaud, *Cambodia: Year Zero*, Allen Lane, 1978.

The administrative authority called Pou Song to Buriram. A group of Seventh-day Adventists and other priests asked him to accompany them to a Thai prison outside the Buriram refugee camp to serve as a translator. A Cambodian refugee had killed another refugee. This scenario repeated itself many times in these refugee camps. Pou Song did not stay in Buriram long, even though life there was pleasant enough. He wanted to join us in Chonberi and managed to get the administrators to transfer him there.

We stayed in Chonberi for several months. Chonberi served as the transit centre for assessment and interviews. Only families with a real possibility of leaving for a third country were taken to Chonberi. The United States' Immigration and Naturalization Services (INS) turned some people back if they failed to answer questions to establish true relationships.

Nonetheless, loopholes existed and people tagged on the names of non-relations to their paper. For example, a couple who have only three children would tell the INS that they have five children. The two available places went to friends or distant relatives. They took our pictures in Chonberi.

In Kao-I-Dang, Aunt Rey had enrolled me in a Khmer classical dance troupe. I loved it. The daily morning exercises made my body even more supple and pliable, and soon after I became the lead ballerina in my age group. I continued with my dance lessons in Chonberi.

During my spare time – and there was plenty of spare time for every refugee – I would spin myself into a dizzying state in the corner of our shelter and would try to run in a straight line. Grandpa Kuy was not amused and grunted for me to stop. From then on, I would only spin myself into the dizzying state when he was not around. I challenged my other brothers to do it as well. Only Daravuth took up the challenge. He didn't do it right and ran into the wall, bumped his head and broke into a scream. Everyone blamed me for his lack of coordination and bruised head.

Other times, I played hopscotch with the other girls my age. The boys were too macho to join us; they intervened only to disrupt us and force us to scream and curse them. Rather they devised different games with marbles, kicked shuttlecocks and hit badminton which over time convinced me that they were having more fun than the girls because they generated more frequent and louder outbursts of laughter.

I learnt to laugh like them – a laugh that was uproarious and bellyaching – but I was told it was not befitting a lady, as the family frequently reprimanded me for 'neighing like a horse on the loose'. But I would forget myself and repeatedly 'neigh like a horse on the loose'. The family would try to shame me into obedience by scolding me in front of other people. Their public shaming of course worked its effect on me and fuelled in me a burning anger, which I added to my private collection of each individual's past offences. *I hate it when they exaggerate and publicise my errors. I don't do it to them.*

I liked the various games we played with rubber bands. For unknown reasons we seemed to have unlimited supply of rubber bands from which we made long ropes. We received great exercise jumping through and over them as the other team twirled or held them in place. I had as much fun connecting the rubber bands together, learning by trial and error that the two big toes could be used to quicken the rope making process.

Lundi daily followed the postman around. Also, he continued to keep us abreast by his frequent visits to the bulletin board of our status as refugees. Lundi recalls: 'Pou Song bought me ice cream even though he didn't have enough money. He wanted to save the little bit he managed to save to attend school once he reached the United States.'

The barb-wired fence was already erected when we arrived into Chonberi. Sina again decided to venture beyond the camp to the nearby Thai village. He took Mardi along with him. The first time, they exchanged the can of oil the aid organisations passed out to us for fruits. For the second trip, they decided to be clever. They divided the can of oil into two cans, filling the bottom of these cans with water, knowing that the oil would float to the top. Their deception quickly came to an end when several days later they overheard the Thai merchants selling along the barb-wired fence discussing the mendacity of the Cambodian refugees. The boys walked away in shame.

Their shame quickly dissipated. Survival mentality once again took hold. One day, a Thai family drove up to the front gate of Chonberi with a truckload of watermelons to sell to the refugees inside. Mardi and Sina volunteered to help sell the watermelons. The couple welcomed the extra help with apparent joy. A crowd rushed in to buy the special treat. Mardi and Sina sold many, gave away many and pocketed some of the change. The Thai family had complete trust in the boys. Afterwards, they even paid the boys for their help.

In June 1980, Aunt Ry, Seng Hok, baby daughter Visal, and Seng's younger brother Tith, were called to a refugee camp in Surin. It was formerly Cambodian territory that had been annexed by Thailand. Many Cambodians lived there. The Hok family encountered a good life there. Aunt Ry went to exchange gold in order to buy the various tropical fruits that existed there in abundance.

Each refugee camp had a defined boundary. Uncle Seng's curious brother Tith several times ventured beyond the barb-wired fence. One time, the Thai security caught, beat and made him sleep with chickens directly on top of him. By the time of his release, the chickens had done their work and he left with droppings splattered all over him from head to toe. After this incident, either he had short-term memory or he did not mind the humiliation, Tith again ventured beyond the restricted border.

The paperwork for the Hok family went through smoothly. The authority transferred the family to Lumpini, a transit camp outside of Bangkok. The family toured Bangkok for one day. One week later, the administration called the family to the United States. They flew via Hong Kong, where they stayed overnight in a hotel.

From Hong Kong, they flew to the United States with a layover in Seoul. There, Aunt Ry fell ill and asked a stranger to *koh kchal* for her, literally, to 'scratch the wind' out of her system. The condition of the 'wind' denotes an imbalance in the body, resulting in illnesses, caused by social, psychological or biological environments or the mischief of evil spirits.

This is a Khmer tradition still practiced by many Cambodians to this day whereby a sick person has her full back and the upper part of her chest scratched by a coin smeared with an alcoholic lotion. The scratches are short motions, repeated at the same area until the skin turns blood red. The motion starts at the centre of the back or chest and is pulled in a slanted downwards motion to the side. Many marks in the same stroke are made but in different areas of the back or upper chest until all are marked. By the end, the marks formed the veins of a leaf in red.

(I had the 'wind scratched' out of my system countless times, often against my will, as the process is incredibly painful.)

The family arrived in Grand Rapids, Michigan, several months before we did.

The Thai authority and the INS refused to process Grandpa Kuy's paper. He could not leave the camp for the United States because of his medical condition. Enter Bob Houskamp, also an elder at Millbrook Church. He contacted a state senator, Bob Vander Laan, a member of the same church. He in turn contacted his friend, the US Senator for Michigan who attended a neighbouring church. The issue reached Washington, DC.

The name and contact number for the US ambassador to Thailand landed in the hands of Bob Houskamp. He directly contacted the embassy, requesting the good office of the ambassador to pressure the INS to release and expedite the paperwork for my family, in particular, to resolve the dilemma surrounding Grandpa Kuy's medical condition.

The INS finally relented on the condition that the sponsor found a doctor in the US who would claim responsibility for Grandpa Kuy. A Dr. Miller volunteered his medical services. The agreement converged around the beginning of December. A few more phone calls went to the embassy to get the Seng family to Grand Rapids in time for Christmas.

During this time as well, church members pooled their resources and expertise to transform Uncle Eng's basement into our living quarters. Uncle Eng preferred for us to stay with his family rather than to live in a separate apartment.

Church members had also arranged housing for Ta Ân's family. However, the INS became suspicious of Ta Ân's background. They queried how he managed to return from France via communist China without problems. His background and explanation posed too great a risk in an era of strong anti-communist sentiments. However, the French government accepted his family's application to France, where the family eventually ended up.

From Chonberi the authority transferred us to Lumpini, a transit camp close to the US embassy in Bangkok. We stayed there for one month. Amidst our preparation to leave for the United States, Grandma Hao fell gravely ill, vomiting and coughing up blood. Aunt Rey accompanied her to a hospital in Bangkok.

Here, my dance troupe was asked to perform for the Thai king.

Unfortunately, the performance was scheduled for the week after our departure date. As the lead dancer, I felt the missed opportunity. But the despondency lasted only briefly, especially as the time neared for us to board the 747 that would take us to 'heaven'.

Pou Song had also been transferred to Lumpini around the same time we arrived. The situation took a volatile turn at times as none of the refugees trusted the Thai; the Thai reciprocated our sentiments. They almost locked Pou Song up in prison. But then he was allowed to go to Bangkok to treat Grandma Hao.

Pou Song remembers: 'The day I arrived in Bangkok marked the happiest day in my life. I knew there was no turning back and that I was safe. I bribed the security guards to let me outside into the city. I had a bowl of noodle soup – the most delicious bowl of noodle soup I had ever tasted.'

Pou Song left on the Boeing 747 with 500 other refugees, including Hmong refugees from Laos, a few days before us. The airline people asked him to help out with translation.

My family arrived in the United States on 22 December 1980. We had a layover of a few hours in Hong Kong. The head stewardess over the intercom requested the assistance of anyone who knew English to serve as a translator. Aunt Rey volunteered when she realised no one else was. Long and the relatives of King Sihanouk, whose daughter was one of the dance teachers, flew with us on the Boeing 747. All the seats were filled. We had another layover in Anchorage, Alaska. From Alaska, the plane landed in San Francisco. Whereas everyone else had at least an overnight layover in San Francisco, our family immediately boarded a connecting flight for Michigan.

Chapter Nine

Acclimatising to American Freedom
(23 December 1980 – January 2004)

Our plane landed in Grand Rapids, Michigan on the eve of Christmas Eve 1980. An entourage of church members, news cameras and relatives greeted us as we deplaned. I was confounded and amused by the strange white hair and blue eyes of these friendly people. Everyone, both male and female, looked alike.

Outside, the wind howled and the cold pierced through bulky jackets to chill our bony frames. There were light flurries of snow that night as the van transported us from Kent County International Airport to our new life, our new home, our new country. As we huddled inside Uncle Eng's striped black van and peered outside, a grey, leaden film covered the world, bespeckled with soft fallen white fuzz. A mixture of numbness and controlled elation at having reached 'paradise' prevented us from processing the implications of this new life. Our six-year journey appeared surreal in the context of this new-found safety.

We spent our first evening in the United States eating apples in the basement of Uncle Eng's house on Chamberlain Street, which Millbrook Christian Reformed Church had turned into our home. In Cambodia, apples are an expensive import that did not exist during the Khmer Rouge regime. To welcome us, it seemed my uncle Eng had bought us nothing but apples.

Watching our arrival on the news that night and again the next day evoked much merriment and laughter. It amused us greatly to experience the airport scene all over again, but this time to be more coherent about it. (In later years, our 'developed' sense of humour would have us laughing fondly at ourselves as refugees, swimming in the refugee winter jackets, holding plastic bags loudly emblazoned with UNHCR, IOM and the like.)

That first week we frequented the mall, enthralled by the holiday decorations. Beautiful Christmas decorations adorned the doors and ceilings of each boutique. My family never ventured anywhere in our much-used van without everyone going along: Grandma Hao, Grandpa Kuy, Aunt Rey, Uncle Eng and his wife Lan and their seven-month-old Jeanette, my brothers Mardi, Sina, Lundi, Daravuth and myself. Often trailing behind the van in a church-donated blue Opel were Aunt Ry, her husband Seng, two-year-old daughter Visal, three-month-old son Donald and Seng's brother Tith, who had now been in the United States a few months.

Imagine this sight: a large clan of Cambodian refugees in a mostly white suburban mall, dressed in mismatched hand-me-downs, excitedly pointing in awe at things, uttering dissonant sounds and blocking traffic to pose for pictures. If there were many stares and remarks from passers-by, we were oblivious to them.

Grocery shopping was another major outing. I remember running up and down the aisles the first time we went to the supermarket. The abundance was incomprehensible. My brothers and I often got into heated discussions while deciphering the contents of things. In one aisle we recognised the familiar face of Gerber. While living in refugee camps, relief organisations handed out Gerber baby food; we loved it. You can imagine our thrill to find Gerber there in Grand Rapids! Our elation greatly increased when I reached into my church-donated coat pocket to find a quarter there. And how fortuitous that Meijer only charged a quarter for a jar of Gerber! A great commotion arose as to the flavour. Apple won out.

My siblings and I were enrolled in Millbrook Christian Elementary School the following January, less than two weeks after our arrival in the United States. Tingling sensations of anticipation fluttered through me. I detected similar sentiments on the faces of my brothers. A tall, light-haired girl came to our house to guide us to the bus stop, located at the end of our block. All of us shivered in our cumbersome winter coats at the assault of the cold Michigan winter air. Brrrr! I hated the cold. To this day, given a choice between extreme heat and cold, I prefer extreme heat.

What a strange, incongruous world! Could it be the same one that I lived in just a few weeks ago? A most wonderful white cotton-covered earth had suddenly replaced the squalid waste of the refugee camps. Cold replaced hot. Layers of clothes replaced patchwork rags. A schedule replaced idleness. Hope replaced despair. As I discovered one change, another one soon attracted my attention. I could hardly absorb and digest each new change without an overwhelming sense of gratitude and awe.

Uncle Eng told us we would probably need to bring our own lunch to school. My oldest brother Mardi packed our lunches of rice and a Cambodian meat dish into a huge, brown grocery bag. We did not know that each of us would be in separate classrooms, spread across a gigantic building. Much confusion arose during lunchtime. The other students had no problem locating their lunch pails, except for me. Frustration with my inability to communicate, coupled with deep shame in having to be in such a sorrowful state, triggered hot streams of tears. Finally, Mardi rescued me, coming down the hall, collecting our family along the way to congregate for lunch.

Another time, I followed the examples of other classmates and grabbed a carton of milk placed by the door. To my great embarrassment and chagrin, I took someone else's pint for the duration of that week until someone explained to me that the milk had been pre-ordered and paid for. I would have to wait until the next semester to place my order. That explained my classmates' whispering, curious glances among themselves and the beseeching looks towards the teacher.

I was intrigued by television. My brothers and I constantly argued over what was and was not real. I remember the snickering and bewildered looks we gave each other the first time we saw actors and actresses open-mouthed kissing.

'Do you think they're really doing that?' Lundi asked incredulously.

'I don't think it's real,' I answered categorically.

I could not believe that people would actually do that; how utterly disgusting! Some things have changed. (In public, a Cambodian kisses by gently rubbing her nose against the cheek of another; this is symbolic of taking the scent of the loved one with her.)

A trip to the neighbourhood Burger King was considered a very special family outing. 'Everyone into the van,' Uncle Eng ordered the group, as he slipped into the driver's seat. 'Do we have everyone? And who has my camera?'

'Let's take a group picture now in front of the house?' suggested Lundi.

'Yeah!' I chimed in. I had on my favourite yellow spring coat that I had picked out of the pile of clothes church members had dropped off.

'No. Let's just go and we can take pictures while we're there, and possibly when we get back,' decided Grandma.

We greatly anticipated this bi-monthly trip. Although I initially hated the taste of burgers and anything else on the menu, the Burger King crown and getting dressed up made the trip treasured.

*

My brothers, relatives and I each went through our own unique socialisation process in the States according to the age group we fit into. Each person, young or old, had to learn to deal privately with the specific dilemma each faced given the newness of every experience; we did not have a model from which to draw answers. We stumbled along in the dark in hope that one day life would make sense.

As young children we put on many different affectations to disguise our awkward immigrant status, naively believing we could and that it was necessary. We were constantly comparing who had acquired the more fluid American accent, and furtively poked fun at our older relatives who continued to speak with a heavy accent.

During one recess that first year at school, two boys from Daravuth's kindergarten class wondered out loud why our eyes were set so far apart. Then one of them gave Daravuth a push. Instinctively, I jumped into the fray and pushed the boy back. I would have followed the push with a punch and a kick, but instead I retreated to comfort my little brother. The other children surrounded us with words of comfort and eventually, by the next year, these boys became two of Daravuth's closest friends.

In hindsight, I believe those two boys were initially scared of the differences until they realised the similarities we shared with them. Unfortunately, I see many adults caught in this fear. But it is more unbecoming for an adult than a child.

On the home front, the older relatives wanted to ingrain us in culture and tradition. When entering a room, we had to *oun*, lower our head, so as to keep our head below the adults while passing them. And, it would be inconceivable that we should even accidentally touch the head of an older person. This act of irreverence would be fodder for weeks of gossip if ever witnessed by an outsider. Also we were prohibited from taking pictures with only three people, for this would invite bad omens.

While at school we were taught the rights and value of equality and individuality. The apparent contradiction was battled out at home. 'I'll sue you,' I yelled out while being whipped by one of my aunts, who naturally resorted to the very popular and customary form of discipline in many societies. I had been in the States only a few months, but my utterance was telling of how quickly the American mentality permeated my thinking.

≈ ≈ ≈

From an early age my siblings and I were branded orphans and immediately felt the consequences of that fact. Our bond then and now was our identity, our sorrow and our unspoken exhortation to each other to care for one another.

Being the oldest, Mardi imposed on himself the heaviest burden. He possesses a big heart for the poor and, at times, a martyrdom complex. Constant restlessness consumes him as he searches for ways to use his Master's degree in economics for Cambodia's gain. In 1996 he founded Plant Hope In Cambodia (PHIC), a US-registered non-profit organisation that funds humanitarian projects in Cambodia, from the digging of wells to the building of schools. In his spare time he helps the Cambodia's pro-democracy Sam Rainsy Party to organise and raise funds in the United States.

Mardi is married to godly Jennifer, and they have the cute, gentle-souled Samuel and the most adorable, ebullient daughter Chantal. (One day, the parents found Chantal eating ants in their nice secluded Sudbury, MA backyard. Having heard so many sad stories of her dad's history and the plight of those less fortunate around the world, she wanted to empathise with them. On her first visit to Cambodia, an older cousin dared her to eat fried grasshoppers, which she did without a moment's hesitation.)

Sina exudes quiet strength. There in the cold basement of Chamberlain Street, I remember his gentleness consoling me to sleep many times when the horrors of Cambodia were still fresh imprints on my young mind. (Nightmares disrupted my sleep nightly during those initial years in the States. It was not uncommon for me to kick and scream in my sleep. Because I shared a bed with my grandma, she was often the recipient of my flailing arms and legs. A few times she had to smack me to stop my violence. Not all of my dreams were nightmarish. At times, in my sleep, I saw apparitions of my mom, always in a crowd of people, smiling or calling for me.)

Sina is a man of few words, but nevertheless quite a prankster. He and his wife Nancy are the proud parents of precocious Gabriel (whose best friends now are snakes in his large backyard) and his equally precocious younger brother Jared and beautiful baby sister Isabel Grace. Having always been very good with his hands, he carved and chiselled much of his furniture. In March 2003, he quit his engineering job to start his own business, Conceptual Site Furnishings, Inc.

Sina recalls his childhood: 'In our house near Wat Koh, all the children slept in one room. Maman had bought a huge piece of property near Kbal Khnal and Bung Trabaek to build a villa. But she never got around to building it because of her frequent field visits to be with Papa and then the capture of Phnom Penh by the Khmer Rouge.'

My mother took the blueprint for the villa with her when we evacuated Phnom Penh, believing the evacuation temporary.

Sina continues: 'I think Maman was pregnant with Asrei when she craved this incredibly spicy and salty beef stew. I enjoyed going to the *psah*, market, with her. On one trip, a robber came and snatched a gold necklace off her neck as we were strolling past the different stalls. We chased after him but failed to overtake him.'

Early on, Lundi knew he wanted to pursue medicine. He was placed third in the regional Spelling Bee having only been in the United States a few years and graduated third from Valley Christian High School. He developed a (needed, off-the-wall) sense of humour while in the University of California at Irvine medical school. Initially he wanted to become a paediatrician like his mentor Dr. Song Tan. However, his work with Cambodian-Americans at the Los Angeles Department of Mental Health convinced him to pursue psychiatry.

Lundi explains why he chose psychiatry: 'Cambodians to this day are haunted by their Khmer Rouge experience. Many of us experience PTSD, post-traumatic stress disorder. Before diagnosis, we think it is normal to be always irritable, angry, have nightmares, hear voices. About one to two per cent of Cambodians I see have schizophrenia. These are the effects of the Khmer Rouge atrocity, even after almost 30 years.'

I ask: 'Have you had some of those symptoms? And if not, what distinguishes you or us from other Cambodians with PTSD?'

He explains: 'Until a few years ago, I underwent great stress and can sympathise. So, we are not exempt. Cambodians, in light of their social stresses, poverty, relatively lower level of education and support, their functioning level is not as high as another person without PTSD. They also have what we called "hyper-vigilance". For example, some Cambodian patients tremble at the sound of sirens; others fear to go outside their house.'

Lundi has encountered countless obstacles which makes his academic accomplishments taste that much sweeter.

He is the most pragmatic of us five – too much so at times: 'Why go to the Grand Canyon, when we can view pictures of it at home?' In June 2005 he married Sophanita Denis.

Daravuth is the artist-poet, the good-looking one and our conscience. His deep sensitivity beautifully contrasts with his bulky physique. Although the 'baby' of the family, Vuth possesses integrity very few men can claim. I smile with unabashed pride reflecting on how God mercifully yet powerfully chipped and moulded him from a small bite-scarred child, sleeping all alone in that cold and damp corner of the basement on a fold-out lawn chair and never knowing a mother's touch, into an intelligent, gifted and godly man.

As the fourth child in the family, I separate Daravuth from our three older brothers who had each other as playmates. Consequently, I tend to be overly protective of Vuth. And because of his love of art, poetry and things aesthetic, I am more drawn to him.

He aspired to be in medicine, and volunteered one year at Angkor Children's Hospital in Siem Reap, Cambodia, after graduation from university. But after (just a little) coaxing from his sister, he pursued law at the University of San Francisco School of Law in the fall of 2002 and is now a lawyer.

Wherever my brothers find themselves, I am certain of their contribution to society. For us, I believe, the sense of social obligation stems from our Christian upbringing and Cambodian past.

My mom's mom was the inspiration and catalyst for any academic accomplishments my brothers and I may have. She singularly, deeply instilled in us the value of education. If I were to name one person most responsible for my pursuit of higher education, the credit all goes to Grandma Hao. Her strength is further realised when one knows that she herself never had one minute of formal instruction in her 80 years.* An 'X' stands for her signature. Nevertheless, she spoke three languages and held high aspirations for her children and grandchildren, that they should be learned. She often quipped, 'A thief can steal material wealth, but not an education.'

Coupled with being a consummate pragmatist, Grandma lived her life in self-sacrifice and devotion to family. She glued us together.

* No one knows Grandma Hao's date of birth.

Often she took the sting of life's hardship on herself in order that her family might experience a more bearable existence. We basked in her love. She appointed herself guardian to her orphaned grand-children; she nursed her war-paralysed and often difficult husband with unreserved thoroughness. What little she had went first to her children and grandchildren.

She derived her joy from the welfare of her family. She would beam with immense pride at grandson Andy Ung's vigil care and concern for her failing health, or at little granddaughter Jenny Ung's academic achievement, or at the birth of a great-grandchild. A beautiful smile would greet little granddaughter Vanessa Hok from school or Daravuth's teasing.

She possessed unparalleled foresight and tenacity for life.

She instilled in her family the importance of knowing one's roots and culture. In December 1993, Grandma, along with Mardi and Lundi, returned to Cambodia for the first time since they escaped in 1979 and visited her birthplace. She held a big celebra-tion, with gifts to family, friends and former enemies as an expres-sion of the good blessings her family had received since leaving Cambodia. Grandma was always armoured in compassion and for-bearance.

Grandma Hao held steadfastly to her Buddhist beliefs. After her husband passed away in 1984, she set up a little shrine in a corner of her room in memory of him. Inside the swinging-door wooden cupboard his picture loomed in the centre among miniature Buddhist icons and burning incense sticks. On special occasions, an anniversary of his birth or death for example, she would cook special cuisine to offer as a food sacrifice to the gods to feed her husband in his afterlife. Daily, she meditated, prayed and chanted along with recorded voices of Buddhist monks. *'Sam ma, sam put …'* She attended regularly all Buddhist holidays and celebrations and never failed to offer the requisite sacrifices of food or money.

In her dedication to follow the path of goodness she came into contact with others who pursued similar paths. It was not the suffering but the kindness of people, particularly church members towards her children and grandchildren, that would break her heart with inexpressible gratitude. For that she encouraged us to attend church activities even though she held on to a different faith.

Amidst intense suffering, she displayed immeasurable strength and courage. No matter how many of sorrow's piercing darts came her way, they could not break her spirit. She bore offences with unparalleled grace and dignity. One can only surmise the costs to her, for rarely did she betray any expression of defeat. Rarely would she allow tears to be part of her makeup.

Her life attests to the maxim that adversity is the mother of virtue.

On 19 February 1999, she slipped away into another world and took with her countless untold secrets. It was time for her to rest.

*Endure, my heart, for you have endured worse than this.**

Grandma Yi Hao was the fragrance of my life. Now life is less beautifully scented without her presence.

Grandma constantly implored us to do our best. Our admiration, respect and love for her keep us trying.

The two people after Grandma Hao who have moved and shaped me most are Marge and Wally Boelkins. Early on, they befriended my family and to this day remain close to all my relatives. They call me best friend; I call them my godparents. They exemplify 'the good Samaritan' and Christian love in action. From when we first came till only recently, many of my relatives, beginning with Aunt Rey to Uncle Seng to all my brothers, have worked at one point or another for Wally's manufacturing company, Unist, Inc. I spent all my high school and college summer holidays working for Unist,

---

* Homer's *The Odyssey*.

Inc. and living with Marge and Wally in their beautiful estate, where I was given my own car and own wing of the house. For Thanksgiving, Christmas and various other holidays they would fly me either to see them or visit my relatives in California. Through these many years their prayers and support have sustained me in the valleys as on the peaks. Marge drove me to Washington, DC and settled me into my first week of university. They flew out for my university and law school graduations. Upon my first trip to Cambodia, they came to visit me for five days to make sure that I was really healthy and safe. Again in 2004, when I decided to move to Cambodia to live as a resident, they visited for three days, to make sure that I was well situated. (On these two visits, how did I repay them but to take them on harrying adventures on dilapidated motorbike rides and visits to remote villages.) Incredibly, their generosity and love extend not only to me but to so many other friends and strangers, not to mention their sizeable family of six children and 22 grandchildren. Grandma Hao and Marge are the mothers I never had. Wally is the father I never knew.

My brothers and I owe much to our aunts and uncles, who unexpectedly fell into the role of our caretakers. To this day, their unconditional love, generosity and forbearance continue to sustain us. As each of us is a work in progress, I can only imagine the pains I caused them as I groped along those earlier years into adulthood. How easy, natural and self-righteous it was to concentrate disproportionately on how I'd been wronged and to overlook my fits and tantrums.

We witnessed their struggles, perseverance and tenacity in adapting, painfully yet successfully, to this foreign culture America. While they felt the condescension, felt people talking to them as if they were not their social or economic equals, they learnt the secret of not taking on others' problems.

Nonetheless, we are all prideful people and they were no different. As a nine-year-old I remember casting my eyes down while the cashier snickered at the food stamps my aunts and uncles handed her. How much more for them who felt the full impact of this shame! The days of domestic help and drivers flicker dimly as bittersweet memories of an irreversible era.

But to their credit, welfare was only a temporary crutch. Soon after, my aunts and uncles were working days, including as a janitor in a jail, and attending classes at night. We learnt from their experiences and came away with a strong sense of responsibility to strive since they had given so much to pave a smoother road for us. To my young eyes, my aunts and uncles were very mature when we first arrived in the States – I did not realise that they were hardly over their teenage years and deeply traumatised from the war.

Through the years, people – Cambodians and non-Cambodians alike – have commented on my good fortune to have loving and understanding relatives to raise me. Particularly among fellow Cambodians, I detect a mixture of envy and admiration in their tone. The implicit understanding is that human nature when caught in a dire situation will exploit those around them for self-interest, especially those deemed the most vulnerable. Growing up, I remember responding sarcastically to myself, 'Yeah, if they only knew what I had to put up with.'

Only recently have I come to a better understanding of these people's observation. My relatives do possess immense forbearance, compassion and generosity borne from personal experience, life's harshest teacher. It was and is within this incredible familial support that I have been allowed to pursue higher education and travel places not normally open to someone of my social status.

≈ ≈ ≈

For the first six years we lived in the heart of a Christ-fearing community. I believe we were the only Asians in the area and triggered much curiosity. Living in Michigan gave us the time and space to thaw from our numbness of having lost our parents (for my brothers and I) and being uprooted from our country. This was our period of 'incubation' as we were lavished with warmth and kindness.

However, resilience necessitates independence so it was opportune that my relatives decided to relocate in a quest for a warmer climate and other Cambodians. Southern California proved to be the right move. We were half an hour away from the largest Cambodian community in the world outside Cambodia, Long Beach, and many miles away from the Michigan snowstorms.

For my family and me, at some level it was easier to handle the extraordinary events of our past than the ordinary day-to-day chores. Our adrenaline was constantly pumping when survival preoccupied our thoughts. I believe this paradox holds true for many people who have undergone prolonged horrific circumstances. To survive is part of our natural human instinct, as intrinsic as breathing. But when the dust has settled and issues of mere survival no longer exist, we had to learn to programme our mentality from one of reactionary living to that of willed, purposeful existence. Before we lived to 'get by' as we were constantly uprooted from one location and culture to another. This mentality was no longer needed.

The process of transition and recovery can be profoundly excruciating because often the wounds require surgery rather than a temporary Band-Aid. If the eyes are the windows to the soul, then the blood-shot veins that webbed across our lenses those first few years must have reflected deeply and privately held anguish and inexpressible sorrows.

Failure to break the bondage of past horrors can lead to a life of stagnation and may spiral into other emotional traumas. No one likes to be around an angry person; someone who seizes upon another's kindness as an entitlement rather than undeserved grace; someone who revels in his own victimisation. No one desires to be Alyosha's father in Dostoevsky's *The Brothers Karamazov*.

This is easier said than done. I believe healing requires a very conscious, deliberate and honest processing of one's circumstance; it involves utilising tools that are not readily available to a people who attribute everything to karma reflexively and who are generally unaccustomed to self-reflection and introspection. It seems a fatiguing discipline deemed too individualistic and emotionally exhausting.

But I am making a gross generalisation that may need a qualifier. For me personally, ever since I can remember, I possessed a heightened need to comprehend the unintelligible elements of my experience. I believe all survivors (in the all-encompassing sense of the term) have this desire for interpretation of their experiences. Each Cambodian privately and Cambodia collectively must work towards closure of the past. For me personally, I found closure in forgiveness, for to dwell in hatred levied too heavy a toll.

Emotional turmoil marked my high school years. A teenager faces enough problems without having to deal with the private pain of loss and loneliness. Nightly, I soaked the pages of the *Book of Psalms** with tears. I allowed low self-esteem to infect my physical and emotional health. I was deeply and chronically depressed and gained a lot of weight. It did not bring much comfort to be reminded how I used to have a pretty face.

I lived in a state of grogginess, almost a hallucination. Stated differently, life then can be likened to daily overeating on greasy Chinese food, where a sickened feeling accompanies each movement or act. Clarity of thought and freedom of soul were not to be

---

* Through the years, I have calligraphied verbatim the whole *Book of Psalms* onto 11 x 14 parchment papers, half of them illustrated by my brother Daravuth.

had. It was something similar to the time during my first year in college when I pulled four consecutive all-nighters. During these four days and nights I was aware and functioning, but only as a zombie is aware and functioning. My relatives each had their own emotional demons that they encountered, but they did so more quietly than I.

As I am a product of two classes, I am also a product of two cultures, very opposed in nature. The upshot of this has led to identity issues; 'where do I belong?' I understand other young Cambodian-Americans have similarly struggled with this. Understandably, a notable number found expression in membership of a gang. The parents too busy making ends meet and struggling with the aftershock of the genocide to understand the problems facing their children in the new culture. The children, on the other hand, were too embarrassed by their background and their parents' awkward transition in the new land. One can hear the kids groan, *We're such fobs!* ('Fresh off the boat', an acronym to denote the lack of language or fashion savvy of a new immigrant.)

Growing up in Michigan, I was embarrassed to invite friends home after school because I did not want to expose them to the pungent smell of fish sauce or whatever else we would be having for dinner that evening. Or how could I forget the times my adult relatives pointed to things or gave directions with their middle finger! As I cringed with embarrassment, desperately avoiding my friends' eyes, the thought resonated, *Don't they know that you just don't do that here in America?*

Additionally, a language barrier exists, exacerbating communication. The parents do not speak English, and the children did not know Cambodian well enough to accommodate. The result is Cambodianglish, a mixture of a few Cambodian words sprinkled into a very broken English-structured sentence. Consequently, it is easier to replace a Cambodian for an English word, and vice versa, in a sentence. Even to this day, despite my English fluency, I often speak with my relatives in 'Cambodianglish'. Moreover, the Cambodian vocabulary used at home is very limited to honorifics and household terms. We lacked the rich vocabulary of middle-class America. One can imagine the frustration of not having a voice, not being heard. In situation like this, it is easier for my relatives to issue directives and for me to yell back, 'You don't know what you're talking about!' And the door slams.

The familial discord is compounded by the general societal distrust of communities on the wrong end of the economic spectrum. (Even many years later, my aunt fumed at a church lady's unsolicited remarks to her to teach her nephews about sexual mores. My brothers had not done anything to precipitate such distrust.) Naturally, these young people will find resonance with their friends who are similarly marginalised and in turn will forge identity based on regional or national turfs. When we lived in Michigan, my siblings and I were financially cared for by the privately-run Bethany Christian Services. When we moved to California, the Los Angeles Department of Children's Services became our patron and we became 'wards of the court'. The Christian Education Fund financed our private schooling. I basked in people's kindness but I despised pity. My sensor quickly and acutely detected the difference. The suffocating social hierarchy afforded an Asian, an immigrant and an orphan reinforced my poor image. Where lies the content of one's character?

Having escaped hell on earth, I did not gain strength in one dosage; health came in stages. Twilight precedes the arrival of dawn. But there existed a definite period in time, even though I cannot pinpoint it exactly, when I know I passed into full health.

I graduated third in my class and decided to attend Georgetown for its notable School of Foreign Service and its distance. I needed the space to grow up. My four years in Washington, DC gave me the tools to do so. The academic courses articulated concepts and principles that resonated with me. They opened a door to my past by providing me a framework from which to understand my history, a broader perspective than just my limited personal experiences. The diverse backgrounds of my friends and classmates (those of royal blood and world famous names) affirmed my understanding of how similar we all are in spite of our posturing to appear otherwise. I found spiritual revival at Fourth Presbyterian Church.

For me, the fact that I grew up away from the Cambodian community and in a very non-Asian community, served advantageously for two reasons. First, it strengthened my desire and curiosity to know my roots. Second, my different traits and circumstances contrasted starkly with the surrounding environment and drew attention I needed during those formative years. People found me 'exotic' (as if I was a bird! As my little cousins would retort today, 'Whatever!').

During my years at Washington, DC, I learnt to celebrate my biculturalism. All in all, I find it more a boon than a bane to be able to extract certain qualities from each culture and to temper American individualism with Asian communalism, American assertiveness with Asian demure passivity. Ever since I can remember, almost everything I do has Cambodia as its focal point.

And ever since I can remember, I always wanted to go to law school. Most of the people I admire – for example Martin Luther, John Calvin, the American founding fathers, Gandhi and Nelson Mandela – had a legal education. I admired their sense of right and wrong, and of social justice, but even more I admired them for their talents of rhetoric and clarity of expression. Growing up I felt entangled in my expressions, I had an angst for better communication but lacked the thoughts and words to translate the surges growing inside me. And for some reason, I just knew the study of law would train me to make sense of the bungled feelings and turbulence inside me. I could not be more ecstatic when the University of Michigan Law School at Ann Arbor accepted me into its Juris Doctor programme beginning in fall 1997. I passed the New York Bar Examination in July 2001.

Prior to and during law school, I had several opportunities to work extensively in Cambodia. Immediately after graduating from Georgetown University, I spent a year volunteering with a programme funded by the US Agency for International Development called CANDO or Cambodian-American National Development Organization. I taught English and basic legal vocabulary to officials at the Ministry of Justice and judges from the various Municipal, Appeals and Supreme Courts. After my stint with CANDO, I volunteered with a legal aid organisation in the area of juvenile justice. I travelled to 20 provincial prisons and interviewed juveniles detained there and the relevant aid workers, judges and prison officials. The research was consolidated in a report that I wrote for the national and international community on the (lack of a) juvenile justice system. During my spare time, I presented the news in English on Cambodian national television, TVK, off and on for several months over the course of a couple of years.

I returned again to Cambodia in 1998 to witness the country's second national elections and volunteered with the Ebert Stiftung Foundation to assist Cambodia's embryonic labour movement.

Again, I found myself in Cambodia in 2001–2002 for the country's first commune elections. I travelled all over Cambodia again to train political party agents from the three main political parties on procedures and regulations.

The time and opportunity for me to move back to Cambodia to live as a permanent resident came in January 2004, where I was offered a position to work with an American law firm as a legal consultant. As soon as I can transfer my Juris Doctor and New York Bar membership to become a member of the Cambodian Bar Association, I will establish the law firm Chiv Seng & Associates.

For now, I am content to work in association with Mr. Songhak Chiv of the Cambodia International Law Firm, to be one of the founders and the vice-president of the unique Women's Association of Small & Medium Businesses (WASMB), to serve as the local director of Santa Clara Law School's summer abroad programme and to sit on the board of the international organisation Cambodia Living Arts (or Silapak Khmer Amatak), founded by my dear friend and celebrated human rights activist Arn Chorn-Pond.

People constantly enquire why I want to live in Cambodia when there's not much here to absorb my talents and energy. I strongly believe that Cambodia needs to build a critical mass of genuine and talented professionals, be they from the existing local community or ethnic Cambodians from overseas, like myself, to live simple and ordinary lives as responsible citizens. Before, when I visited Cambodia as a temporary volunteer or as a visitor, I put on my activist cap. Now, I am a simple citizen of Cambodia.

My two cultures have not only altered my perspective but also physically affected my vision. If you remember, one day during the Khmer Rouge era I was one of a group of children who were ordered to carry muddy branches from one location to another. When cleaning us up, one of the men poked my right eye with a long-nailed finger. My eye ballooned to the size of a baseball. For the next month, my mother ground different herbs and applied them to my eye. It worked, leaving only a scar.

One-and-a-half decades later, a fall during a high school ski trip left a scar on my left eye, even after many stitches. Half-inch marks on both my eyelids continue to bear testament to both cultures.

CHAPTER TEN

Meeting Khieu Samphan and the Mixed KR Tribunal
(December 2001 – to date)

On 20 August 2001, the well respected, English-language *Cambodia Daily* published an open letter by the former Khmer Rouge head of state, Khieu Samphan. The seven-page letter stated he was shocked to hear from his wife that people had suffered while he was head of state. He apologised, but said he had had no authority to determine arrests and killings and was out of touch with the real situation. He also questioned the benefit of a war crimes tribunal. The letter generated news around the world. The *Washington Post* in the District of Columbia where I lived covered it. That same day, the director of the Documentation Center of Cambodia, Youk Chhang, emailed me the non-*mea culpa* epistle.

During my last semester of law school I had written a seminar paper on the need for the International Criminal Court. Upon reading Khieu Samphan's letter, I found myself contesting the words set before me as the fresh arguments in my paper percolated in my mind; his letter injected life to my academic theories. I immediately transferred my thoughts to paper in response to the former head of state. One week later, the *Cambodia Daily* published an edited version of my open rebuttal.

In sum, I argued that the apprehension of Mr. Khieu Samphan is necessary for the following three principal reasons: first, it is a moral imperative. For us to remain silent and inactive in the presence of such evils would strike at who we are as moral beings, a violent assault on human dignity. Only when we have properly voiced our disgust by publicly repudiating these gross transgressions can we begin to restore the moral order within the system and ourselves.

Privy to our moral outrage and revulsion is the concept of justice. Justice demands retribution. In apportioning just desserts to the perpetrators, certain desirable values inevitably flow to the respective actors involved. For example, punishment administers accountability and responsibility on the perpetrators. Even if the perpetrators escape arrest, the warrant for their arrest stigmatises them and brands them as pariahs. The values of stigmatisation and shame, although intangible, should not be underestimated. Additionally, the community, e.g. Cambodia, is restored when justice is meted out. Also, I argued, the administration of justice redresses the survivors' rights as legal citizens. Personal autonomy presumes every Cambodian a 'legal person', that is, a carrier of formal rights and obligations. Notably, the criminal process lends legal recognition that justice is not a privilege but a right that is redressable for all Cambodians. Finally, respect is bestowed upon the victims when a concerned community takes concrete steps on their behalf and in their memory. Therefore, a legitimate trial allows for individual and collective closure, the sense of finality that all that could have been done has been done. This closure in turn provides a necessary precondition for meaningful growth and development.

I continued, stating that another aspect of justice reasons that punishment contributes to the general deterrence of future crimes. Implicit in the argument is that potential violators are put on notice. Absent notice and punishment, a moral hazard exists – in effect creating a *de facto* license to kill at will and with impunity.

Second, I argued that twinned to our moral obligation is our legal obligation. A legal system is based on the rule of law. Meaning results when concepts are translated into function. To be sure, Cambodia is not lacking in laws; on the contrary, it has a rich compendium of concepts; the problems lie in their lack of implementation. As we know, it is action that breathes life and texture to abstract principles.

Lastly, I reasoned with Mr. Khieu Samphan that his apprehension gives meaning to 'democratic governance'. A democratic government guarantees the law to be the equaliser in content and application among its citizens. However, when the law punishes petty and common crimes but allows mass murderers, like Mr. Samphan, to circulate freely and comfortably among its citizens, democratic peace and stability are undermined and the law is relegated to meaninglessness. Unfortunately, as is often the case in Cambodia, to quote a known saying, 'For my friends, whatever they want; for my enemies, the law.' A failure to punish is then a clear abdication of democratic authority. The response of inaction serves as a reminder that the other side of the sins of commission is the sins of omission and directs one to privilege a more active response.

I concluded my rebuttal saying that I may have forgiven him but that does not mean I do not think he need not be tried in the court of law.

In November that year, the International Republican Institute (IRI) asked whether I would be interested in working as a short-term consultant in Cambodia for the first multi-party commune elections in February 2002. Knowing of IRI's laudable democracy work in Cambodia, I could not resist such an opportunity to be in the country again (to the ire of my concerned relatives, 'Are you crazy? Make something of your life first, before you can help others.').

For the next few months, the IRI Cambodia staff and I met with high-ranking officials from the three main political parties and the National Election Commission to invite them and their party agents to our 80-plus seminars planned throughout the provinces. The one-day seminars taught the rules and regulations of democratic elections and trained the political party agents to monitor fraud and irregularity on Election Day. We also located suitable training venues (mainly in pagodas for political neutrality) and created and printed 60,000 *IRI Training Handbook*s for distribution.

I was the only foreign trainer, working with two or three local Khmer professional trainers who fanned out into the communes across the country teaching for a month and a half. Each of my 18 seminars had between 60 and 100 attendees; the other trainers sometimes had up to 140 participants. For my protection and assistance, IRI local staff Chan travelled with me. I taught in Khmer.

After my seminar in Battambang, Chan and I hired a local driver for $25 per day to take us to Pailin, a two-hour drive through remote terrain, to my next seminar, scheduled for early the next morning. The one-year-old paved road already had potholes, but nonetheless proved a 100 per cent improvement from what it was when I travelled it in 1998. My eyes took in the open fields surrounded by mountains; at times, I rolled down the window so the fresh mountain air could caress my face. As we neared Pailin, the scenery was replaced by closed-in jungle.

We arrived into the town of Pailin early that afternoon. We checked into the only noticeable hotel in town, an island towering in open fields for people who could afford the $20- to $40-per-night accommodation. As we had the rest of the day free, I asked to see the border post between Thailand and Cambodia, several miles away from town. The driver took the shorter road. Ten minutes later, the dirt path sloped into a stream. In it, a pick-up truck struggled to cross to our side of the river. A few of the men had got out and made the crossing by foot. The water came up to their armpits. After determining that we didn't want to risk death our rusty car, we retraced our steps and took an alternative road.

Several miles later, passing scattered huts along the way, we crossed a one-car swinging bridge that amazingly carried our weight despite our initial misgivings. The fall would have been long and fatal, even if the stream below was shallow. From our raised perspective we attempted to admire the remarkable panorama of jungles and mountains. We arrived at the border post five minutes later. A market sprawled to our left, several Thai-owned casinos sat to our right and the Cambodian and Thai border posts loomed visibly up ahead, manned with soldiers carrying machine guns.

We parked about 300 metres from the border and walked towards the Cambodia guard post. We attracted a few stares as Chan, the driver and I walked along the wide-open road. We stopped to chat with the soldiers and informed them that we would be wandering further ahead to view the Thai's side. Two or three times chills ran down my spine as I remembered the border's history; also, we were open targets should a soldier on either side decide to act up. I decided to talk loudly and act like I had every right to be there. The Thai soldiers looked in our direction, probably wondering what three Cambodians were doing ambling and conversing on the wide borderline.

Afterwards, we walked back and entered the market; I bargained for a scarf but turned it down when the seller refused to be paid in Khmer riel; only Thai baht or US dollars were acceptable currency. On the way back to town, we drove through the parking lots of the glittering casinos. We arrived in Pailin in time for dinner and our charismatic seminar facilitator, a political operative, joined us. Halfway through dinner, he asked me whether I would like to meet

Khieu Samphan, whom he knew relatively well, having met with him on numerous occasions.

Khieu Samphan,* one of the aging and shrinking number of remaining top leaders of the Khmer Rouge, was born in Svay Rieng province and was the eldest son of a provincial judge. Samphan is described by his contemporaries as intelligent, ambitious and aloof. He studied at College Sihanouk in Kampong Cham, then at the prestigious Lycée Sisowath in Phnom Penh, before heading to the University of Paris where he did his doctoral thesis on industrialisation, entitled 'Cambodia's Economy and Industrial Development'. Finishing it four years later in 1959, he returned to Phnom Penh and began publishing a French-language, left-wing newspaper *L'Observateur*.

Initially Prince Sihanouk lauded Khieu Samphan for his patriotism and integrity, and in 1962 he was urged to stand for parliament. However, this favour, subjected to the Prince's capricious disposition, did not last as Samphan's openly-leftist stance soon clashed with that of the Prince's; Sihanouk ordered Samphan beaten and imprisoned, and shut down his newspaper.

In 1966, this time without the aid of the Prince, Khieu Samphan regained his seat in parliament. In April 1967, the government's army violently cracked down on demonstrators in Battambang; Prince Sihanouk approved of the government's repressive measures and blamed Khieu Samphan and other leftists for instigating the Samlaut uprising. Khieu Samphan fled the capital with two other prominent leftists; the population mythologised their disappearance and they became known as the 'Three Ghosts'. They did not appear publicly again until Sihanouk was ousted in 1970.

---

* This background information is culled mainly from David Chandler's *Brother Number One*, Westview Press Inc., 1992 and Elisabeth Becker's *When the War Was Over*, Public Affairs, 1998.

In February 1973, Prince Sihanouk and his wife Monique met the Three Ghosts and other top Khmer Rouge leaders in a jungle hamlet along the Lao-Cambodian border.

In October 1975, six months after the fall of Phnom Penh, a Central Committee meeting affirmed Khieu Samphan's position as liaison officer with the National Front (ostensibly headed by Prince Sihanouk), and throughout the duration of the Khmer Rouge regime Samphan served as the head of state.

After the Vietnamese invasion in 1979, for political palatability, Pol Pot handed over the title of prime minister to his lieutenant, Khieu Samphan. During the Cold War the Khmer Rouge continued to have support on the international stage, as the West (i.e. the US), Thailand and Singapore wanted, among other reasons, to contain Vietnamese expansion. One decade later, at a preparatory meeting for the Paris Peace Agreement, French foreign minister Roland Dumas welcomed Khieu Samphan as the Khmer Rouge's president, among other top Cambodian factional leaders (Hun Sen, Prince Sihanouk and Son Sann).

On his return to Cambodia on 27 November 1991, Khieu Samphan became the first of his Khmer Rouge brothers and sisters to enter Phnom Penh. A crowd mobbed and assaulted him. He was rushed out of Cambodia as his head streamed with blood.

In 1998, Pol Pot died of old age in Anlong Veng, now an emerging tourist destination. As well as Khieu Samphan, former deputy prime minister Ieng Sary survives today, living and partying in a gaudy but expensive mansion in Phnom Penh.

My meeting with Khieu Samphan in Pailin was one of the most surreal events of a lifetime. It was a polite hour-and-ten-minute conversation.

Immediately after my training in Wat Kaong Kang, the course facilitator, Chan, the driver and I went on the brief five-minute car ride to Khieu Samphan's house. On the way, we picked up an older man walking, Pol Choeun (I believe), who I was told was very close to Samphan. He had confirmed the meeting when attending my seminar earlier that day. He had told me, informally, that I could not record the conversation or take pictures.

Khieu Samphan came outside as we pulled up to his two-story wooden house, the ground floor unusually enclosed. My heart skipped a beat as I immediately recognised him as someone I had met many times before – of course, the familiarity came from public pictures – and he appeared not to have aged. He was my height or a bit taller (between 5'3 or 4), smoothed skinned, fair and well-built – more stocky than average Cambodian men. He dressed in an informal, comfortable *ä cha* outfit.*

I was in formal Khmer costume. I pressed my palms together to greet him in the customary Khmer manner and commented on the lack of security. The facilitator thought this too direct and blunt a statement and apologised on my behalf, explaining that I was Cambodian-American. I couldn't read what Samphan initially thought of me, as he reacted little.

There was nothing in the room except for two green American-style cushioned armchairs and three regular wooden Khmer chairs, separated by a coffee table. We were served hot water, of which I took several sips. He sat in one of the armchairs nearest to the window, looking out into the front yard and dirt road. I sat directly across from him on a wooden chair that made me noticeably higher than him.

Besides mentioning enough facts about him to illustrate my deep interest, I also interspersed the conversation with information about myself in order to demonstrate that I was genuinely trying to understand the Khmer Rouge period: that I had lived in Svay Rieng province during the Khmer Rouge period; that my father was a

---

* A casual outfit usually worn by old men or religious ministers.

teacher like him; and that I was the author of the response to his open letter (his eyes steeled up upon hearing this, a fact he did not anticipate). I did not tell him that I was a lawyer but did mention that I had studied 'a little bit of law'.

When I asked direct questions the other people in the group continued to soften the impact and deflect them by trying to answer for him: for instance, when I asked if 'Lauk Pol Pot' was the 'they' (Khmer: *kae*) he referred to as ordering the killings – amidst the different voices and uneasy, covered-up laughter, one answer was 'the organisation'.

I asked for his thoughts and feelings about the period of 1975–78 – about the deaths of so many people and how it was the first time in world history that a people systematically killed their own people. True to form, he proclaimed his ignorance of the killings. I asked whether he travelled outside of Phnom Penh at all at that time – if he had gone to the provinces, had he suspected at all that there were killings during the almost four-year period? He mentioned *chae-ta-na*, and seeing the confusion on my face he translated it as 'intention' in French. Criminal law requires *acteus reus* (an act) and *mens rea* (intent) before a person can be found guilty. He mentioned how difficult it would be to prove intent – his writings in his papers, referring to the newspaper *L'Observateur* he started in the 1960s, would absolve him. I softly retorted that intent can change, especially during different periods of one's life.

He asked rhetorically whether he looked like a mass murderer, violent and capable of committing the gross, inhuman acts, as if alluding to the characteristics that have been attributed to him, that of an affable, modest, intelligent man. He said that many in the international community compare him to a Hitler, but Hitler would throw lavish parties and drink whenever he conducted killings – he asked if he looked like anything like that? I wanted to respond more directly by saying that profiles of serial killers in the West often included nice-looking and intelligent men, but instead I responded that a person doesn't have to actually have done the killing himself – under law he would still be guilty if he had given the order.

Very quickly we both understood each other's position, but in this polite surreal conversation, Khieu Samphan and I talked past each, treading very carefully so as not to break the fragile moment. I would ask him a question and he would veer to talking about something else. He gave simple facts and denied any responsibility, which on one level irritated me (but I couldn't show my irritation in fear of losing the conversation with him) but on another level didn't surprise me, because I had no expectation of a revelation. I wanted to hear him talk and to form my own impression of him in light of the accounts I had read of him. I went into the conversation with the upper hand in that I had moral authority (relative to him) and my calm presence and actions allowed him to know it.

I asked whether he has a defence lawyer in the event the war crimes tribunal took place. He said he did not want to nor did he think about such details or else he wouldn't have his health.

His mention of William Shawcross' book *Sideshow* and other comments lead me to think he genuinely believed he was an agent of the time period – the Cold War and the strong geopolitical current swirling around Cambodia. And I think, to a degree, he still believes Cambodia is not free of its geopolitical problems. I mentioned my dismay to see only Thai bahts and dollars used in Pailin, and asked what he thought of the foreign influences on both the eastern and western boundaries of Cambodia. It is a very difficult situation, he said, because first there are internal problems and then geopolitical influences that are too strong for weak Cambodia. He sounded very hopeless. I defiantly told him I would never take this stance of resignation.

When discussing *Sideshow* and when I mentioned I was from Svay Rieng he stated how Svay Rieng suffered severely. Yes, I know, I told him: the US carried out concentrated bombing raids there, on neutral Cambodia. I said 'another tribunal should be created' to try former US secretary of state Kissinger for crimes against humanity. Khieu Samphan remained unresponsive – no agreement or disagreement. This was probably wise on his part because to agree to 'another tribunal' he would have implicitly agreed to a tribunal for himself. I added to fill in the silence that, yes, the creation of a tribunal really depends on whoever has power. He mentioned how the United States 'may know everything'.

I told him that he must know so many different societies and have witnessed a lot. Did he have any advice for the future of Cambodia? He said, again, to think too much ahead would give him headaches, so he didn't. And also that no one would want his advice anyway.

Towards the end, he added that it was good that I was not a journalist. No, I assured him, but I mentioned again that I had studied a bit of law and impressed upon him my deep curiosity that has haunted me ever since I could remember.

I told him how I really didn't know what to think of the situation: whether Cambodia should follow South Africa's model of a truth and reconciliation commission or have a tribunal. I told him how the ghosts of the Khmer Rouge era continued to haunt every Cambodian individually and the country as a whole, and how closure was needed for a brighter future.

When things got heavier than the already heavy conversation, he changed the conversation to talk about lighter things so that I may 'laugh a little': his days in France, his visits to the States and the different characteristics of different societies. How New Yorkers could not care less whether someone bumps them on the street, but not so in Montpelier, especially the older ladies – that they expected you to move out of the way, even when it is their sharp umbrellas that are in your way and poking you. How no one recognises you as Khmer abroad, it is always 'Chinese'.

I did not join in the laughter and kept my solemnity. The person to my right also lost both his parents to the Khmer Rouge, and I'm certain the other two people suffered personal losses as well, but there was no personal animosity placed on Khieu Samphan by them.

I wished I could have pushed him harder for more direct answers, for example whether he could honestly say he didn't receive reports during the four-year period of killings, how it could be possible that all the killings were done unbeknownst to him by underlings.

I can honestly say I felt no anger towards him and I was surprised at how calm I was. I was a bit teary-eyed at times, but the whole situation was so incredibly surreal – a twilight zone experience.

I told him I still had to make the trip back to Battambang that evening. Oh, it's all right now, he reassured us, the road is smooth so it shouldn't take that long. He did not seem in a rush for us to part for he kept the conversation going a bit, until the person to my left said we should say goodbye. I again pressed my palms together and again thanked him for taking the time to meet with me. He walked us to the door and took several steps outside as the four of us got into the white sedan to leave.

Once inside the car, I noticed concern spread across Chan's and the driver's faces, which made me check the time on my wrist. No one said anything. It was long past the hour we had scheduled to leave for Battambang, a lonely two-hour drive across remote terrain. I gathered they were concerned to be caught shrouded in darkness along the way. Moreover, I regretted the fact that I revealed to Khieu Samphan that we were leaving that evening instead of staying overnight, and chided myself for the stupidity. I frequently looked back to see whether anyone was following. My heart simultaneously throbbed from the past encounter and potential unwanted encounters along the way. We rode on in silence, all lost in our individual thoughts.

≈ ≈ ≈

In January 2004 I moved back to Cambodia to live as a citizen, which makes me now an American-Khmer (rather than Cambodian-American). As I have always wanted to study law, so I have always wanted to move back to Cambodia to live. The issue was always one of time and opportunity, not whether or not I would. I feel so compelled to be here; this feeling stems partly from my sense of obligation in light of the blessings thrown my way. But this is not the complete picture, for I have received more than I have given to this society. If anything, it is sufficient that I am one among a growing few here who are trying to be the critical mass of simple ordinary citizens to counterbalance the dark side of society. Everywhere else, I feel a restlessness that I need to be in Cambodia. Mind you, I often feel restless here, but it's a different type of restlessness: of not doing enough, never of location.

In early 2004, Khieu Samphan's book *Cambodia's Recent History and the Reasons Behind the Decisions I Made*, published in the Khmer language, hit the news stands. It sold like *k'teauv pi seh*, Khmer noodles on a Saturday morning in Phnom Penh, and became an instant bestseller. I bought a copy and had my Khmer-language teacher use it for my classes.

An uncle – a long-time resident of Phnom Penh and husband to Mieng Maly – immediately bought a copy and devoured its contents. While riding with them to the seaside Sihanoukville, he proceeded to lecture me on the history and geopolitics of Cambodia from information he drew from Khieu Samphan's book. He had read it as if it were a history book, to be taken at face value. I do not believe that he, as part of Cambodia's emerging middle and educated class, is unique in his sympathy with Khieu Samphan. There are enough facts in the book to resonate with the experiences he remembers from his youth, so much so to make the propaganda and misinformation that he encountered but has no way of verifying also palatable and believable.

When picking up the book to read I recalled my conversation with Khieu Samphan. I had asked him if he would write a book for posterity's sake and he categorically rejected the possibility.

In law, we are taught that the less one says publicly before a trial the better – it allows less ammunition for the prosecution. This principle is enshrined in the Fifth Amendment of the US Constitution, whereby an arrested individual has 'the right to remain silent …' Here, however, Khieu Samphan has shrewdly calculated that the court of law will most likely find him guilty and he is writing to sway the court of public opinion, that is 'his compatriots', the Cambodian population. He has calculated wisely.

The book opens with a preface from his French attorney, Jacques Vergès. A long time friend of Samphan from their school days in Paris in the 1950s, Jacques Vergès has gained notoriety for representing German war criminal Klaus Barbie, Venezuelan terrorist Carlos the Jackal and Iraq's Saddam Hussein.

Samphan begins his foreword with a tribute of 'respect and esteem' for compatriots he has spoken to who had overcome the grief and pain caused by the Khmer Rouge revolution. Did any thought of a Khmer-American woman he met a little over a year earlier factor into the salvo in defence that is this book?

The main themes in the book are similar to the themes Samphan raised in his article in the *Cambodian Daily* and in his conversation with me – in chief that he was only a figurehead of the Khmer Rouge regime, who was forced into this unexpected and unwanted position of leadership. He also mentioned the need to protect Cambodia's sovereignty several times with me; in his book this is a more pronounced defence that he weaves throughout. In the book, as in his conversation with me, he makes frequent references to William Shawcross' *Sideshow*. Khieu Samphan dedicates one whole chapter to his writings in *L'Observateur*, with me, he mentioned that these writings are indicators of his intention which would absolve him of culpability. Similar to his conversation with me, he mentions favourably Cambodian patriarch Son Sann.

Khieu Samphan's repeated claims of ignorance ring loud and false on several occasions. In Chapter Seven where he discusses the evacuation of Phnom Penh, there's a particularly infuriating paragraph where he attempts at empathy, where his 'heart skipped a beat' upon being told that the evacuation order had been given to include 'old men, pregnant women, children and sick people'. He wonders out loud for us:

> Were they able to take many of their belongings? How did they know where to go? How many could actually reach their destination? What happened to my brothers and sisters, my parents, and my close friends? How could it be that, just as I was hoping to see them, they were again so far from me? What ordeals would they face? Could they overcome them? How many would give up? All these questions tormented me. Why such measure? When had it been decided?'*

Maybe, it is only me who find this false compassion to be particularly irksome and offensive, especially in the Khmer version.

In another paragraph, I wonder his thoughts when he crafted these words, that is, as one coerced and kept in the dark from policies:

---

* *Cambodia's Recent History*, Ponleu Khmer Printing & Publishing House, Cambodia, p. 55. Translated by Puy Kea.

... despite my nomination as president of Democratic Kampuchea, my work didn't change during the years of 1976–78. Of course, I had to make declarations on official dates, such as the commemoration of the April 17 victory ... to receive letters of credit from ambassadors ... participated in – and even presided over – receptions for various Heads of State. But my relationship to the real authority remained exactly the same ...*

I am struck by the gall and simplicity of such pronouncements in light of the destruction of a culture and his prominent and trusted position in a very brutal regime.

Having met him and read his book, I am amazed time and again at Khieu Samphan's ability to live with himself, at his ability to convince himself of the rightness of his cause to a degree where he is still functioning well. What is it that makes my prison mate – the woman who had her head crushed – go mad, while Khieu Samphan – who is responsible for the death of two million – remains sane? What is the lesson to us human beings in this matter? That it is better to be hardened and not feel, for to feel deeply, we risk being a few mangoes short of a dozen?

Many foreign Cambodian-watchers and academics put a lot of stock in a war crimes tribunal as a vehicle to usher in justice for Cambodians, and are often frustrated with the apparent apathy of Cambodians in not fighting harder for a tribunal's establishment. However, many Cambodians continue to face injustices perpetrated on them. It is a luxury for me to have the energy to hone in on the Khmer Rouge issue.

I believe that the tribunal proposed by the Cambodian government and accepted by the United Nations for a domestically-controlled trial will not do. It will inevitably lead to a parody of justice that

* Chapter 8, *Cambodia's Recent History*, op. cit p. 71.

would curdle even the blood of the dead. Recently, the Royal Government of Cambodia lobbied the nebulous 'international community' – i.e. the United Nations and donor countries – to contribute the initial US$56 million to jumpstart the UN-backed 'mixed' tribunal comprising of local and international judges. At the time of writing, the Cambodian government has obtained the needed initial funding. In light of universal criticism of the judiciary as lacking independence and often being used as a political tool, I highly doubt the legitimacy of any trial, especially one as highly-charged politically as this one, when the established mechanism falls far short of universal legal standards of justice. The condescension and arrogance of some Westerners will never cease to amaze me in thinking that Cambodians should settle for a 'different' standard of justice – meaning, second-class justice.

Of course, the ultimate responsibility rests on the shoulders of the Cambodian leaders who lobby for such meniality. I believe the population at large has resigned to the inevitability that a legitimate trial will not happen and come to accept any scraps thrown their way. They reason, 'If we don't do something, the Khmer Rouge leaders will die out. Closure and justice must be had.' I understand and even agree to a degree with this mentality. For Cambodians, I see the issue of lobbying on two planes – a public stance and a private stance. Publicly, Cambodians should not accept anything less than first-class justice and we should fight for such standard. But now in light of the tribunal's inevitability, I believe this tribunal is not without benefits, mainly the addition of new information to enlighten our understanding, international focus on Cambodia and the collateral scrutiny on the current government, and generating much-needed discussions by the population at large, allowing them to focus on their horrific history and their individual roles in it. However, we are fooling ourselves if we think justice or collective closure will be had.

I do not believe the tribunal itself will bring about personal healing. That takes place in the quietness of one's soul. For me, there has been no tribunal but nonetheless I have emotional health. Healing came with time, grace, space, distance and an incredible support structure of loving family members, friends and community. Many Cambodians have not been as fortunate in the opportunities given to them. A new form of dire poverty, domestic violence, social dysfunction, hopelessness and lack of opportunities have replaced the cruelty they experienced by the Khmer Rouge.

I continue to mourn the loss of lives due to the Khmer Rouge. Today, I also mourn the loss of human potential. How many Khmer Mozarts, Einsteins and Da Vincis will never be realised because there are no infrastructures to encourage and absorb a Khmer child's human potential? I mourn when I meet a little girl on the street begging. I see my face in her face. The only difference between us is in our opportunities. At one point in my life, an opportunity existed which led to other opportunities that nurtured and encouraged my budding potential. In this little girl's situation, in light of the current infrastructure and framework, the odds are stacked against her.

Since my encounter with Khieu Samphan, I have spoken with my relatives about their reactions towards Khieu Samphan and Khmer Rouge justice (or lack thereof).

Over the phone with Uncle Seng, I asked: 'You returned to Prey Roka village for the first time in the summer of 2002. Did you feel hatred or revenge towards your former persecutors? For example, Mok?'

Uncle Seng quietly and thoughtfully responded: 'No sense of revenge. I felt sorry for them. They don't know anything. They have no sense of justice. A long time ago, I felt anger. But after having lived in a civilised world, I only feel pity for them. Their only thought, to this day, is survival, how to have the next meal. Their lives are lived in a pitch-black prison – no electricity, so remote from all things civilised – nothing. What is past is past.'

Aunt Ry shares a similar inevitability: 'I did not grab Mok's hand, during our short visit to Prey Roka; she seemed a bit uncomfortable and we were there for such a short time, as we wanted to return to Phnom Penh that same day. She busied herself with the children – Andy, Vanessa, Jenny. I guess I may have felt anger towards her, but not as one in ignorance. Like Uncle Seng, I mainly felt pity for them and a deep sadness at everything. Before Pol Pot, our family lived a very comfortable, happy life. But everything is in the past now.

'You know, during the Khmer Rouge years, the expectation was death. During the four years, I was only waiting to die. Each day prepared us for death. Each week we would see a group of familiar faces disappear. After weeks and months of this, my mind was so conditioned for the arrival of death that nothing was shocking anymore. One day, the authority had a group of 30 men who were kept temporarily under Mok's house when we were still living there. The next day, they all disappeared. Because we worked in *kang chalot* with other base people, they would discuss with great amusement the dismemberment of these victims. Even at the dining hall, they laughed at the various body parts of these *khmang*, enemy. Because death was always a constant for us, not a sudden event, I took it as a given that one day I would be next to disappear. For example, I only came under extreme shock the evening we were scheduled to die. The day before when we dug our own grave, I had little reaction.'

I asked her: 'Why didn't you resist, if you had nothing to lose, if you knew for certain you were going to die at their hands?'

Aunt Ry reflected: 'Yes, Uncle Seng and I asked ourselves that same question sometimes. You know in that group of 30 men, only one gun guarded them. Fear is the only answer. We couldn't communicate with each other. I remember Grandma Hao had told us to learn how "to plant a dumb tree", that is to say, to keep silence, to be *kor*, mute, like this particular Khmer tree with cotton inside the seed.'

'And your thoughts on Khieu Samphan?' I asked.

Aunt Ry deviated to talking about a visit of another Khmer Rouge leader, Chhun Mom,* to Aunt Renee's house in Cypress, Southern California. It was as if she didn't want to have an opinion on this topic of Khieu Samphan and Khmer Rouge justice, an association too impersonal for her. She experienced direct cruelty by Mok, but not Khieu Samphan. Or it could be that having been raised in a culture that teaches one, especially a woman, not to have an individual voice, she genuinely did not know what to think of Khieu Samphan and other top Khmer Rouge leaders.

I posed the same question to my brothers. Lundi responded, 'If you had asked me this question ten years ago and I had been face-to-face with Khieu Samphan, I would have ripped his neck off! But part of the healing process is the ability to forgive. So, personally, I have forgiven, but legally, he must still be prosecuted.'

It never even entered Sina's mind to be given an opportunity to confront Khieu Samphan. If he had been in my position, he would have liked to know in particular whether there is remorse: 'They're responsible, because they were in the leadership. Many people were killed, so his response of ignorance is not believable. And how, as a human being, could you have done that?'

Through the years, I have tried to grapple with the insanity of the Khmer Rouge. People have often asked me, 'How can such evil have occurred?' I believe the answer is rooted in human nature. I have thought often of the contorted face of the crazy woman crushed to death, the disappearance of my father, the agony of my mother that

---

* Although not in the top ten considered culpable, his name has been changed to preserve anonymity. He had returned to Cambodia via Beijing with Ân and Nan. He was also visiting California during the time that Ân and Nan were visiting my relatives. He admitted, like Khieu Samphan, that he also became a fool for the Khmer Rouge.

lonely night long ago, my newly-wed aunt and uncle who were killed hugging each other on a stake, the blood-drenched fields that were my work and play grounds, my relatives' Dang Rek experience, and then the smiling, grandfatherly face of Khieu Samphan.

And I have read about the inhumanity of slavery, of apartheid, of the Jewish Holocaust, of the Rwandan genocide, of Nero, of Stalin, of Mao Zedong, among other atrocities throughout history, across all cultures, by all manners of personality.

And I have demanded to know: if hell is the complete separation from God, and this earth is the buffer zone, dear abominable Adam, father of mankind, what have you done with your freedom?

But is there not an ember within me also capable of such barbarity? What if I had been fanned, not by love and mirth, but the right inflammatory rhetoric, social environment and time? What if, instead of being a 'new' person from the city, I grew up a child of Angkar, emboldened with an AK-47, with the awesome power to determine the life or death of another?

Who is this savage, the Khmer Rouge? Is she not I, but only one degree removed at birth? Is her baseness not within my capability? Do we at times not find ourselves standing at the edge of a precipice?

Life is but a breath.
Live passionately. Love deeply. Pray unceasingly.

About the Author

Theary Seng was born in Phnom Penh, Cambodia, in early 1971. Under the Khmer Rouge, she lived in Svay Rieng province bordering Vietnam, where the killings were most intense and where she spent five months in prison. She and her surviving family trekked across the border for Thailand in November 1979 and emigrated to the United States one year later. After graduation from Georgetown University in 1995 and during summer breaks from the University of Michigan Law School, she returned to volunteer in Cambodia with various human rights and labour organisations. In January 2004, she moved permanently to live and work in Cambodia as a commercial lawyer. Theary is a member of the New York Bar Association and American Bar Association, and is awaiting membership to the Cambodian Bar Association. When Theary is not busy contemplating whether she should learn how to cook and be a good Khmer girl, how to introduce the world to Khmer cheese *prahok* or how to maintain some semblance of privacy, she can be found whizzing around town on a motodop (taxi), reading, practising calligraphy, sleeping, teasing the neighbourhood kids, sitting on the board of Cambodia Living Arts, working with Khmer entrepreneurs via the Women's Association of Small & Medium Businesses (which she co-founded with several friends and is vice-president) or being a groupie to Bona's band at the Memphis Pub.